Medieval Europe:

A SHORT HISTORY

Medieval Europe:

A SHORT HISTORY

SECOND EDITION

C. WARREN HOLLISTER

JOHN WILEY & SONS, INC.

NEW YORK, LONDON, SYDNEY

Library of Congress Catalog Card Number: 68-19334

Printed in the United States of America

TO MY PARENTS

Preface

In this new edition of *Medieval Europe: A Short History* the fundamental goals of the original edition remain unchanged, but the format has been altered on the basis of suggestions by instructors and students who have used the book in their classes. It remains a core book that endeavors to be trustworthy, lively, and brief. Much of the material in the original edition dealing with the Roman Empire at its height and early Christianity has been deleted because such material is more appropriate to ancient history than to medieval history. But a significant amount of material has been added to the remainder of the book, especially on the subjects of manorialism, high medieval Christianity, literature, thought, and the arts. More important still, Eastern Europe is now given more attention, and two chapters have been added to the end of the book which carry the history through the Late Middle Ages—from A.D. 1300 (where the first edition ended) to A.D. 1500. It is hoped that the addition of these chapters on the fourteenth and fifteenth centuries will be helpful to instructors who use this book together with one of the standard Modern Europe texts, most of which start in 1500. The added chapters should also make the book more suitable to the many medieval survey courses which extend to the eve of the Reformation.

A number of instructors in Western Civilization courses have been using this book in tandem with my *Roots of the Western Tradition: A Short History of the Ancient World*. These two books, indeed, were conceived as a pair, covering briefly the ancient and medieval world. But each of the two was designed also to stand on its own as a survey of its respective era. Since courses in ancient history often cover the period terminating around A.D. 500, and since courses in medieval history often begin with the period around A.D. 300, a certain amount of overlapping between the two books was unavoidable. In this new edition the overlap has been reduced to a minimum by the device of handling the late Roman Empire as background rather than subjecting it to narrative chronological treatment. In the future, instructors who adopt the sequence of *Roots of the Western Tradition* and *Medieval Europe* need merely instruct their students to begin their reading in *Medieval Europe* with Chapter Three.

Santa Barbara, California   C. WARREN HOLLISTER
1968

Preface to the First Edition

This brief survey of medieval Western Europe is intended for the beginning college student or for the general reader who wishes a compact summary of the period. When used in college or university courses in Western Civilization or World History, its brevity will allow ample time for collateral readings in the sources or in the more advanced and interpretive secondary literature. It was written to meet a need that I have encountered in my own teaching: for a core book around which diverse supplementary readings could be clustered — a review of the medieval period that is neither a bare outline nor a small encyclopedia.

It is my conviction that such a book must be trustworthy, literate, and brief. The student must be able to depend on the interpretations in the book as representing sound conclusions of modern scholarship rather than brilliant but untested hypotheses of the author. The student should, if at all possible, enjoy the book — drawing from it a lucid organization of the historical data and a sense of liveliness and excitement as well. Finally, he should not be obliged to spend the bulk of his reading time on a narrative survey. The book must be sufficiently long to present a coherent overview of a great historical epoch and to suggest its economic, intellectual, and cultural achievements as well as its political developments, but it must be sufficiently short to permit the student to read widely in supplementary works — to explore special topics in depth, to become familiar with the controversial literature on great historical issues, and to examine some of the contemporary sources. A good sampling of appropriate collateral readings, many of them in paperback, is provided in the annotated bibliographies at the ends of each of the three sections of this book.

For the sake of brevity, much has been omitted. I have seldom been able to probe very far beneath the surface of events. Had I done so consistently, the book would have been far too long to serve the purpose for which it is intended. Historians will inevitably disagree as to what should be included and what excluded in a compact summary of this sort, and the final choice must always rest on the judgment of the individual author. In particular, the careful reader will notice two major omissions in the present book: (1) Eastern Europe has been treated only sketchily, because I believe that its evolution in the Middle Ages was less essential to the making of Western Civilization than was the development of medieval culture in Germany, Italy, France, and England. (2) The narrative closes early in the fourteenth century, thereby excluding the period commonly known as the Late Middle Ages. I have chosen to leave this period to historians of the Renaissance, who quite rightly lay claim to the era of Petrarch and Boccaccio. The teacher of Western Civilization might wish to supplement this book with one of several excellent brief surveys of the Renaissance Age that are available in paperback, for example, Wallace K. Ferguson's splendid volume in the Berkshire Series.

To the several anonymous readers who were selected to evaluate and criticize the present work, I express my thanks. All these readers are well-known historians whose styles clearly betray their identities, but I am not permitted to mention them here by name as I would wish. I also thank Professors Brian Tierney and Richard C. Dales, who provided perceptive suggestions on Chapters 14 and 15, respectively. I am indebted to my wife and my parents, who read the manuscript in full, pruning it of many infelicities and ambiguities. More objective readers could be found, but none more devoted.

Santa Barbara, California   C. WARREN HOLLISTER
August 1964

Contents

xii   Contents

List of Maps

Maps by Russell H. Lenz and John V. Morris

List of Illustrations

Medieval Europe:

A SHORT HISTORY

Introduction

A few generations ago the medieval centuries of European history were widely regarded as "The Dark Ages." Western man was thought to have dropped into a deep slumber at the fall of the Western Roman Empire in A.D. 476, awakening at length, like Rip Van Winkle, in the bright dawn of the Italian Renaissance. Indeed, it was the humanists of fifteenth-century Renaissance Italy who first created this dismal image of their medieval forebears, and the condemnation was echoed by the sixteenth-century Protestant reformers and by the philosophers of the eighteenth-century French Enlightenment. The term "Middle Ages" was coined to denote a prolonged era of spiritual and cultural intermission separating classical antiquity from the Renaissance and unworthy of a name of its own. It was an age whose art was barbaric or "Gothic"—a millennium of darkness—a thousand years without a bath.

Today this ungenerous point of view stands discredited, although it persists among the half-educated. Several generations of rigorous historical scholarship have demonstrated clearly that the medieval period was an epoch of immense vitality and profound creativity. The age that produced Thomas Aquinas and Dante, Notre Dame de Paris and Chartres, Parliament and the university, can hardly be described as "dark" or "barbaric."

Still, one is reminded endlessly in textbooks that life in medieval Europe was vastly different from life in modern America and that the medieval intellectual climate was far removed from our own. Countless students have been taught to contrast feudalism with democracy, the medieval mind with the modern mind, the "Age of Faith" with our own age of technology, or doubt, or cybernetics, or whatever it might be. These are truths that few would be inclined to doubt, and it seems unnecessary to belabor the point that the political and cultural leaders of today are not very much like St. Bernard or Pope Gregory VII. The chief pitfall in understanding medieval Europe is not a failure to recognize its all too obvious contrasts with modern society. Rather, it is the danger that in dwelling too intently upon these alien qualities we may overlook the all-important fact that the Middle Ages constituted the earliest phase of our own civilization. One of the great benefits in the study of medieval history is the opportunity it affords to examine the birth, youth, and early maturity of Western European society. As we investigate the Middle Ages we are scrutinizing our own cultural origins. By the twelfth and thirteenth centuries Western Civilization had succeeded in attaining a cultural level comparable to that of the great civilizations of the past, but it also possessed an enormous potential for further development. It was destined, in later centuries, to transcend by far the achievements of the past and, for good or ill, to transform the world.

Part 1

THE EARLY MIDDLE AGES:

The Genesis of Western Civilization

Part 1

THE EARLY MIDDLE AGES:

The Genesis of Western Civilization

1

The Christian Empire

THE MOOD OF THE LATE EMPIRE

During the three centuries following the end of the Roman imperial line in the West in A.D. 476, the Mediterranean world underwent a profound transformation. Where once a single state had encompassed the far-flung lands of the Mediterranean basin, now three distinct civilizations were established on the ruins of the old Empire. These three—Byzantium, Western Europe, and Islam—differed sharply from one another in style and outlook; all had broken appreciably from the traditions of Old Rome. Yet each, to a different degree, was a product of the Greco-Roman past. Although no longer Roman, all were deeply indebted to the legacy of classical antiquity.

Each of Rome's three heirs was animated by a powerful transcendental faith based on the Hebrew religious tradition. Each, in its own way, was shaped by the intense religious experience of the late Empire itself. Accordingly, our examination of these three successor civilizations must begin with a study of the Roman Empire's Christian phase, that is, of the crucial decades between Constantine's conversion and the fall of the Western Empire. In these decades Church and Caesar worked together toward the Christianization of the ancient world.

As Rome grew old, the allegiance of her people gradually shifted from the traditional gods of hearth, field, and city to potent tran-

5

scendental deities of the Orient such as Isis, Mithras, and the Great Mother, who promised the priceless gifts of personal redemption and eternal life. Even in the buoyant years of the second century A.D., imperial culture and prosperity had failed to affect a vast, wretched substratum of the population. And as the peace of the second century gave way to the turbulence and disintegration of the third, an ever-increasing portion of the Empire's inhabitants was reduced to a state of grinding poverty and futility. To men such as these the shining dreams of classical humanism—an ordered universe, an ideal republic, a good life—were cruel illusions. For them, the world was not enough, and the salvation cults became their one hope.

The older pagan cults of Jupiter, Minerva, and the other deities of the classical pantheon survived the turmoil of the third century but only in profoundly altered form. They, too, were transformed by the great transcendental upsurge of the age, for during the third century all that was vital in the traditional pagan cults was incorporated into a vast philosophical scheme known as Neoplatonism. One of the most influential philosophers of the Roman era, Plotinus, taught this doctrine of one god, infinite, unknowable, and unapproachable except through a mystical experience. Plotinus' god was the ultimate source of all things, physical and spiritual. All existence was conceived as a vast hierarchy radiating outward from God, like concentric ripples in a pond, diminishing in excellence and significance in proportion to its distance from the divine source. Human reason, which the Greeks had earlier exalted, was now reduced to impotence, for the nexus of reality was an unknowable god that lay beyond reason's scope.

Despite their mystical doctrine of monotheism, the Neoplatonists allowed a place in their system for the manifold deities of paganism. The pagan gods were interpreted as symbols of the Neoplatonic god—crude symbols, but useful nevertheless. The pagan pantheon, so radically unsuited to the deepening mood of otherworldliness, was now galvanized and given new relevance by the overarching structure of Neoplatonic philosophy. So it was that the deities of Old Rome came to participate increasingly in the new trend toward mysticism and monotheism. The distinction between Jupiter and Mithras was steadily fading.

CHRISTIANITY AND THE EMPIRE

It was in this atmosphere of mysticism and the supernatural that Christianity won its final victories. By Constantine's reign (A.D. 306–337) the age of questing rationalism and fallible, anthropomorphic deities had long passed, and with Constantine's conversion and his subsequent victory at the Milvian Bridge (312), the triumph of Christianity over its mystical rivals was all but assured.

The Christians were deeply grateful to Constantine, their first imperial convert. But had they possessed the broad, retrospective view available to the modern historian they might have expressed a kind of gratitude also toward Diocletian (284–305), their last imperial persecutor. For the ruthless, authoritarian measures by which Diocletian and Constantine revived the faltering Empire had the effect of postponing imperial collapse in the West for nearly two centuries, and the Christians put this borrowed time to good use. Indeed, Constantine's founding of Constantinople provided the foundation for the Christian Byzantine Empire that endured for a millennium. Had Rome collapsed at the end of the third century— had there been no experience of a Christian Roman Empire—the subsequent history of Europe, North Africa, and Western Asia would surely have been substantially altered.

The fourth-century Empire witnessed mass conversions to Christianity under the benevolent support of Christian emperors. From a vigorous, dedicated minority sect, Christianity expanded during the fourth century to become the dominant religion of the Mediterranean world. No longer persecuted and disreputable, Christianity became official, conventional, respectable. And of course it lost much of its former spiritual élan in the process. Moreover, total victory was accompanied by a new surge of internal dissension. The fourth century was an age of bitter doctrinal struggle, and here, too, the Christian emperors played a commanding role. It was only through imperial suppression that Arianism, the most powerful of the fourth-century heresies, lost its hold on the inhabitants of the Empire. The Arians, who followed Christ's teachings but denied his full divinity, constituted a potent force in the Church until Emperor Theodosius I (378–395) condemned them and broke their power, making orthodox Christianity the official religion of the Roman state. Indeed,

Theodosius proscribed paganism itself and, deprived of imperial sanction, the old gods of Rome gradually passed into memory.

Orthodox Christianity now dominated the Empire; yet old heresies lingered on and vigorous new ones arose. And although Arianism was dying in the Empire by the late fourth century, it survived among the Germanic peoples along the frontiers. These barbarians had been converted by Arian missionaries around the middle of the century, at a time when Arianism was still strong in the Empire, and the persecutions of the orthodox Emperor Theodosius had no effect on the faith of the Germanic tribes. Consequently, when in time the barbarians built their successor states on the debris of the Western Empire they were divided from their Roman subjects not only by culture but also by the bitter antagonisms that have traditionally separated rival faiths.

Christianity gained much from Constantine's conversion but it also lost much. The post-Constantine Church was less fervent, less dedicated than before; it was also less independent. For the gratitude of Christians toward Constantine almost reached the point of adulation. He was regarded as a thirteenth Apostle, as the master of all churches, as a monarch whose office was commissioned by God. His regal presence dominated the great Ecumenical Council of Nicaea in 325, and it was at his bidding that the Council denounced Arianism. In the decades that followed, the Arian-orthodox struggle swayed back and forth according to the inclinations of the emperors. First the Arian leaders were condemned to exile, then the orthodox, until finally, late in the fourth century, Arianism subsided under the pressure of the sternly orthodox Emperor Theodosius I. Good Catholics rejoiced when Theodosius banned Arianism, but they might well have been apprehensive of a situation in which such crucial matters of faith depended upon imperial fiat.

A situation of this sort is traditionally called "Caesaropapism." It arises from a political structure in which Church and state are both controlled by a single individual—a "Caesar-pope." Caesaropapism was a significant characteristic of the Christian Empire, and in the East it became a fundamental ingredient in the organization of the Byzantine state throughout its age-long history. For a thousand years Church and state tended to merge under the encompassing authority of the emperor at Constantinople. His subjects regarded him not merely as a Caesar but as the supreme ruler of a

Christian state (or rather, in the eyes of the East Romans, *the* Christian state). As such, he was usually able to depend on the fervent support of his Christian subjects, and their support gave the Eastern Empire the strength to endure. On the other hand, the Eastern emperor's orthodoxy evoked a spirit of uncompromising hostility in districts where heterodox views held sway. The religious disaffection of these districts—most notably Egypt and Syria— resulted in their eventual loss during the opening stages of the seventh-century Islamic conquests.

Dominant in the East, Caesaropapism failed in the West, for the fifth century brought renewed turbulence and, ultimately, political catastrophe to the Western Empire; Western Christians began to doubt the wisdom of placing all their hope in the imperium. Gradually they came to realize that the disintegration of the Empire did not mean the end of the world or the collapse of the Church. Eastern Christians might indeed regard their Empire as the Ark of Christ, but those in the West wisely refused to bind themselves to a sinking ship. Accordingly, the Western Church slowly began to assert its independence of imperial authority, thereby laying the foundation for the Church-state tension that became such a dominant theme in the evolution of European civilization.

THE LATIN DOCTORS

The conversion of Constantine was merely one event in the long and significant process of fusion between Christianity and Greco-Roman civilization. This process had been at work among the early Christian apologists who sought to present their faith in the intellectually respectable context of Greek philosophy. The classical-Christian synthesis was carried still further by great third-century theologians such as Origen of Alexandria who produced a masterful fusion of Christian doctrine and Platonic philosophy. The process reached its climax in the Western Empire during the later fourth and early fifth centuries with the work of three Christian intellectuals, St. Ambrose, St. Jerome, and St. Augustine, who wrote with such erudition and insight that they have come to be regarded as "Doctors of the Latin Church." Working at a time when the Christianization of the Empire was proceeding apace, yet before the intellectual vigor of classical antiquity had faded, these three scholar-saints applied all the sophisticated wisdom of their fine classical educations to the elucidation of the Christian faith. Nearly seven centuries were to pass before Western Europe regained the intellectual level of late antiquity, and the writings of these three Latin Doctors therefore exerted a powerful influence on the thought of the succeeding ages.

Although Ambrose, Jerome, and Augustine made their chief impact in the realm of intellectual history, all three were deeply involved in the political and ecclesiastical affairs of their day. Saint Ambrose (c. 340–397) was bishop of Milan, a great city of northern Italy that in the later fourth century replaced Rome as the imperial capital in the West. Ambrose was a superb administrator, a powerful orator, and a vigorous opponent of Arianism. Thoroughly grounded in the literary and philosophical traditions of Greco-Roman civilization he enriched his Christian writings by drawing heavily from Plato, Cicero, Virgil, and other great figures of the pagan past. And as one of the first champions of ecclesiastical independence from the authority of the Christian Empire he stood at the fountainhead of the Church-state controversy that was to affect Western Europe for more than a millennium. When the powerful orthodox emperor, Theodosius I, massacred the rebellious inhabitants of Thessalonica, St. Ambrose excommunicated him from the Church of Milan, forcing Theodosius to humble himself and beg forgiveness. The Emperor's public repentance set a momentous precedent for the principle of ecclesiastical supremacy in matters of faith and morals—a precedent that would not be forgotten by churchmen of later centuries.

Saint Jerome (c. 340–420) was the most scholarly of the three Latin Doctors. A restless, troubled man, he roamed widely through the Empire, living in Rome for a time, then fleeing the worldly city to found a monastery in Bethlehem. Jerome's monks in Bethlehem devoted themselves to the copying of manuscripts, a task that was to be taken up by countless monks in centuries to come and which, in the long run, resulted in the preservation of important works of Greco-Roman antiquity that would otherwise have vanished. The modern world owes a great debt to St. Jerome and his successors for performing this humble but essential labor.

St. Jerome himself was torn by doubts as to the propriety of a Christian immersing himself in pagan literature. On one occasion

Jesus appeared to him in a dream and banished him from paradise with the words, "Thou art a Ciceronian, not a Christian." For a time thereafter Jerome renounced all pagan learning, but he was much too devoted to the charms of classical literature to persevere in this harsh resolve. In the end he seems to have concluded that Greco-Roman letters might properly be used in the service of the Christian faith.

Jerome's supreme achievement lay in the field of scriptural commentary and translation. It was he who produced the definitive Latin translation of the Bible from its original Hebrew and Greek— the so-called Latin Vulgate Bible, which Catholics have used ever since. By preparing a trustworthy Latin text of the fundamental Christian book he made a notable contribution to the civilization of Western Europe.

St. Augustine of Hippo (354–430) was the towering intellect of his age. His achievements exceeded those of St. Ambrose, the ecclesiastical statesman, and St. Jerome, the scholar. For St. Augustine too was a statesman and a scholar, and he was a great philosopher as well. As bishop in the important North African city of Hippo he was deeply immersed in the affairs of his day, and his writings were produced in response to vital contemporary issues. Augustine's thought combines profundity and immediacy—the abstract and the human. In his *Confessions* he describes his own intellectual and moral Odyssey through paganism and Manichaeism into the orthodox Christian fold. He writes with the hope that others, lost as he once was, might be led by God to the spiritual haven of the Church.

Augustine wrote voluminously against the various pagan and heretical doctrines that threatened Christian orthodoxy in his age. Out of these diverse writings there emerged a lofty system of speculative thought that served as the intellectual foundation for medieval philosophy and theology. Like so many of his predecessors and contemporaries he worked toward the synthesis of classical and Christian thought, but more than any before him he succeeded in welding the two cultures into one. He was disturbed, as Jerome was, by the danger of pagan thought to the Christian soul. But, like Jerome, he concluded that although a good Christian ought not to *enjoy* pagan culture he might properly *use* it for Christian ends. Accordingly, Augustine used the philosophy of Plato and the Neoplatonists as a basis for a new and thoroughly Christian philosophical scheme.

It has been said that Augustine baptized Plato. As the thirteenth-century philosopher St. Thomas Aquinas observed, "Whenever Augustine, who was imbued with the philosophy of the Platonists, found in their teaching anything consistent with faith, he adopted it; those things which he found contrary to faith, he amended."

Thus Augustine stressed the Platonic notion of ideas or archetypes as the models of tangible things, but instead of placing his archetypes in some abstract "heaven," as Plato did, he placed them in the mind of God. For Augustine, the Platonic archetypes were "divine ideas." These ideas constituted the highest form of reality—the only true knowledge—and the human mind had access to the archetypes through a form of God's grace that Augustine called "divine illumination." Augustine was much too good a Christian to fall into the Zoroastrian notion that matter was worthless or that the human body was evil. But by emphasizing the superiority of ideas over particulars he was led to the conclusion that the material world was less important—less real—than the spiritual world. He concluded that man's body was a prison for his soul, and that the soul's escape from its material body was the chief goal of the Christian life. And he insisted that man, corrupted by the original sin of Adam's fall, was incapable of escaping the prison of his body except through God's grace. Hence man could not earn his own way into heaven; he was predestined to salvation or damnation by the will of God.

These and other doctrines were developed in the process of St. Augustine's long struggle against the various heretical sects that flourished in his age. In the course of his arguments he examined many of the central problems that have occupied theologians ever since—the nature of the Trinity, the existence of evil in a world created and governed by an omnipotent God, the special power and authority of the priesthood, the compatibility of free will and predestination.

When pagan critics ascribed the Visigothic sack of Rome in 410 to Rome's desertion of her former gods, Augustine met the challenge by writing his profoundly influential *City of God* which set forth a complete Christian philosophy of history. Human development was interpreted not in economic or political terms but in moral terms. Kingdoms and empires rise, prosper, and decline according to a divine plan, ordained from the beginning, yet forever beyond human comprehension. But even though the pattern of history must always elude us, we do know this: God is not interested in the fate of tribes and empires except insofar as they affect the destiny of individual men; the chief business of history is the salvation of human souls. And the salvation of souls depends not on the victories of Caesar but on the grace of God. Therefore true history has less to do with the struggles of states than with the struggle between good and evil that rages within each state and within each soul. The human race is divided into two distinct classes: not Romans and barbarians as the pagan writers would have it, but those who live in God's grace and those who do not. The former are members of the "City of God," the latter belong to the "City of Evil." The two cities are hopelessly intertwined in this life, but their members will be separated at death by eternal salvation or damnation. The divine plan for human history therefore has one fundamental purpose: the growth and welfare of the City of God. As for the city of Rome, perhaps, in the long run, its decline will be beneficial—perhaps even irrelevant!

The Romans had never excelled in the realm of speculative thought, but with the Christian Augustine, Roman philosophy came into its own at last. He was the Western Empire's greatest philosopher and, indeed, one of the two or three foremost minds in the history of Christianity. His theory of the two cities, although often simplified and misunderstood in later generations, influenced Western thought and politics for a thousand years. His Christian Platonism dominated medieval philosophy until the mid-twelfth century and remains a significant theme in religious thought to this day. His distinction between the ordained priesthood and the laity has always been basic to Catholic theology. And his emphasis on divine grace and predestination was to be a crucial source of inspiration to the Protestant leaders of the sixteenth century.

As a consequence of Augustine's work, together with that of his great contemporaries, Ambrose and Jerome, Christian culture was firmly established on classical foundations. At Augustine's death in 430 the classical-Christian fusion was essentially complete. The strength of the Greco-Roman tradition that underlies medieval Christianity and Western civilization owes much to the fact that these three Latin Fathers, and others like them, found it possible to be both Christians and Ciceronians.

2

The Decline of Rome and the Germanic Invasions

DECLINE AND FALL

The catastrophe of Rome's decline and fall has always fascinated historians, for it involves not only the collapse of mankind's most impressive and enduring universal state but also the demise of Greco-Roman civilization itself. The reasons are far too complex to be explained satisfactorily by any single cause—Christianity, disease, slavery, soil exhaustion, or any of the other master keys that have been proposed from time to time. We must always bear in mind that the Roman Empire "fell" only in the West. It endured in the East, although there, too, Greco-Roman civilization was changed significantly. The civilization of the Eastern Empire during the medieval centuries is normally described not as "Roman" or even "Greco-Roman" but as "Byzantine," and the change in name betokens a profound alteration in mood. In other words, Greco-Roman culture was gradually transformed in both East and West, but its transformation in the West was accompanied by the dismemberment of the Roman state, whereas its transformation in the East occurred despite an underlying political continuity in which emperor followed emperor in unbroken succession.

In the West, then, we are faced with two separate phenomena—

political breakdown and cultural transformation. The political collapse culminated in the deposition of the last Western emperor in A.D. 476, but the real period of crisis was the chaotic third century. The recovery under Diocletian and Constantine was merely partial and temporary; the impending death of the body politic was delayed, but the disease remained uncured. The impoverished masses in town and countryside had never participated meaningfully in Roman civilization, and the third-century anarchy resulted in the spiritual disengagement of the middle classes as well. Initiative and commitment ebbed in the atmosphere of economic and political upheaval and were stifled by the autocracy that followed. Fourth-century Rome was a totalitarian police state that robbed its subjects of their independence and watched over them by means of a vast network of informers and secret agents. The collapse of such a state cannot be regarded as an unmitigated disaster. To many it must have seemed a blessing.

The West had always been poorer and less urbanized than the East, and its economy, badly shaken by the political chaos of the third century, began to break down under the growing burden of imperial government and the defense of hard-pressed frontiers. Perhaps the fatal flaw in the Western economy was its inability to compensate for the cessation of imperial expansion by more intensive internal development. There was no large-scale industry, no mass production; the majority of the population was far too poor to provide a mass market. Industrial production was exceedingly inefficient and technology progressed at a snail's pace. The economy remained fundamentally agrarian, and farming techniques advanced very little during the centuries of the Empire. The Roman plow was rudimentary and inefficient; windmills were unknown and water mills exceptional. The horse could not be used as a draught animal because the Roman harness crossed the horse's windpipe and tended to strangle him under a heavy load. Consequently, Roman agriculture was based on the less efficient ox and on the muscles of slaves and *coloni*.

Economic exhaustion brought with it the twin evils of population decline and creeping poverty; and at the very time that the manpower shortage was becoming acute and impoverishment was paralyzing the middle classes, the expenses of government were soaring. The army and bureaucracy steadily expanded until at length the state payroll contained more names than the tax rolls. One result of these processes was the deurbanization of the West. By the fifth century the once vigorous cities were becoming ghosts of their former selves, drained of their wealth and much of their population. Only the small class of great landowners managed to prosper in the economic atmosphere of the late Western Empire, and these men now abandoned their town houses, withdrew from civic affairs, and retired to their estates where they often assembled sizable private armies and defied the tax collector. The aristocracy, having now fled the city, would remain an agrarian class for the next thousand years. The rural nobility of the Middle Ages had come into being.

The decline of the city was fatal to the urbanized administrative structure of the Western Empire. More than that, it brought an end to the urban-oriented culture of Greco-Roman antiquity. The civilization of Athens, Alexandria, and Rome could not survive in the fields. It is in the decay of urban society that we find the crucial connecting link between political collapse and cultural transformation. In a very real sense Greco-Roman culture was dead long before the final demise of the Western Empire; the deposition of the last emperor in 476 was merely the faint postscript to a process that had been completed long before. By then the cities were moribund. The rational, humanist outlook had given way completely to transcendentalism and mysticism. The army and even the civil government had become barbarized as the desperate emperors, faced with a growing shortage of manpower and resources, turned more and more to Germanic peoples to defend their frontiers and keep order in their state. In the end, barbarians abounded in the army, entire tribes were hired to defend the frontiers, and Germanic military leaders came to hold positions of high authority in the Western Empire. Survival had actually come to depend on the success of half-hearted Germanic defenders against plunder-hungry Germanic invaders.

Despite the deurbanization, the mysticism, and the barbarism of the late Empire, it is nevertheless true that in a certain sense Greco-Roman culture never died in the West. It exerted a profound influence, as we have seen, on the Doctors of the Latin Church and, through them, on the minds of the Middle Ages. It was the basis of repeated cultural revivals, great and small, down through the centuries—in the era of Charlemagne, in the High Middle Ages, in the Italian Renaissance, and in the neoclassical eighteenth century. And if in one sense the Roman state was dead long before the line of Western emperors ended in 476, in another it survived long thereafter—in the ecclesiastical organization of the Roman Catholic Church and in the medieval Holy Roman Empire. Roman law endured to inspire Western jurisprudence; the Latin tongue remained the language of educated Europeans for more than a millennium while evolving in the lower levels of society into the Romance languages, Italian, French, Spanish, Portuguese, and Roumanian. In countless forms the rich legacy of classical antiquity was passed on to the Middle Ages. Europeans for centuries to come would be nourished by Greek thought and haunted by the memory of Rome.

THE GERMANIC PEOPLES

Medieval civilization owed much to its Greco-Roman heritage, but it drew sustenance also from the Judaeo-Christian and the Germanic cultural traditions. We have already observed the fusion of Greco-Roman and Christian culture in the Roman Empire, culminating in the work of Ambrose, Jerome, and Augustine. By the fifth century the fusion of these two traditions was essentially complete, but their integration with Germanic culture had only begun. Throughout the turbulent centuries of the Early Middle Ages the Greco-Roman-Christian tradition was preserved by the Church, whereas the Germanic tradition dominated the political and military organization of the barbarian states which established themselves on the carcass of the Western Empire. The Germanic invaders soon became at least nominal Christians, but for centuries a cultural gulf remained between the Church, with its Greco-Roman-Christian heritage, and the Germanic kingdoms with their primitive, war-oriented culture. The Church of the Early Middle Ages was able to preserve ancient culture only in a simplified and debased form, for as time went on ecclesiastical leaders and aristocratic laymen came more and more to be drawn from the same social milieu. Still, it remained the great task of the early medieval Church to civilize and Christianize the Germanic peoples. In the end the Classical-Christian-Germanic synthesis was achieved and a new Western European civilization came into being.

Most of the tribes that invaded the Western Empire seem to have come originally from the Scandinavian area, the homeland of the later Vikings. Gradually they migrated into Eastern and South-eastern Europe and began to press against the Rhine and Danube frontiers. It is hazardous to make broad generalizations regarding their culture and institutions, for customs varied considerably from tribe to tribe. The Franks, the Angles, and the Saxons, for example, were agrarian peoples whose movements were slow, but who, once settled, were difficult to displace. Little influenced by Roman civilization they came into the empire as heathens. The Visigoths, Ostrogoths, and Vandals, on the other hand, were far more mobile. All three had absorbed Roman culture to some degree before they crossed the frontiers, and all had been converted in the fourth century to Arian Christianity.

A good contemporary account of early Germanic institutions is to be found in a short book entitled *Germania* written by the Roman historian Tacitus in A.D. 98. This work is not entirely trustworthy; it is a morality piece written with the intention of criticizing the "degeneracy" of the Romans by comparing them unfavorably with the simple and upright barbarians. Nevertheless, it is an invaluable source of information on early Germanic customs and institutions. We can certainly accept Tacitus' description of the Germans as large men with reddish-blond hair and blue eyes, living in simple villages, but his eulogy of their virtue and chastity is a gross exaggeration. On the whole they appear to have been drunks, liars, and lechers, whose vices were certainly no less numerous than those of the Romans, only cruder. Their standards of personal hygiene are suggested by the observation of a fifth-century Roman gentleman: "Happy the nose that cannot smell a barbarian." *

Although the Germans used iron tools and weapons, their social and economic organization was in many ways reminiscent of the Neolithic culture stage. Their chief activities were tending crops or herds and fighting wars. The key social unit within the tribe had traditionally been the kindred group or clan, which protected the welfare of its members by means of the blood feud. When a man

---

* The author, some of whose best friends are of Frankish and Anglo-Saxon descent, disclaims any sort of ethnic bias. The crudeness of the barbarians was due entirely to their lack of social and educational opportunities.

was killed, his clan was bound to avenge his death by conducting a feud—declaring war, as it were—against the killer and his clan. In the boisterous atmosphere of the tribe, killings were only too common, and in order to keep the social fabric from being torn asunder by blood feuds it became customary for the tribe to establish a *wergeld*, a sum of money that the killer might pay to the relatives of his victim to appease their vengeance. Wergeld schedules became quite elaborate, the amount of money to be paid by the killer varying in accordance with the social status of his victim. Smaller wergelds were established for lesser injuries such as the cutting off of a victim's arm, leg, thumb, or finger. There was no guarantee, however, that the man who did the killing or maiming would agree to pay the wergeld, or that the victim or his clan would agree to accept it. In spite of the wergeld system, blood feuds continued far into the Middle Ages.

The ties of kinship were strong among the early Germans, but they were rivaled by those of another social unit, the war band or *comitatus*. Kinship played no part in this institution; it consisted rather of a group of warriors bound together by their loyalty to a chief or king. The comitatus was a kind of military brotherhood based on honor, fidelity, courage, and mutual respect between the leader and his men. In warfare the leader was expected to excel his men in courage and prowess, and should the leader be killed, his men were honor-bound to fight to the death even if their cause should appear hopeless. The heroic virtues of the comitatus persisted throughout the Early Middle Ages as the characteristic ideology of the European warrior nobility.

The comitatus and the clan were subdivisions of a larger unit, the tribe, whose members were bound together by their allegiance to a king and by their recognition of a body of customary law. Germanic law was arbitrary and childish compared with the majestic legal edifice of Rome. Procedural formalities were all important, and guilt or innocence was often determined by requiring the accused to grasp a bar of red-hot iron or to plunge his hand into a cauldron of boiling water. Nevertheless, throughout the Early Middle Ages the legal structure of the Western European states tended to be Germanic rather than Roman. It was not until the twelfth century that Roman law was revived in the West and began to make its influence felt once again. In the meantime, Germanic law, for all its crudeness, implanted one singularly fruitful idea in the Western mind: that law was a product not of the royal will but of the immemorial customs of the people. And if law could not be altered by the king, then royal authority could not be absolute. In the Early Middle Ages a number of Germanic kings had the customs of their people put into writing, but they rarely claimed the power to legislate on their own.

The centuries immediately preceding the invasions witnessed the development of relatively stable royal dynasties among many of the Germanic tribes. Perhaps an unusually gifted warrior with a particularly large comitatus might start such a dynasty, but before many generations had gone by the kings were claiming descent from some divine ancestor. When a king died, the assembly of the tribe chose as his successor the ablest member of his family. This might or might not be his eldest son, for the tribal assembly was given considerable latitude in its power to elect. The custom of election persisted in most Germanic kingdoms far into the Middle Ages. Its chief consequence during the fifth-century invasions was to insure that the barbarian tribes were normally led by clever, battle-worthy kings or chieftains at a time when the Western Empire was ruled by weaklings and fools.

Historians of previous centuries made much of the fact that certain Germanic institutions seemed to contain the seeds of constitutionalism and popular sovereignty. Democracy, so it was said, had its genesis in the forests of Germany. It should be obvious, however, that the veneration of a customary "law of the folk" or the political prominence of a tribal assembly is not uniquely Germanic but is common to many primitive peoples. The noteworthy thing about these institutions is not their existence among the Germanic barbarians but their endurance and development in the centuries that followed.

THE BARBARIAN INVASIONS

The Germanic peoples had long been a threat to the Empire. They had defeated a Roman army in the reign of Augustus; they had probed deeply into the Empire in the late second century and again in the mid-third century. But until the later fourth century the Romans had always managed eventually to drive the invaders out. Beginning in the mid-370s, however, an exhausted Empire was confronted by renewed barbarian pressures of an unprecedented magnitude. Lured by the relative wealth, the good soil, and the sunny climate of the Mediterranean world, the barbarians tended to regard the Empire not as something to destroy but as something to enjoy. Their age-long yearning for the fair lands across the Roman frontier was suddenly transformed into an urgent need by the westward thrust of a ferocious tribe of Asiatic nomads known as the Huns. These fierce horsemen conquered one Germanic tribe after another and turned them into satellites. The Ostrogoths fell before their might and became a subject people. The other great Gothic tribe, the Visigoths, sought to avoid a similar fate by appealing for sanctuary behind the Roman Danube frontier. The Eastern emperor Valens, a fervent Arian, sympathized with the Arian Visigoths, and in 376 the entire tribe crossed peacefully into the Empire.

There was trouble almost immediately. Corrupt imperial officials cheated and abused the Visigoths, and the hot-tempered tribesmen retaliated by going on a rampage. At length Emperor Valens himself took the field against them, but the emperor's military incapacity cost him his army and his life at the battle of Adrianople in 378. Adrianople was a military debacle of the first order. Valens' successor, the able Theodosius I, managed to pacify the Visigoths, but he could not expel them. When Theodosius died in 395 the Roman Empire was split among his two incompetent sons, and, as it happened, the Eastern and Western halves were never again rejoined. A vigorous new Visigothic leader named Alaric now led his people on a second campaign of pillage and destruction that threatened Italy itself. In 406 the desperate Western Empire recalled most of its troops from the Rhine frontier to block Alaric's advance, with the disastrous consequence that the Vandals and a number of other tribes swept across the unguarded Rhine into Gaul. Shortly thereafter the Roman legions abandoned distant Britain, and the defenseless island was gradually overrun by Angles, Saxons, and other barbarian war bands. In 408 the only able general in the West was executed by the frantic, incompetent Emperor Honorius who then abandoned Rome and took refuge behind the marshes of Ravenna. The Visigoths entered Rome unopposed in 410 and Alaric permitted them to plunder the city for three days.

The sack of Rome had a devastating impact on imperial morale, but in historical perspective it appears as a mere incident in the disintegration of the Western Empire. The Visigoths soon left the city to its feeble emperor and turned northward into Southern Gaul and Spain where they established a kingdom that endured until the Moslem conquests of the eighth century. Meanwhile other tribes were carving out kingdoms of their own. The Vandals swept through Gaul and Spain and across the Straits of Gibraltar into Africa. In 430, the very year of St. Augustine's death, they took his city of Hippo. A new Vandal kingdom arose in North Africa, centering on ancient Carthage. Almost immediately the Vandals began taking to the sea as buccaneers, devastating Mediterranean shipping and sacking one coastal city after another. Vandal piracy shattered the age-long peace of the Mediterranean and dealt a crippling blow to the waning commerce of the Western Empire.

Midway through the fifth century the Huns themselves moved against the West, led by their brilliant and pitiless leader Attila, the "Scourge of God." Defeated by a Roman-Visigothic army in Gaul in 451, they returned the following year, hurling themselves toward Rome and leaving a path of unimaginable devastation behind them. The Western emperor abandoned Rome to Attila's mercies, but the Roman bishop, Pope Leo I, traveled northward from the city to negotiate with the Huns on the wild chance that they might be persuaded to turn back. Oddly enough, Pope Leo succeeded in his mission. Perhaps because the health of the Hunnish army was adversely affected by the Italian climate, perhaps because the majestic Pope Leo was able to overawe the superstitious Attila, the Huns retired from Italy. Shortly afterward Attila died, the Hunnish empire collapsed, and the Huns themselves vanished from history. They were not mourned.

In its final years the Western Empire, whose jurisdiction now scarcely extended beyond Italy, fell under the control of hard-bitten military adventurers of Germanic birth. The emperors continued to reign for a time, but their Germanic generals were the powers behind the throne. In 476 the barbarian general Odovacar, who saw no point in perpetuating the farce, deposed the last emperor, sent the imperial trappings to Constantinople, and asserted his sovereignty over Italy by confiscating a good deal of farmland for the use of his Germanic troops. Odovacar claimed to rule as an agent of the Eastern Empire, but in fact he was on his own. A few years later the Ostrogoths, now free of Hunnish control and led by a brilliant king named Theodoric, advanced into Italy, conquered Odovacar, and established a strong state of their own.

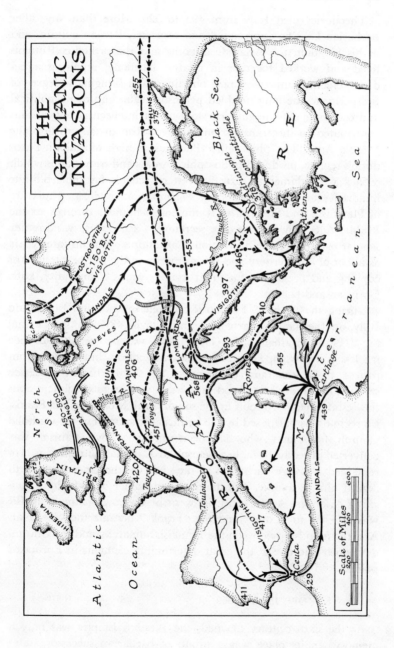

THE GERMANIC INVASIONS

Black Sea
Adrianople 378
Constantinople
Athens
Mediterranean Sea

HUNS 455
HUNS 375
453
446
VISIGOTHS 397
410
455
Rome 493
Visit Carthage
439
460
Italy 568
LOMBARDS
VANDALS 406
Troyes 451
FRANKS 420
Tours 507
Toulouse
VISIGOTHS 417
Ceuta
VANDALS 429
412

OSTROGOTHS C. 150 B.C.
VISIGOTHS
VANDALS
SUEVES
HUNS
SCANDIA
ANGLES 450–500
SAXONS
BRITAIN
PICTS
HIBERNIA

North Sea
Atlantic Ocean
Danube R.
EMPIRE

Scale of Miles
0   200   400   600

23

Theodoric ruled Italy from 493 to 526. More than any other barbarian king he appreciated and respected Roman culture, and in his kingdom the Arian Ostrogoths and the orthodox Romans lived and worked together in relative harmony, repairing aqueducts, erecting impressive new buildings, and bringing a degree of prosperity to the long-troubled peninsula. The improving political and economic climate gave rise to a minor intellectual revival that contributed to the transmission of Greco-Roman culture into the Middle Ages. The philosopher Boethius, a high official in Theodoric's regime, produced philosophical works and translations which served as fundamental texts in western schools for the next five hundred years. His *Consolation of Philosophy*, an interesting mixture of Platonism and Stoicism, was immensely popular throughout the Middle Ages. Theodoric's own secretary, Cassiodorus, was another scholar of considerable distinction. Cassiodorus spent his later years as abbot of a monastery and set his monks to the invaluable task of copying and preserving the great literary works of antiquity, both Christian and pagan.

During the years of Theodoric's beneficent rule in Ostrogothic Italy, another famous barbarian king, Clovis (481–511), was creating a Frankish kingdom in Gaul. Clovis was far less Romanized, far less enlightened, far crueler than Theodoric, but his kingdom proved to be the most enduring of all the barbarian successor states. The Franks were good farmers as well as good soldiers, and they established deep roots in the soil of Gaul. Moreover, the Frankish regime was buttressed by the enthusiastic support of the Catholic Church, for Clovis, who had been untouched by Arianism, was converted directly from heathenism to Catholic Christianity. He remained a savage barbarian to the end, yet the Church came to regard him as another Constantine, a defender of orthodoxy in a sea of Arianism. As the centuries went by the royal name "Clovis" was softened to "Louis" and the "Franks" became the "French." And the friendship between the Frankish monarchy and the Church developed into one of the great determining elements in European politics.

EUROPE IN A.D. 500

As the sixth century dawned, the Western Empire was only a memory. In its place was a group of barbarian successor states

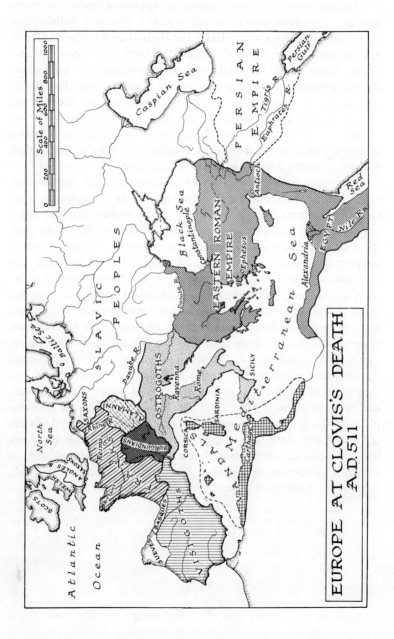

EUROPE AT CLOVIS'S DEATH
A.D. 511

that foreshadowed in certain respects the nations of modern Western Europe. Theodoric headed a tolerant and relatively enlightened Ostrogothic-Arian regime in Italy. The barbaric but orthodox Clovis was completing the Frankish conquest of Gaul. The Vandal monarchy, Arian in religion and increasingly corrupt and intolerant, lorded it over the restive population of North Africa. The Arian Visigoths were being driven out of southern Gaul by the Franks, but their regime continued to dominate Spain for the next two centuries. And the Angles and Saxons were in the process of establishing a group of small heathen kingdoms in Britain that would one day coalesce into "Angleland" or England.

At the very time that the Germanic kingdoms were establishing themselves in the West, the Roman papacy was beginning to play an important independent role in European society. We have seen how the great mid-fifth century pope, Leo I (440–461), assumed the task of protecting the city of Rome from the Huns, thereby winning for himself the moral leadership of Italy. Leo and his successors declared that the papacy was the highest authority in the Church, and, following the example of St. Ambrose, they insisted on the supremacy of Church over state in spiritual matters. In proclaiming its doctrines of papal supremacy in the Church and ecclesiastical independence from state control, the papacy was hurling a direct challenge at Byzantine Caesaropapism. In the fifth century these papal doctrines remained little more than words, but they were to result in an ever-widening gulf between the Eastern and Western Church. More than that, they constituted the opening phase of the prolonged medieval struggle between the rival claims of Church and state. The mighty papacy of the High Middle Ages was yet many centuries away, but it was already foreshadowed in the bold independence of Leo I. The Western Empire was dead, but eternal Rome still claimed the allegiance of the world.

CHRONOLOGY OF THE LATER EMPIRE

All Dates A.D.

 96–180: The age of the great second-century emperors
235–284: Height of the anarchy
185–254: Origen
205–270: Plotinus
284–305: Reign of Diocletian
306–337: Reign of Constantine
    325: Council of Nicaea
    330: Founding of Constantinople
354–430: St. Augustine of Hippo
    376: Visigoths cross Danube
    378: Battle of Adrianople
378–395: Reign of Theodosius I
    395: Final division of Eastern and Western Empires
    410: Alaric sacks Rome
    430: Vandals capture Hippo
451–452: Huns invade Western Europe
440–461: Pontificate of Leo I
    476: Last Western emperor deposed by Odovacar
493–526: Theodoric the Ostrogoth rules Italy
481–511: Clovis rules Franks, conquers Gaul

3

Byzantium Endures

THE SURVIVAL OF THE EAST ROMAN EMPIRE

By the opening of the sixth century the Western Empire had dissolved into a group of barbarian successor states, but the Eastern Empire continued to hold sway over a vast territory stretching from the Balkans to Asia Minor, Syria, Palestine, and Egypt. Many of the same forces that had weakened and demoralized the West operated in the East as well, yet imperial authority collapsed in the West and survived in the East. Why was this so?

For one thing, the East had always been more populous than the West. Its civilization was far older and more deeply rooted; its cities were larger and more numerous. The East had remained the commercial and industrial center of the Empire even in the great days of Rome, and when disaster struck it proved to be far more resilient than the West.

Asia Minor was the Eastern Empire's great reservoir of manpower and revenues (see map, p. 00). For many centuries it was to remain the chief recruiting ground for the Byzantine army and the most dependable source of imperial taxes. During the cataclysmic fifth century, while barbarians were conquering the Western provinces, Asia Minor was a bulwark of the empire. Its tough loyal troops provided the Eastern emperors with an invaluable alternative to the ruinous policy of complete dependence on hired Germanic armies.

28

Asia Minor was protected against the Germanic onslaught by impenetrable Constantinople. This great city, the New Rome, was the heart of the Eastern Empire. As long as it remained inviolate behind its great landward and seaward walls the Empire lived on. In later centuries enemies would sweep across the Empire to the very gates of Constantinople only to fall back in rage and frustration. In the seventh century Constantinople withstood a great Persian siege; in the eighth century it repelled the full fury of the all-conquering Moslems. Little wonder that the Germanic barbarians preferred the more vulnerable West. More than once, the East Roman government relieved itself of Germanic pressure by suggesting to the barbarians that if they moved West they might have better luck and easier conquests. Doubtless cynical, this suggestion was also true.

The Eastern Empire had the further advantage during the crucial fifth century of being much better governed than the Western Empire. A series of able Eastern emperors carefully husbanded their resources, fattened their treasury, and strengthened the fortifications of Constantinople while the Western Empire was collapsing. Superior leadership undoubtedly helped the East weather the storm, but its emperors could have accomplished little had it not been for the superb strategic location of their capital and the enduring commercial and human resources of the lands they ruled. The cradle of ancient civilizations had the strength to survive the barbarian flood that submerged the more recently civilized West.

BYZANTINE GOVERNMENT

The civilization of the Byzantine Empire was a synthesis of three elements: Roman government, Christian religion, and Greco-Oriental culture. From Rome the Eastern Empire drew its legal system, its bureaucracy, and its principles of administration. Indeed, Byzantine government was a direct offspring of the third- and fourth-century Roman political system. Byzantine autocracy had its roots in Diocletian's glorification of the emperor; Byzantine Caesaropapism evolved out of the Christian Empire of Constantine and Theodosius I. The heavy taxation of the late Roman emperors continued, and life in the Byzantine Empire remained burdensome and insecure.

The prevailing Byzantine mood was defensive and conservative. The state, oppressive though it was, had to be preserved at all costs. The swollen, tradition-bound bureaucracy abhorred novelty. It took no risks, resisted the bold policies of imaginative emperors, yet held the state together in eras of anarchy and incompetent rule. Corrupt and wasteful, the bureaucracy nevertheless contributed to the Empire's remarkable stability and endurance.

More efficient than the bureaucracy, the army was a relatively small but highly effective force, thoroughly trained and usually well led. In many wars the very survival of the Empire was at stake, and Byzantine generals, like Byzantine bureaucrats, took few risks. They preferred caution to daring, cunning to brute force. War was both an art and a science to the Byzantines, and although frequently outnumbered in the field they were seldom outmaneuvered or outfought. Still, the Empire often chose to pacify its enemies with tribute rather than take its chances against them in battle.

BYZANTINE CHRISTIANITY

It was Christianity that created the widespread dedication to the state so essential to Byzantium's age-long endurance. The orthodox Christians of the empire, although taxed to the ears and tormented by the arbitrary tyranny of the government, remained fervently committed to the sacred emperor. No mere secular sovereign, the emperor was the viceroy of God, and his state was the province of Christ. When Constantine founded Constantinople in 330 he dedicated the city to the Holy Trinity and the Blessed Virgin Mary, and the Byzantine Empire throughout its long history regarded itself as under their special protection. As the state went, so went the Church of Christ, or so the Byzantines believed. Their armies fought not merely for the Empire but for Almighty God; every war was a crusade. The fires of patriotism, nourished by the Christian Faith, burned more fiercely in Christian Byzantium than they ever had in pagan Rome.

The Byzantine emperors continued the tradition of Caesaropapism that began with Constantine. The Eastern Church worked in close partnership with the state, and the patriarch of Constantinople often took his orders from the sacred emperor. Even the decisions of general councils of the Church required imperial approval. But although the emperor's control of the Church magnified his power and earned for him the allegiance of the orthodox, it also multiplied his problems and responsibilities. Religious disputes became matters of imperial concern, and heresy was a threat to the state.

As it happened, the Eastern Church of the fifth and sixth centuries was torn by doctrinal controversies. The most prominent heresy of the age was a doctrine known as *Monophysitism* that arose in Egypt, spread to Syria and Palestine, and created in these regions a feeling of bitter hostility toward the orthodox emperors whose policies ranged from ineffective attempts at conciliation to naked persecution. The Monophysites were concerned above all with the nature of Christ. It had already been established, as a result of the Arian controversy, that Christ was fully human and fully divine, but the question remained, what precisely was the relationship between Christ's humanity and Christ's divinity? Was Christ in fact two persons, was he a single person with two natures, or was he one person with one nature in which humanity and divinity were blended? Each of these views had its adherents among the Christians of the fifth and sixth centuries. Orthodoxy was represented by the middle view—that Christ was one person with two natures— whereas the Monophysites clung passionately to the doctrine of a unified Christ with a single, blended nature. The Monophysites tended to regard Christ as more divine than human, and their doctrine has therefore been interpreted as a swing toward the spiritualism of the ancient Orient which scorned human nature and the physical universe. These "Christological" disputes may seem remote and meaningless to the twentieth-century mind, but they were enormously important in their day, and they created insoluble difficulties for the Eastern emperors. Religious unity was essential to the survival of their state, and as masters of the Eastern Church they were responsible for achieving and maintaining it. Several emperors sought to work out a compromise doctrine that would satisfy everyone—for example, that Christ had two natures but one *will*—but in fact they satisfied no one.

The West, which the emperors hoped one day to reconquer, was firmly orthodox and refused to accept any doctrinal formula that smelled even slightly of Monophysitism. In 451 a general council of the Church was held at Chalcedon, which fell under the influence of the great Roman pope, Leo I, and declared firmly in favor of the orthodox view of Christ, as one person with two natures. As a result, the Monophysites in Egypt formed a separate Church with its own hierarchy, traces of which exist to this day. In the years that followed, the emperors sought to win back the Monophysites, sometimes by compromise, sometimes by persecution. But Monophysitism remained an anti-imperial nucleus—a rallying point for nationalist separatism. When, in the seventh century, Moslem armies swept into the Empire they were welcomed by the Monophysites of Syria and Egypt, who preferred the relative tolerance of Arab rulers to the militant orthodoxy of the Christian emperors. Only when these rich but troublesome provinces were lost forever to the Empire could a final doctrinal settlement be achieved.

BYZANTINE CULTURE

From Rome the Eastern Empire drew its principles of law and government; from the Hellenized Christianity of the fourth-century Empire it drew its theology, its popular faith, its Caesaropapism; and from Greece it drew its language and its philosophical and literary inspiration. To the end, the Byzantines preserved and cherished their Greek heritage, but their enduring Hellenism was strongly modified by Christian and Oriental influences, particularly in the field of art, where they achieved a brilliant fusion of Hellenistic and Near-Eastern styles. The classical ideal of Greek and Roman antiquity—the massive, straightforward, marvelously proportioned buildings, the muscular, realistic sculpture—had been profoundly modified by the spiritual transformation of the third and fourth centuries. Throughout the fourth-century Roman Empire, the new mood of otherworldliness gave rise to new artistic values which deemphasized the earthly and the concrete, stressing instead religious symbolism and spiritual exaltation. The hero of the new age was the saint, and the artistic representation of human beings stressed their holiness rather than their physiological perfection. Typical of the new Christian art was the heavily robed, emaciated figure with slender, solemn face and deep eyes. Lost or ignored were the traditional Greco-Roman techniques of perspective, but in their place the Christian artists employed glittering, exuberant colors to convey a feeling of transcendental radiance akin to the glory of paradise. This new art, with its Oriental splendor and solemn grandeur, was ideally suited to the Byzantine spirit, and it dominated the Eastern Empire for the remainder of its history. Magnificent domed churches adorned the cities of the Empire, their interiors aglow with richly colored mosaic decorations worked on backgrounds of gold. The Byzantine artist strove not to portray nature but to transcend it, and even to this day a visitor stepping inside one of the great Byzantine churches—Sancta Sophia in Constantinople, St. Mark's in Venice—is struck with the feeling that he has suddenly stepped beyond this world altogether and into another. In short, the art of Byzantium was just as successful in achieving its objectives as was the very different art of Periclean Athens or Augustan Rome.

THE AGE OF JUSTINIAN

In the preceding pages we have been using the terms "Byzantine" and "East Roman" more or less interchangeably. It might well be asked, when did the Empire cease to be "East Roman" and become "Byzantine"? The question is impossible to answer since, as we have seen, the key elements of Byzantine civilization developed gradually out of the Roman political system of the fourth century. In general, the "Byzantinization" of the Eastern Empire involved a slow but steady shift from a westward to an eastward outlook, from Latin to Greek, and from classical to Oriental. Yet Byzantine art was Orientalized from the beginning and retained elements of Greco-Roman classicism to the end. The Byzantines never forgot their Greco-Roman heritage, nor did they forget that their ruler was a "Roman emperor." But as time progressed they became increasingly involved in their struggles with Eastern enemies—the Persians, the Moslems, and various tribes of Asiatic nomads. They forgot their Latin. They ceased to be seriously concerned with the Roman pope or the lost Western provinces. They turned their backs on Europe and their faces toward Asia.

In many respects the Emperor Justinian (527–565) was Constantinople's last Roman. Although his reign marks the first Golden Age of Byzantine art and the apogee of Byzantine Caesaropapism, Justinian was nevertheless a Latin-speaking emperor who was driven by the dream of reconstructing the old Roman Empire in all its former grandeur. The two great missions of his life were the codification of Roman law and the reconquest of the West.

Interior of San Vitale, Ravenna (526–547).

Female Martyrs, mosaic from S. Apollinare Nuovo, Ravenna
(493–525).

St. Mark's in Venice (begun in 1063).

When Justinian came to the throne in 527 the Eastern Empire was stronger than it had been for many decades. His predecessors had weathered the worst of the Germanic invasions and had accumulated a sizable financial reserve in the imperial treasury. Theodoric, the able ruler of Ostrogothic Italy, had died the year before, and several of the barbarian successor states in the West seemed to be losing their early vigor. A man of iron convictions, boundless energy, and intellectual distinction, Justinian renounced traditional Byzantine conservatism for a policy of bold resolution and audacity. The accomplishments of his reign were spectacular—and his empire almost perished from the strain.

Justinian received invaluable support and encouragement in the realization of his plans from his brilliant and beautiful wife—the ex-prostitute Theodora—and from a remarkable group of talented subordinates in the fields of law, administration, architecture, and warfare. But Justinian himself was the consummate genius of his age, the tireless executor of imperial policy, the "Emperor who never sleeps." He was a learned theologian who grappled energetically but vainly with the insoluble problem of reconciling orthodoxy and Monophysitism. He administered the *coup de grace* to dying paganism by closing the pagan schools at Athens, which had been in operation ever since the days of Aristotle and Plato. He was a great builder who lavished his resources on the beautification of Constantinople. Under his direction the most gifted architects of the age produced Byzantium's greatest artistic triumph—the Church of Sancta Sophia (the Holy Wisdom) in Constantinople. The interior of this magnificent structure, opulent with gold, silver, ivory, blazing mosaics, and precious gems, was crowned by a vast dome, an architectural marvel that seemed to float on air. The total effect was indescribable. Justinian is reported to have exclaimed at Sancta Sophia's dedication, "Glory to God who has judged me worthy of accomplishing such a work as this! O Solomon, I have outdone thee!"

Justinian was also one of the great creative figures in the history of law. He ordered that the vast body of precedents, juridical opinions, and imperial edicts of the Roman legal tradition be brought together into a single definitive body of civil law—the *Corpus Juris Civilis*. This monumental work, the product of a prodigious collective effort, thenceforth governed Byzantine jurisprudence. More

Sancta Sophia (The Church of Holy Wisdom) in Constantinople (532–537). The minarets are from a much later period.

than that, it was the vehicle through which Roman law was revived in twelfth-century Western Europe to inspire the legal systems of the European states. In Justinian's hands, Roman law became more rational and systematic than ever before, but it also took on an autocratic tone characteristic of his own age that would one day contribute to the growth of authoritarianism in the nations of the West. The monarchs of late medieval and early modern Europe were able to challenge the medieval Germanic notion of custom-based limitations on royal sovereignty by turning from the legal crudities of Germanic law to the sophisticated but autocratic principles of Justinian's great codification. For in the *Corpus Juris Civilis*, the collective legal wisdom of ancient Rome was colored by Jus-

37

tinian's own doctrine that law was the product of the ruler's will.

Obsessed with the glories of the Roman past, Justinian almost inevitably turned his attention to the reconquest of the West. He sent a small but well-trained army into North Africa, which, under the brilliant leadership of his general Belisarius, crushed the rotting Vandal regime in two quick battles. In 534 Belisarius occupied the former Vandal capital of Carthage, and two years later he led his forces into Italy hoping for an equally easy victory over the Ostrogoths. But Ostrogothic resistance proved unexpectedly tenacious. Only after an agonizing struggle of twenty years (535–555) were the Ostrogoths crushed and Italy returned to the Empire. Ironically, the devastation wrought by these "Gothic Wars" virtually annihilated the old civilization of Italy. The peninsula had thrived under the Ostrogoth Theodoric; now it was a desert. Rome had changed hands again and again during the long struggle and was now depopulated and demolished. Justinian, hoping to recapture the past, had only succeeded in destroying it.

Justinian's forces enjoyed some success against Visigothic Spain, occupying a large strip of land along the Mediterranean shore, but they were powerless to push back the entrenched Frankish regime in Gaul. In the end Justinian won control of most of the Mediterranean coastline but at tremendous cost. The conquered lands were too exhausted and impoverished to pay the heavy taxes necessary to support the protracted wars, and the imperial treasury was soon depleted. Justinian's greatest shortcoming was his inability to match ambitions to resources, and he left his Empire overextended and exhausted. In retrospect the reconquest of the West was a momentous blunder, yet it would be fatuous to criticize Justinian for seeking to re-establish Mediterranean unity and to recapture Rome. As a Roman emperor in the tradition of Augustus and Diocletian he was bound to make the attempt.

THE EASTWARD ORIENTATION

Justinian's later years were darkened by the increasing economic exhaustion of his Empire, the onslaught of a devastating plague, and growing bitterness between the orthodox and the Monophysites. The decades following his death in 565 saw a gradual transformation of imperial policy as the tottering Empire abandoned

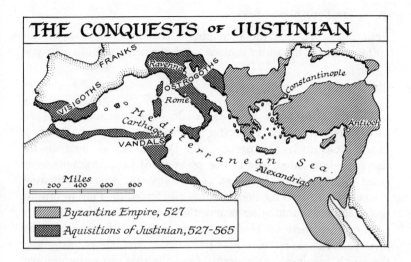

THE CONQUESTS OF JUSTINIAN

FRANKS
VISIGOTHS
Ravenna
OSTROGOTHS
Rome
Constantinople
Carthage
VANDALS
Mediterranean Sea
Antioch
Alexandria

Miles
0   200   400   600   800

Byzantine Empire, 527
Aquisitions of Justinian, 527-565

many of its newly conquered Western territories and summoned its remaining strength to ward off dangerous enemies from the north and east. Latin gave way to Greek as the language of the imperial administration, and the emperors were thenceforth known by the Greek title *Basileus* rather than *Caesar* or *Augustus*. The dream of a reconstituted Western Empire slowly dissolved. Three years after Justinian died, a savage Germanic tribe, the Lombards (Long Beards), broke into Italy and brought renewed devastation to the tormented Roman homeland. The Byzantines continued to hold much of southern Italy and a few coastal cities to the north, including their provincial capital of Ravenna, but elsewhere the Lombards raged unchecked. Within a few decades of Justinian's death the Visigoths had destroyed Byzantine power in southern Spain. North Africa remained in Byzantine hands for well over a century but fell eventually to the Moslems in the 690s.

In the meantime, Justianian's beleaguered successors were faced with the task of restoring the treasury and coming to grips with Eastern problems. Persia, relatively quiescent under Justinian, reasserted its dangerous pressure on the Eastern frontier, and from the seventh century onward Slavic tribes were pouring into the Balkans. A new tribe of Asiatic nomads, the Avars, looked hungrily at the wealth of Byzantium, and only heavy tribute payments succeeded in keeping them at bay. The preoccupation with the East and gradual abandonment of the West, the disappearance of Latin

39

from the court, and the increasing Orientalization of Byzantine
culture and the Byzantine outlook mark the beginning of a new era.

CRISIS AND SURVIVAL

The threat from the East reached its climax in the reign of the
able warrior-emperor Heraclius (610–641). For years Heraclius
fought desperately against powerful Persian armies bent on the
Empire's destruction, and at one point (626) Constantinople withstood a ferocious double siege of Persians and Avars. Ultimately
Heraclius destroyed the Persian army and forced the Persian Empire
to conclude a humiliating peace. But no sooner had the Persians
been crushed then the Moslems, fired by the new faith of Mohammed (d. 632), burst into Palestine, Syria, and Egypt, detaching
these rich provinces permanently from the rule of Constantinople.
Heraclius died exhausted and broken, and the Byzantine Empire
was reduced to Asia Minor, the Balkans, and a few scarcely defen-
sible territories far to the west, which would be lost during the
next century or so.

With the indispensable resources of Asia Minor still at its disposal
Byzantium survived. Constantinople underwent a fierce Moslem
siege in 717–18 but held firm. Indeed, in later centuries the Byzantines recovered their balance and extended their influence. They
converted the Slavs to Christianity and brought them into the fold
of the Eastern Church. They fought the Arabs to a standstill and
drove the nomads from the Balkans. They experienced new Golden
Ages of art and learning. Indeed, at the very moment of Constantinople's fall to the Turks in 1453, the empire was undergoing a
great classical-humanist revival that made a significant impact on
the culture of the Italian Renaissance.

THE BYZANTINE LEGACY

Throughout the Middle Ages Constantinople remained Europe's
eastern bastion against the Moslems. Its impregnable walls protected
not only the Byzantine Empire but Western Europe as well from
the ravages of Asiatic invaders. And the West was indebted to
Byzantium for far more than its soldiers and its walls. The Eastern
Empire served Western Europe and the world as a custodian of

classical culture. The writings of the Greek philosophers, for example, were with a few exceptions unknown in the early medieval West but were preserved and studied in Constantinople. The Byzantines systematized and perpetuated the great Roman legal heritage. Byzantine art influenced the work of Carolingian architects and medieval and Renaissance painters. Byzantine missionaries Christianized and civilized the Slavs and laid the political and theological foundation for Czarist Russia. Indeed, when Constantinople fell in 1453, Moscow became the third Rome: its rulers assumed the Byzantine mantle as Caesars or Czars, lording it over both Church and state just as their Byzantine predecessors had. It has even been suggested that the present rulers of Russia, with their control of both the State and the Communist ideological apparatus, are carrying on the tradition of Byzantine Caesaropapism in a secularized form.

Yet the Byzantine achievement had its limitations. Byzantium remained an autocracy to the end, and its creative genius was stunted by its profound conservatism. Its originality was limited largely to the realms of art and heresy. For most of its long history it was a society under siege, and so much of its energy was devoted to its own survival that little was left for social, political, or technological experimentation or bold philosophical speculation. It performed the priceless service of preserving the thought and letters of Greco-Roman antiquity, but to this magnificent legacy it added little of its own. Perhaps its heritage from classical antiquity was too complete; perhaps the Byzantines were so awed by the achievements of their Greco-Roman forebears that they were psychologically incapable of surpassing them or striking out in new directions. In this sense the Byzantines were prisoners of their own past. The sophistication of Constantinople stands in sharp contrast to the ignorance and barbarism of the early medieval West, but the West, for all its barbarism, had the inestimable advantage of a fresh start. Its relapse into intellectual twilight and semi-savagery resulted ultimately in its liberation from the dead hand of the past. The spirit of Greco-Roman antiquity inspired and enriched Western Christendom but did not shackle it.

4

The Barbarian West

TOWN AND COUNTRY

In the aftermath of the Germanic invasions Western Europe found itself cut adrift from the government of the Roman Empire. The Church survived to carry on much of the old classical legacy. But Germanic kings and nobles were generally incapable of preserving the political and economic institutions of the Roman past. Towns had been declining in Western Europe ever since the third century; by A.D. 600 they were shrunken phantoms of what they once had been. North of the Alps the municipal governments of antiquity had disappeared without a trace. But many of the towns themselves managed to endure, after a fashion, as centers of ecclesiastical administration. They remained the headquarters of episcopal government and the sites of the bishops' cathedral churches. Many towns became important pilgrimage centers, for the more important cathedral churches possessed relics—bones of dead saints for the most part—that were regarded as agents of spiritual and physical healing. The cathedral at Tours, for example, possessed the bones of the noted miracle-worker, St. Martin, which were said to heal any who touched them.

These episcopal centers played only a minor role in the culture and economy of the barbarian successor states. Far more important were the monastery, the peasant village, and the great farm or villa owned by some wealthy Roman or Germanic aristocrat and divided into small plots worked by semi-free tenant farmers. A small-scale luxury trade persisted, but by and large the economy of the sixth and seventh centuries was local and self-contained. Small agrarian communities produced most of their own needs, for their life was meager and their needs were few.

Except in Britain and northeastern Gaul the barbarians tended to become absorbed into the older indigenous population. Previously free Germanic farmers often descended into the ranks of the semi-servile *coloni*. But at the aristocratic level the pattern of life was set by the barbarian warrior nobility, and consequently the civility of the Roman villa gradually disappeared. The Roman and barbarian nobility were fused through intermarriage into one class— hard-bitten and warlike—far more Germanic than Roman.

GOVERNMENT; INTELLECTUAL LIFE

With the exception of Theodoric, the barbarian kings proved incapable of perpetuating the Roman administrative traditions that they inherited. They allowed the Roman tax system to break down completely; they permitted the privilege of minting coins to fall into private hands. The power and wealth of the state declined accordingly, not because the kings were generous but because they were ignorant. They lacked the slightest conception of responsible government and regarded their kingdoms as private estates to be exploited or alienated according to their whims. They made reckless gifts of land and public authority to nobles and churchmen and regarded what remained as their personal property, to be exploited for the sole purpose of their own enrichment. In brief, they succeeded in combining the worst features of anarchy and tyranny.

During the late Roman Empire Western Europe had been ruthlessly overgoverned; now it was radically undergoverned. The Germanic monarchs did precisely nothing to enliven the economy or ameliorate the general impoverishment. The Church strove to fill the vacuum by dispensing charity and glamorizing the virtue of resignation, but it was ill-equipped to cope with the chaos of the barbarian West. Its organization was confined largely to the defunct towns and walled monasteries. Only gradually were rural parishes organized to meet the needs of the countryside. Not until after the eighth century did the country parish become a characteristic feature of the Western Church. In the meantime a peasant was fortunate if he saw a priest once a year. The monarchy and the Church, the two greatest landholders in the barbarian states, were better known among the peasantry as acquisitive landlords than as fountains of justice and divine grace. Rural life was harsh, brutish, and short, and the countryside was politically and spiritually adrift.

The intellectual life of the barbarian West was almost as backward as its political and economic life. The culture of old Rome was rotting, and the new civilization of Western Europe had scarcely begun to develop. The intellectual level of the sixth and seventh centuries can best be appreciated by looking at a few leading scholars of the period. Bishop Gregory of Tours (d. 594), whose *History of the Franks* is our best source for the reigns of Clovis and his successors, must be counted one of the leading historians of his age. Yet Gregory's *History* is written in barbaric, ungrammatical Latin and is filled with outrageous and silly miracles. The world portrayed by Gregory of Tours was dominated by savage cruelty and naked force and beclouded by magic and superstitious fantasy. Both the story that he presents and the way in which he presents it attest to the radical decline of civilization in sixth-century Gaul.

Pope Gregory the Great (d. 604) was awarded a place alongside Ambrose, Jerome, and Augustine as one of the four Doctors of the Latin Church. But his writings, although marked by the profound practical wisdom and psychological insight of a potentially brilliant man, suffered from the cultural decadence of his age and are incomparably below the level of the fourth-century doctors in philosophical and scholarly sophistication. Pope Gregory's works had the effect of oversimplifying Augustinian theology and watering it down for the benefit of his own naive contemporaries. The lofty theological issues with which Augustine grappled are overshadowed in Pope Gregory's thought by a concentration on such matters as angels, demons, and relics.

Bishop Isidore of Seville (d. 636) was known as the foremost intellectual of his generation. His most impressive work, the *Etymologies*, was intended to be an encyclopedia of all knowledge. It was a valuable work for its time and was studied for many generations thereafter. But its value was vastly diminished by Isidore's remarkable lack of critical powers. He seems to have included every scrap of information that he could find, whether likely or unlikely, profound or absurd. It can perhaps be said that he was victimized by the credulity of the ancient writers on whom he depended, and left adrift by the weakness of the Roman scientific tradition. Nevertheless, as the greatest mind of his age, he was astonishingly naive. On the subject of monsters, for example, he writes as follows:

> The Cynocephali are so called because they have dogs' heads and their very barking betrays them as beasts rather than men. These are born in India. The Cyclopses, too, hail from India, and they are so named because they have a single eye in the midst of the forehead . . . . The Blemmyes, born in Lybia, are believed to be headless trunks, having mouth and eyes in the breast; others are born without necks, with eyes in the shoulders . . . . They say the Panotii in Sythia have ears of so large a size that they cover the whole body with them . . . . The race of the Sciopodes is said to live in Ethiopia. They have one leg apiece, and are of a marvelous swiftness, and . . . in summertime they lie on the ground on their backs and are shaded by the greatness of their feet.

Finally, in a burst of skepticism, Isidore concludes,

> Other fabulous monstrosities of the human race are said to exist, but they do not; they are imaginary.

In fairness to Isidore it should be said that his treatment of monsters fails to show him to best advantage, and that it was drawn from earlier materials dating from the ancient world. But he combined and synthesized these materials with an intellectual abandon typical of his age.

THE BARBARIAN KINGDOMS

The century between A.D. 500 and 600 witnessed important changes in the political structure of Western Christendom. In A.D. 500 Theodoric's Ostrogothic regime dominated Italy, the Vandals ruled North Africa, the Visigoths governed Spain, Clovis and his Franks were conquering Gaul, and the Anglo-Saxons were beginning their settlements in Britain. A century later, two of these states had been destroyed by Justinian's armies: North Africa was now

EUROPE AROUND 600

North Sea

SCOTS
PICTS
BRITONS
ANGLO SAXONS
SAXONS

Atlantic Ocean

BRITTANY
KINGDOM OF THE FRANKS
Rhine R.
Loire R.
Danube R.
AVARS

Rhone R.
Pavia
Genoa
KM. OF THE LOMBARDS
Venice
Ravenna

SUEVI TO 584
BASQUES

KINGDOM OF THE VISIGOTHS

BALEARICS

CORSICA
Rome
Naples
SARDINIA

Mediterranean
Carthage
SICILY
Sea

███ *Byzantine Empire*

Scale of Miles
0   200   400   600

Byzantine rather than Vandal, and the Ostrogothic kingdom of Italy had collapsed.

By 600 the Anglo-Saxon tribes had occupied much of Britain, enslaving many of the indigenous Celtic inhabitants and driving the rest into the western mountains of Wales. Anglo-Saxon Britain was now a confused medley of small, independent heathen kingdoms in which the process of Christian conversion was just beginning.

Gaul in 600 was thoroughly dominated by the Franks under the cruel and incompetent successors of Clovis, founder of the *Merovingian* dynasty.* This dynasty followed the Germanic custom of dividing the kingdom among the sons of a deceased ruler. Often the sons would engage in bitter civil war until, as it sometimes happened, one

* Named after Clovis' half-mythical ancestor, Merovech.

46

of them emerged as sole monarch of the Franks. He would then die, dividing the kingdom among *his* sons, and the bitter comedy would be repeated. Merovingian government was predatory and unenlightened; the Merovingian Church became disorganized and corrupt.

Corruption was also paralyzing Church and state in Visigothic Spain. The monarchy, converted in 589 from Arianism to Catholicism, was able at length to reconquer its Mediterranean shore from feeble Byzantium (*c.* 624). But the inept Visigothic kings allowed their power to slip little by little into the hands of a greedy and oppressive landed aristocracy. The worm-eaten regime was an easy prey for the conquering Moslems in the early 700s.

The century since Theodoric's reign had been a disastrous one for Italy. The horrors of Justinian's Gothic wars were followed by the invasion of the savage Lombards. By 600 the decimated peninsula was divided between the Byzantines in Ravenna and the south, and the Lombards in the north. The papacy, under nominal Byzantine jurisdiction, dominated the lands around Rome and sought to preserve its fragile independence by playing Lombard against Byzantine.

CREATIVE FORCES

Such was the condition of Western Europe in 600. At first glance one can see little to hope for in the all-prevailing gloom. Yet this was the society out of which Western civilization was born. This was the formative epoch—the age of genesis—in which apparently minor trends would one day broaden into the powerful traditions that would govern the course of European history. Even in 600 there were glimmerings of light in the darkness. Classical culture still survived, if only in a sadly vulgarized form. Isidore of Seville was no Augustine, but he was far more than a mere barbarian. The Church, although tainted by the ignorance and corruption of its environment, still retained something of its power to inspire, to enlighten, and to civilize.

Far to the north, Ireland had been won for Christianity by St. Patrick in the fifth century; by 600 it had developed an astonishingly creative Celtic-Christian culture. Irish scholars were familiar with both Greek and Latin literature at a time when Greek was unknown elsewhere in the West. By the later seventh century Irish artists were producing magnificent illuminated manuscripts in a flowing, curvilinear Celtic style. Irish Christianity, isolated from the continental Church by the heathen Anglo-Saxon kingdoms, developed distinctive customs of its own. It was organized around the monastery rather than the diocese, and its leaders were abbots rather than bishops. Irish monks were famous for their learning, the austere holiness of their lives, and the vast scope of their missionary activities. They converted large portions of Scotland to their own form of Christianity and by the early 600s were conducting missionary activities on the Continent itself.

Monasticism was the most dynamic and significant institution in the Early Middle Ages. The impulse toward monastic life is not peculiar to Christianity but is found in many religions—Buddhism and Judaism, to name but two. The Essenes, for example, whose cult may have produced the famous Dead Sea scrolls, constituted a kind of Jewish monastic order. There have always been religious souls who longed to withdraw from the world and devote their lives to uninterrupted communion with God, but among Christians this impulse was particularly strong. Monasticism came to be regarded as the most perfect form of the Christian life—the consummate embodiment of Christ's own words: "And every man that has forsaken home, or brothers, or sisters, or father, or mother, or wife, or children, or lands for my name's sake, shall receive his reward a hundredfold, and obtain everlasting life" (Matt., XIX, xxix).

The impulse toward withdrawal and renunciation first affected Christianity in the later third century when the Egyptian St. Anthony retired to the desert to live the ascetic life of a godly hermit. In time the fame of his sanctity spread, and a colony of would-be ascetics gathered around him to draw inspiration from his holiness. Saint Anthony thereupon organized a community of hermits who lived together but had no communication with one another, like apartment dwellers in a large American city. Similar hermit communities soon arose throughout Egypt and spread into other regions of the Empire. Hermit saints abounded in the fourth and fifth centuries. One of them, St. Simeon Stylites, achieved the necessary isolation by living atop a sixty-foot pillar for thirty years, evoking widespread admiration and imitation.

In the meantime a more down-to-earth type of monasticism was developing. Beginning in early fourth-century Egypt and then expanding quickly throughout the Roman Empire, monastic communities, based on a cooperative rather than a hermit life, were attracting numerous fervent Christians who found insufficient challenge in the increasingly complacent post-Constantine Church. The holy individualism of the desert and pillar saints thus gave way to a more ordered monastic life. Still, the early communities remained loosely organized and continued to emphasize the ascetic practices of severe fasting, hair shirts, and purifying lashings, which had been pioneered by the hermits.

ST. BENEDICT AND HIS RULE

Saint Benedict of Nursia (*c.* 480–544) changed the course of Western monasticism, tempering its flamboyant holiness with common sense and realistic principles of organization. As a youth, St. Benedict fled corrupt Rome and took up the hermit life in a cave near the ruins of Nero's country palace. In time word of his saintliness circulated and disciples gathered around him. As it turned out, Benedict was more than a mere ascetic; he was a man of keen psychological insight—a superb organizer who slowly learned from the varied experiences of his youth how the monastic life might best be lived. Born of a Roman aristocratic family, he possessed a practical genius and a sense of order and discipline that were typically Roman. He founded a number of monasteries, which drew not only prospective saints but ordinary people as well—even the sons of wealthy Roman families. At length he established his great monastery of Monte Cassino atop a mountain midway between Rome and Naples. For centuries thereafter Monte Cassino was one of the chief centers of religious life in Western Europe. It became a model monastery, governed by a comprehensive, practical, compassionate rule. In the midst of Justinian's Gothic Wars, St. Benedict died, but his rule survived to inspire and transform Western Europe.

Pope Gregory the Great described the Rule of St. Benedict as "conspicuous for its discretion." It provided for a busy, closely regulated life, simple but not excessively ascetic. Benedictine monks were decently clothed, adequately fed, and seldom left to their own devices. Theirs was a life dedicated to God and to the attainment of personal sanctity, yet it was also a life that could be led by any dedicated Christian. It was rendered all the more attractive by the increasing brutality of the outside world. The monastic day was filled with carefully arranged activities: communal prayer, devotional reading, and work—field work, household work, manuscript copying—according to the needs of the monastery and the ability of the monk. The fundamental obligations were chastity, poverty, and obedience; the monk must be celibate; he must discard all personal possessions; he must obey his abbot. The abbot, elected by the monks for life, was unquestioned master of the monastery, but he was to consult the monks in all his decisions. He was strictly responsible to God and was instructed to govern justly in accordance with the Rule. He was cautioned not to sadden or "overdrive" his monks or give them cause for "just murmuring." Here especially is the quality of discretion to which Pope Gregory alludes and which doubtless has been the major factor in the Rule's success.

CONTRIBUTIONS OF THE BENEDICTINES

Within two centuries after Benedict's death the Rule had spread throughout Western Christendom. The result was not a vast hierarchical monastic organization but rather a host of individual, autonomous monasteries sharing a single Rule and way of life but administratively unrelated. Benedict had visualized his monasteries as spiritual sanctuaries into which pious men might withdraw from the world. But the chaotic and illiterate society of the barbarian West, desperately in need of the discipline and learning of the Benedictines, could not permit them to abdicate from secular affairs.

In reality, therefore, the Benedictines had an enormous impact on the world they renounced. Their schools produced the vast majority of literate Europeans during the Early Middle Ages. They served as a cultural bridge, transcribing and preserving the writings of Latin antiquity. They spearheaded the penetration of Christianity into the forests of heathen Germany and later into Scandinavia, Poland, and Hungary. They served as scribes and advisers to kings, and were drafted into high ecclesiastical offices. As recipients of gifts of land from pious donors over many generations they held and managed

vast estates, which became models of intelligent agricultural organization and technological innovation. With the coming of feudalism,
Benedictine abbots became great vassals, responsible for political
and legal administration and military recruitment over the large
areas under their control. Above all, as islands of security and learning in an ocean of barbarism the Benedictine monasteries were the
spiritual and intellectual centers of the developing classical-Christian-
Germanic synthesis that underlay European civilization. In short,
Benedictine monasticism became the supreme civilizing influence in
the barbarian West.

POPE GREGORY THE GREAT (590-604)

The Benedictines carried out their great civilizing mission with
the enthusiastic and invaluable support of the papacy. The alliance between these two institutions was consummated by the first
monk to become a pope, Gregory the Great, who recognized immediately how effective the Benedictines might be in spreading
the Catholic faith and extending papal leadership far and wide
across Christendom.

We have already encountered Pope Gregory as a Dark Age
scholar—a popularizer of Augustinian thought. His theology, although highly influential in subsequent centuries, failed to rise
much above the intellectual level of his age. His real genius lay in
his keen understanding of human nature and his ability as an administrator and organizer. His *Pastoral Care*, a treatise on the duties and
obligations of a bishop, is a masterpiece of practical wisdom and
common sense. It answered a great need of the times and became
one of the most widely read books in the Middle Ages.

Gregory loved the monastic life and ascended the papal throne
with genuine regret. On hearing of his election he went into hiding
and had to be dragged into the Roman basilica of St. Peter's to be
consecrated. But once resigned to his new responsibilities, Gregory
devoted all his energy to the extension of papal authority. Following in the tradition of Pope Leo I, Gregory the Great believed
fervently that the pope, as successor of St. Peter, was the rightful
ruler of the Church. He reorganized the financial structure of the
papal estates and used the increased revenues for charitable works
to ameliorate the wretched poverty of his age. His integrity, wisdom,

and administrative ability won for him an almost regal position in Rome and central Italy, towering over the contemporary Lombards and Byzantines who were then struggling for control of the peninsula. The reform of the Frankish Church was beyond his immediate powers. But he set in motion a process that would one day bring both France and Germany into the papal fold when he dispatched a group of Benedictine monks to convert heathen England.

THE CONVERSION OF ENGLAND

The mission to England was led by the Benedictine St. Augustine (not to be confused with the great theologian of an earlier day, St. Augustine of Hippo). In 597, Augustine and his followers arrived in the English kingdom of Kent and began their momentous work. England was then divided into a number of independent barbarian kingdoms of which Kent was momentarily the most powerful, and Augustine was assured a friendly reception by the fact that the king of Kent had a Christian wife. The conversion progressed speedily, and on Whitsunday, 597, the king and thousands of his subjects were baptized. The chief town of the realm, "Kent City" or Canterbury, became the headquarters of the new Church, and Augustine himself became Canterbury's first archbishop.

During the decades that followed, the fortunes of English Benedictine Christianity rose and fell with the varying fortunes of the barbarian kingdoms. Kent declined, and by the mid-600s political power had shifted to the northernmost of the Anglo-Saxon states, Northumbria. This remote outpost became the scene of a deeply significant encounter between the two great creative forces of the age: Irish-Celtic Christianity moving southward from its monasteries in Scotland, and Roman-Benedictine Christianity moving northward from Kent.

Although the two movements shared a common faith, they had different cultural backgrounds, different notions of monastic life and ecclesiastical organization, and even different systems for calculating the date of Easter. At stake was England's future relationship with the Continent and the papacy; a Celtic victory might well have resulted in the isolation of England from the main course of Western Christian development. But at the Synod of Whitby in 664,

King Oswy of Northumbria decided in favor of Roman-Benedictine Christianity, and papal influence in England was assured. Five years later, in 669, the papacy sent the scholarly Theodore of Tarsus to assume the archbishopric of Canterbury and reorganize the English Church into a coherent hierarchical system. As a consequence of Northumbria's conversion and Archbishop Theodore's tireless efforts, England, only a century out of heathenism, became Europe's most vigorous and creative Christian society.

The Irish-Benedictine encounter in seventh-century Northumbria produced a significant cultural surge known as the Northumbrian Renaissance. The two traditions influenced and inspired one another to such an extent that the evolving civilization of the barbarian West reached its pinnacle in this remote land. Boldly executed illuminated manuscripts in the Celtic curvilinear style, a new script, a vigorous vernacular epic poetry, an impressive architecture—all contributed to the luster of Northumbrian civilization in the late 600s and the early 700s. This Northumbrian Renaissance centered in the great monasteries founded by Irish and Benedictine missionaries, particularly in the Benedictine monastery of Jarrow. Here the supreme scholar of the age, St. Bede the Venerable, spent his life.

Bede entered Jarrow as a child and remained there until his death in 735. The greatest of his many works, the *Ecclesiastical History of England*, displays a keen critical sense far superior to that of Bede's medieval predecessors and contemporaries. The *Ecclesiastical History* is our chief source for early English history. It reflects a remarkable cultural breadth and a penetrating mind, and establishes Bede as the foremost Christian intellectual since Augustine.

By Bede's death in 735 the Northumbrian kings had lost their political hegemony, and Northumbrian culture was beginning to fade. But the tradition of learning was carried from England back to the Continent during the eighth century by a group of intrepid Anglo-Saxon Benedictine missionaries. In the 740s the English monk St. Boniface reformed the Church in Frankland, infusing it with Benedictine idealism and binding it more closely to the papacy. Pope Gregory had now been in his grave for 140 years, but his spirit was still at work. St. Boniface and other English missionaries founded new Benedictine monasteries among the Germans east of the Rhine and began the long and difficult task of Christianizing and civilizing these savage peoples, just as Augustine and his monks had

Cross Page from the *Lindisfarne Gospels* (*c.* A.D. 700), illustrating the artistic illuminations typical of the Northumbrian Renaissance.

once Christianized heathen Kent. By the later 700s the cultural center of Christendom had shifted southward again from England to the rapidly rising empire of the Frankish leader Charlemagne, whose career will be traced in Chapter 6. Significantly, the leading scholar in Charlemagne's kingdom was Alcuin, a Benedictine monk from Northumbria.

THE CHURCH AND WESTERN CIVILIZATION

The barbarian West differed from the Byzantine East in innumerable ways, the most obvious being its far lower level of civilization. But even more important is the fact that the Western Church was able to reject Byzantine Caesaropapism and to develop more or less independently of the state. Church and state often worked hand in hand, yet the two were never merged as they were in Constantinople and, indeed, in most ancient civilizations. The early Christian West was marked by a profound dichotomy—a separation between cultural leadership, which was ecclesiastical and monastic, and political power, which was in the hands of the barbarian kings. This dualism underlay the fluidity and dynamism of Western culture. It produced a creative tension that tended toward change rather than crystallization, toward an uninterrupted series of cultural climaxes, and toward ever-new intellectual and spiritual configurations. Like St. Augustine's two cities, the heroic warrior culture of the Germanic states and the classical-Christian culture of Church and monastery remained always in the process of fusion yet never completely fused. The interplay between these two worlds governed the development of medieval civilization.

5

The Explosion of Islam

ISLAM, BYZANTIUM, AND WESTERN CHRISTENDOM

Islam, Byzantium, and Western Christendom were Rome's three heirs, and of the three, Western Christendom remained for many centuries the most primitive and underdeveloped. Medieval Europe had much to learn from Islam and Byzantium, and its developing synthesis of classical, Christian, and Germanic traditions was shaped in many ways by its two neighboring civilizations. The influence of these neighbors was impeded, however, by Europe's profound hostility toward the "infidel" Moslems and the "effete, treacherous" Byzantines. In the eighth and ninth centuries Western Europe's contacts with Islam were limited largely to the battlefield. Only after the turn of the millennium did the West begin to draw upon the rich legacy of Moslem thought and culture.

MOHAMMED (c. 571–632)

Islam made its unexpected debut early in the seventh century and developed with astonishing speed into a great, cohesive civilization extending from India to Spain. The birthplace of this compelling new faith was the Arabian Peninsula—the modern Saudi Arabia—which for countless centuries had harbored fierce nomadic tribes that erupted periodically into the rich civilized districts of Palestine, Syria, and Mesopotamia to the north. The many Semitic invaders of the Ancient Near East seem to have come originally from the Arabian Desert—the Amorites, the Chaldeans, the Canaanites, even the Hebrews. These peoples quickly assimilated the ancient civilization of the Fertile Crescent and developed it in new, creative ways, but their kinsmen who stayed in Arabia remained primitive and disorganized.

In Mohammed's time most Arabians still clung to their nomadic ways and to their crude, polytheistic religion, but by then new civilizing influences were beginning to make themselves felt. A great caravan route running northward from southern Arabia served as an important link in a far-flung commercial network between the Far East and the Byzantine and Persian Empires. Along this route cities developed to serve the caravans, and with city life came a modicum of civilization. Indeed, the greatest of these trading cities, Mecca, became a bustling commercial center that sent its own caravans northward and southward and grew wealthy on its middleman profits. At Mecca and other caravan cities tribal life was beginning to give way to commercial life, and new, foreign ideas were beginning to challenge old ways and old points of view. It was in Mecca, around the year 571, that the prophet Mohammed was born.

At Mohammed's birth, the Emperor Justinian had been in his grave for six years. Mohammed's contemporaries include such men as Emperor Heraclius, Pope Gregory the Great, and Bishop Isidore of Seville. When the Benedictine mission from Rome landed in Kent in 597 to begin the conversion of England, Mohammed was in his twenties and was as yet unknown outside of his own immediate circle.

He was born of a poor branch of Mecca's leading clan. With little formal education behind him, he became a caravan trader, and his travels brought him into close contact with Judaism, Christianity, and Persian Zoroastrianism. A nervous, sensitive man with a powerful, winning personality, he received God's call while in his late thirties and began to promulgate his new faith by preaching and writing. He won little support in Mecca apart from his wife and relatives and a few converts from the underprivileged classes. The Meccan commercial oligarchy seemed immune to the teaching of this low-born upstart. Perhaps they feared that his new religion would discredit the chief Meccan temple, the *Kaaba*, which housed a sacred meteoritic stone and was a profitable center of pilgrimages. Their belief that Mohammed's faith would ruin Mecca's pilgrim business was an ironic miscalculation, but their hostility to the new teaching prompted Mohammed to flee Mecca in 622 and settle in the town of Medina, 280 miles northward on the caravan route.

The flight to Medina, known among the Moslems as the Hegira (He-jī'-ra), was a momentous turning point in the development of Islam and marks the beginning date of the Moslem calendar. Mohammed quickly won the inhabitants of Medina to his faith and became the city's political chief as well as its religious leader. Under Mohammed's direction, religious and civil authority were fused. The sacred community was at once a state and a church, and in this respect it foreshadowed later Islamic Civilization.

The Medinans made war on Mecca, raiding its caravans and blockading its trade. In 630 Medina conquered Mecca and incorporated it into the sacred community, and during the two remaining years of his life Mohammed, now an almost legendary figure in Arabia, received the voluntary submission of many of the tribes in the peninsula. By the time of his death in 632 he had united the Arabians for the first time into a coherent political-religious group, well-organized, well-armed, and inspired by a powerful new monotheistic religion. The violent energies of these desert people were now channeled toward a single lofty goal—the conquest and conversion of the world.

ISLAMIC RELIGION

Faith was the cement with which Mohammed unified Arabia. The new faith was called *Islam*, the Arabic word for "surrender." Mohammed taught that his followers must surrender to the will of Allah, the single, almighty God of the universe. Allah's attributes of love and mercy were overshadowed by those of power and majesty, and the greatest good was therefore not to love God but to submit to his commands. Mohammed was not regarded as divine. Rather, he was the last and greatest of a long line of prophets of whom he was the "seal." Among his predecessors were Moses, the Old Testament prophets, and Jesus.

Islam respected the Old and New Testaments and was relatively tolerant toward Jews and Christians—the "people of the book." But the Moslems had a book of their own, the *Koran*, which superseded its predecessors and was believed to contain the pure essence of divine revelation. The *Koran* is the comprehensive corpus of Mohammed's writings, the bedrock of the Islamic faith: "All men and jinn in collaboration could not produce its like." Moslems regard it as the word of Allah, *dictated* to Mohammed by the angel Gabriel from an original "uncreated" book located in heaven. Accordingly, its inspiration and authority extend not only to its meaning but also to its every letter, of which there are 323,621, and it loses its inspiration in translation. Every good Moslem must therefore read the *Koran* in Arabic, and as Islam spread, the Arabic language necessarily spread with it.

The *Koran* is perhaps the most widely read book ever written. More than a manual of worship, it was the text from which the non-Arabian Moslem learned Arabic. It was the supreme authority not only in religion but also in law, science, and the humanities, and it therefore became the standard text in Moslem schools for every imaginable subject. Mohammed's genius is illustrated vividly by his success in adapting a primitive language such as seventh-century Arabic to the sophisticated religious, legal, and ethical concepts that one encounters in his sacred book.

Mohammed offered his followers the assurance of eternal bliss if they led upright, sober lives and followed the precepts of Islam. Above all, they were bound to a simple confession of faith: "There is no god but Allah, and Mohammed is his prophet." The good Moslem was also obliged to engage in ritualistic prayers and fasting, to journey as a pilgrim to Mecca at least once in his lifetime, and to work devoutly toward the welfare and expansion of the sacred community. Holy War was the supremely meritorious activity, for service to the faith was identical with service to the state. Public law in Islamic lands had a religious sanction, and the fusion of religion and politics that Mohammed created at Medina remained a fundamental characteristic of Islamic society. There was no Moslem priesthood, no Moslem "Church" apart from the state; Mohammed's political successors, the caliphs, were defenders of the faith and guardians of the faithful. The creative tension between Church and state which proved such a stimulus to medieval Europe was unknown in the Moslem World.

THE EARLY CONQUESTS: 632–655

Immediately after Mohammed's death the explosive energy of the Arabs, harnessed at last by the teachings of the Prophet, broke upon the world. The spectacular conquests that followed resulted in part from the youthful vigor of Islam, in part from the weakness and exhaustion of its enemies. Emperor Heraclius had just defeated the Persians, and both Byzantium and Persia were spent and enfeebled by their long and desperate conflict. And the Monophysites of Syria and Egypt remained deeply hostile to their orthodox Byzantine masters.

The Arabs entered these tired, embittered lands afire with religious zeal, lured by the wealth and luxuries of the civilized world. They had no master plan of conquest—most of their campaigns began as plundering expeditions—but unexpected victories resulted in an ever-accumulating momentum. Moving into Byzantine Syria they annihilated a huge Byzantine army in 636, captured Damascus and Jerusalem, and by 640 had occupied the entire land, detaching it permanently from Byzantine control. In 637 they inflicted an overwhelming defeat on the Persian army and entered the Persian capital of Ctesiphon, gazing in bewilderment at its opulence and wealth. Within another decade they had subdued all Persia and arrived at the borders of India. In later years they penetrated deeply into the Indian subcontinent and laid the foundations of modern Moslem Pakistan. The inhabitants of the Persian Empire gradually adopted the Islamic faith and the Arab language. They were destined in later years to play a central role in Islamic politics and culture.

Meanwhile the Moslems were pushing westward into Egypt. They captured Alexandria in the 640s, thus absorbing the great metropolis that had been a center of Greek culture ever since the Hellenistic Age. With Egypt and Syria in their hands they took to the sea, challenging the long-established Byzantine domination of the eastern Mediterranean. They captured the island of Cyprus, raided ancient Rhodes, and in 655 won a major victory over the Byzantine fleet.

THE CIVIL WAR: 655–661

In 655 Islamic expansion ceased momentarily as the new empire became locked in a savage dynastic struggle. The succession to the caliphate was contested between the Omayyads, a leading family in the old Meccan commercial oligarchy—late to join the Islamic bandwagon but no less ambitious for all that—and Ali, the son-in-law of Mohammed himself. Ali headed a faction that was to become exceedingly powerful in later centuries. His followers insisted that the caliph must be a direct descendant of the Prophet. As it happened, Mohammed had left no surviving sons, and only one daughter, Fatima, who married the Prophet's cousin, Ali.

In 661 the Omayyad forces vanquished those of Ali in battle and initiated an Omayyad dynasty of caliphs that held power for nearly a century. But the legitimist faction that had once supported Ali persisted as a troublesome, dedicated minority, throwing its support behind various of the numerous progeny of Ali and Fatima. In time the political movement evolved into a heresy known as *Shi'ism*, which held that the *true* caliphs—the descendents of Mohammed through Fatima and Ali—were sinless, infallible, and possessed of a body of secret knowledge not contained in the *Koran*. Shi'ism became an occult underground doctrine which occasionally rose to the surface in the form of civil insurrection. In the tenth century it gained control of Egypt and established a "Fatimid" dynasty of caliphs in Cairo. It inspired an infamous band of Moslem desperados known as the "Assassins" and survives to this day in the Ismaili sect led by the Aga Khan.

THE OMAYYAD DYNASTY: 661–750

The intermission in the Moslem expansion ended with the Omayyad victory over Ali in 661. The capital of the growing Islamic Empire, which had been at Medina before the civil war, was now moved to Damascus in Syria, but the old Arabian aristocracy exerted a firm control over Islam. Constantinople was now the primary military goal, but the great city on the Bosporus hurled back a series of powerful Moslem attacks between 670 and 680. The Byzantine defense was aided by a remarkable secret weapon known as "Greek Fire," a liquid which ignited on exposure to air and could not be extinguished by water, but only by vinegar or sand. In 717–718 a great Arab fleet and army assaulted Constantinople in vain, and having expended all their energies and resources without success the Moslems abandoned their effort to take the city. Byzantium survived for another seven centuries, and the Mos-

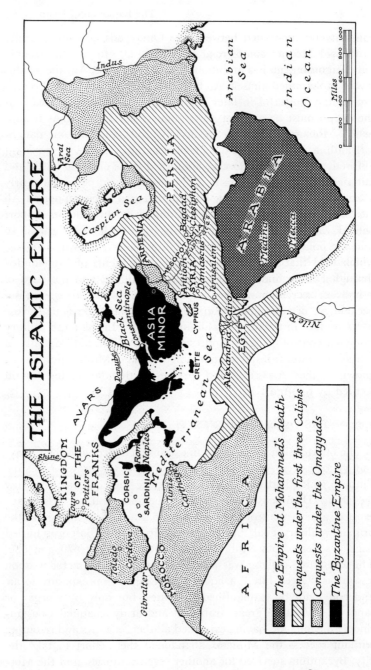

THE ISLAMIC EMPIRE

The Empire at Mohammed's death
Conquests under the first three Caliphs
Conquests under the Omayyads
The Byzantine Empire

Miles
0 200 400 600 800 1000

Indus

Aral Sea

Caspian Sea

PERSIA

ARMENIA

Arabian Sea

Indian Ocean

ARABIA

Medina

Mecca

MESOPOTAMIA

Bagdad

Antioch

Ctesiphon

SYRIA

Euphrates

Damascus

Tigris

Jerusalem

Black Sea

Constantinople

ASIA MINOR

CYPRUS

CRETE

Mediterranean Sea

Alexandria

Cairo

EGYPT

Nile R.

Danube

AVARS

Rhine

KINGDOM OF THE FRANKS

Tours

Poitiers

Rome

Naples

CORSICA

SARDINIA

Tunis

Carthage

MOROCCO

Gibraltar

Cordova

Toledo

AFRICA

lems were effectively barred from southeastern Europe for the remainder of the Middle Ages.

In the meantime, however, Moslem armies were enjoying spectacular success in the West. From Egypt they moved westward along the North African coast into the old Vandal kingdom, now ruled by distant Byzantium. In 698 the Moslems took Carthage. In 711 they crossed the Straits of Gibraltar into Spain and crushed the tottering Visigothic kingdom at a blow, driving Christianity into the fastness of the Pyrenees Mountains. Next the Moslems moved into southern Gaul and threatened the kingdom of the Merovingian Franks. In 733, 101 years after the Prophet's death, the Moslems were halted at last at the battle of Tours* by a determined Christian army led by the brilliant Frankish nobleman, Charles Martel. The Christians at Tours were not the sort that we imagine when singing "Onward Christian Soldiers." They were semi-barbarous Franks clad in wolf skins, their tangled hair hanging down to their shoulders. But they managed to halt the momentum of militant Islam in Western Europe, just as the Byzantines had stopped it in the East.

THE ABBASIDS: 750–1258

In 750, seventeen years after the battle of Tours, the Omayyads were overthrown by a new dynasty, Arabian in family background but with a program of greater political participation for the highly civilized conquered peoples, now converting in large numbers to Islam. Above all it was the Islamized Persian aristocracy whom the Abbasids represented, and shortly after the victory of the new dynasty the capital was moved from Damascus to Baghdad on the Tigris, deep within the old Persian Empire and a stone's throw from the ruins of ancient Babylon.

Baghdad, under the early Abbasids, became one of the world's great cities. It was the center of a vast commercial network spreading across the Islamic world and far beyond. Silks, spices, and fragrant woods flowed into its wharves from India, China, and the East Indies; furs, honey, and slaves were imported from Scandi-

---

* The battle was fought between Tours and Poitiers and is sometimes called the battle of Poitiers. It is traditionally, but incorrectly, dated 732.

navia; and gold, slaves, and ivory from tropical Africa. Baghdad was the nexus of a far-flung banking system with branches in other cities of the Islamic world. A check could be drawn in Baghdad and cashed in Morocco, 4000 miles to the west. The Abbasid imperial palace, occupying fully a third of the city, contained innumerable apartments and public rooms, annexes for eunuchs, harems, and government officials, and a remarkable reception room known as the "hall of the tree," which contained an artificial tree of gold and silver on whose branches mechanical birds chirped and sang. The wealth and culture of Baghdad reached their climax under the Abbasid caliph, Harun-al-Rashid (786–809), whose opulence and power quickly became legendary. Harun was accustomed to receiving tribute from the Byzantine Empire itself. When on one occasion the tribute was discontinued he sent the following peremptory note to the emperor at Constantinople:

> In the name of God, the merciful, the compassionate.
> From Harun, the commander of the faithful, to Nicephorus, the dog of a Roman.
> Verily I have read thy letter, O son of an infidel mother. As for the answer, it shall be for thine eye to see, not for thine ear to hear.
> Salam.

The letter was followed by a successful military campaign that forced the unlucky Byzantines to resume their tribute.

The era of Harun-al-Rashid was an age of notable intellectual activity in which the learned traditions of Greece and Rome and of Persia and India were absorbed and synthesized. Harun's son and successor founded a great intellectual institute in Baghdad—the House of Wisdom—which was at once a library, a university, and a translation center. Thus the Abbasids pushed civilization far beyond the level that it had reached under their Omayyad predecessors. Islamic culture had come of age with remarkable speed. At a time when Charlemagne was struggling desperately to civilize his semi-barbaric Franks, Harun reigned over glittering Baghdad.

The rise of the Abbasids marked the breakdown of the Arabian aristocracy's monopoly on political power. Now the government was run by a medley of races and peoples, often of humble origin. As one disgruntled aristocrat observed, "Sons of concubines have become so numerous amongst us; Lead me to a land, O God, where I shall see no bastards." The Abbasid government drew heavily from the administrative techniques of Byzantium and Persia. A sophisticated and complex bureaucracy ran the affairs of state from the capital at Baghdad and kept in touch with the provinces through a multitude of tax-gatherers, judges, couriers, and spies. The government was enlightened up to a point, although no more sensitive to the demands of social justice than other governments of its day. The Abbasid regime undertook extensive irrigation works, drained swamps, and thereby increased the amount of land under cultivation. But the status of the peasant and unskilled laborer was kept low by the competition of vast numbers of slaves. The brilliance of Abbasid culture had little effect on the underprivileged masses, who, aside from their fervent Islamic faith, retained the same primitive way of life that they had known for the last two millennia.

The Abbasid Revolution of 750 was followed by a long process of political disintegration, as one province after another broke free of the control of the caliph of Baghdad. Even in the palmy days of Harun-al-Rashid the extreme western provinces—Spain, Morocco, and Tunisia—were ruled by independent local dynasties. In the later ninth century the trend toward disintegration gained momentum as Egypt, Syria, and eastern Persia (Iran) broke free of Abbasid control. By then, the Abbasids were slowly losing their grip on their own government in Baghdad. Ambitious army commanders gradually usurped power, establishing control over the tax machinery and the other organs of government. The Abbasid dynasty endured until 1258 when Baghdad was ravaged by the Mongols, but by 950 the caliphs had become the pawns of the supreme military commander and the imperial guard.

ISLAMIC CULTURE

Throughout this epoch of political disintegration the Moslem world remained united by a common tongue, a common culture, and a common faith. It continued to struggle vigorously and often successfully with Byzantium for control of the Mediterranean, and managed for a time to occupy the key islands of Crete, Sicily, Sardinia, and Corsica.

By now most of the inhabitants of Syria, Egypt, and North Africa had converted to Islam, even though these lands had once supported enthusiastic and well-organized Christian churches. The Moslems did not ordinarily persecute the Christians; they merely taxed them, and it may well be that the prolonged tax burden was a more effective instrument of conversion than ruthless persecutions would have been.

The brilliant intellectual awakening of Harun-al-Rashid's day continued unabated. The untutored Arab from the desert became the cultural heir of Greece, Rome, Persia, and India, and within less than two centuries of the Prophet's death Islamic culture had reached the level of a mature, sophisticated civilization. Its mercurial rise was a consequence of the Arabs' success in absorbing the great civilized traditions of their conquered peoples and welding these traditions into a cultural synthesis both new and unique. Islam borrowed, but never without digesting. What it drew from previous civilizations it transmuted and made its own.

The political disintegration of the ninth and tenth centuries was accompanied by a diffusion of cultural activity throughout the Moslem world. During the tenth century, for example, Cordova, the capital of Islamic Spain, acquired prodigious wealth and became the center of a brilliant cultural flowering. With a population of half a million or more, Cordova was another Baghdad. No other city in Western Europe could even remotely approach it in population, beauty, or municipal organization. Its magnificent mosques, mansions, aqueducts, and baths, its bustling markets and shops, its efficient police force and sanitation service, its street lights, and, above all, its splendid, sprawling palace, flashing with brightly colored tiles and surrounded by graceful minarets and sparkling fountains, made Cordova the wonder of the age.

All across the Islamic world, from Cordova to Baghdad and far to the East, Moslem scholars and artists were developing the fruitful legacy of past civilizations. Architects were molding Greco-Roman forms into a brilliant and distinctive new style. Philosophers were studying and elaborating the writings of Plato and Aristotle despite the hostility of narrowly orthodox Islamic theologians. Physicians were expanding the ancient medical doctrines of Galen and his Greek predecessors, describing new symptoms and identifying new curative drugs. Astronomers were tightening the geocentric system of Ptolemy, preparing accurate tables of planetary motions, and

Capilla de Villaviciosa in the Cordova Mosque (961–965).

giving Arabic names to the stars—names such as Altair, Deneb, and Aldebaran, which are used to this day. The renowned astrono-mer-poet of Persia, Omar Khayyam, devised a calendar of singular accuracy. Moslem mathematicians borrowed creatively from both Greece and India. From the Greeks they learned geometry and trigonometry, and from the Hindus they appropriated the so-called Arabic numerals, the zero, and algebra, which were ultimately passed on to the West to revolutionize European mathematics.

But the Moslem scholars and scientists, although masters of the knowledge of past cultures and diligent observers of the world around them, were by and large unsuccessful in superseding their predecessors in any basic way. They tightened, they elaborated, they tinkered, but they produced few fundamental hypotheses— they created no new systems of rational thought to replace those of Aristotle, Plato, and Galen. They knew their Ptolemy backward, yet they produced no Copernicus.

This same inability to think creatively in large systematic terms characterizes Islamic literature. Arab prose is fragmentary and episodic; the individual anecdote takes precedence over the extended narrative. Moslem poets endeavored to perfect individual verses rather than to create long coherent poems. The quatrains of Omar Khayyam's *Rubaiyat* actually seem to have been arranged in alphabetical order; the chapters of the *Koran* itself were assembled in order of decreasing length without the slightest thought of structural unity.

Still, there is no gainsaying Islam's immense achievement. The Arabs conquered their vast territories three times over: with their armies, their faith, and their language. In the end, the term "Arab" applied to every Moslem from Spain to India, regardless of his ethnic background. Within its all-encompassing religious and linguistic framework, Arab culture provided a new stimulus and orientation to the long-civilized peoples of former empires. With its manifold ingredients the rich Islamic heritage would one day provide invaluable nourishment to the voracious mind of the reawakening West.

MOSLEM CHRONOLOGY

```
 c.571–632: Mohammed
      622: The Hegira
  632–655: The First Conquests
  655–661: Civil War: Omayyads versus Ali
  661–750: Omayyad Dynasty: New Conquests
  717–718: Arabs besiege Constantinople
      733: Arabs defeated at Tours
 750–1258: Abbasid dynasty at Baghdad
  786–809: Harun-al-Rashid; Zenith of Abbasid power
```

6

Carolingian Europe

THE SIGNIFICANCE OF THE CAROLINGIAN AGE

In the course of the eighth century Western Christendom began to emerge as a coherent civilization. It did so under the aegis of the Carolingian Empire—a vast constellation of territories welded together by the Frankish king Charlemagne and his talented predecessors. Here for the first time the various cultural ingredients—classical, Christian, and Germanic—that went into the making of European civilization achieved a degree of synthesis. Charlemagne was a Germanic king—of that there could be no question—and he surrounded himself with Germanic warrior-aristocrats. But he also drew churchmen and classical scholars around him and took very seriously his role as protector and sustainer of the Western Church. Although his empire was fundamentally Germanic, its intellectual life, limited though it was, drew heavily from the classical-Christian tradition. The fusion of these cultural ingredients was evident in the life of the Carolingian court, in the rising vigor of the Carolingian Church, and in the person of Charlemagne himself.

Charlemagne's Frankland stood in vivid contrast to contemporary Byzantium and the Abbasid Empire of Islam. Baghdad and Constantinople were the centers of brilliant, opulent, mercantile civilizations. Charlemagne's Franks were a half-barbarized agrarian people struggling toward political and intellectual coherence. But eighth-century Western Europeans were steadily moving toward a life of larger meaning for themselves and for those who came after them. For the first time it began to dawn on a few that they were a people apart. It is hardly likely that they gave over to critical analysis their common heritage rooted in Athens and Jerusalem, Rome and Germany. But some sensed that they were participants in the creation of a new and distinctive civilization; that they were bound together, much as the Moslems, by a common faith and a common scholarly language.

The new Europe was awakened spiritually by the wide-ranging Benedictines and invigorated intellectually by the Bible. It was stirred by the writings of the Latin Doctors and their contemporaries, and by the surviving masterpieces of the Latin literary tradition. And it was bound together politically by a new dynasty of Frankish monarchs, the Carolingians.*

Carolingian Europe differed profoundly from the Western Roman Empire of old. It was a land without large cities, thoroughly agrarian in its economic organization, with its culture centered on the monastery, the cathedral, and the perambulatory royal court rather than the forum. And although Charlemagne extended his authority into Italy, the center of his activities and his interests remained in northern Frankland. In a word, the new Europe no longer faced the Mediterranean; its axis had shifted northward.

AGRICULTURAL TECHNOLOGY

The relative brightness of the Age of Charlemagne was the product of creative processes that had been at work during the preceding dark centuries. From the economic standpoint the most interesting and significant of these processes was the development of a new agrarian technology which increased the productivity of northern European farmlands beyond the level of the old Roman Empire.

By the opening of the eighth century the ineffective scratch plow of Roman times had been superseded throughout the northern districts of the barbarian West by a heavy compound plow with wheels, colter, plowshare, and moldboard that cut deeply into the soil,

---

* Whose family name is derived from that of their most illustrious representative —Charles the Great, or Charlemagne.

pulverized it, and turned it aside, thereby producing ridges and furrows. The development of this heavy plow was complex and gradual; the basic idea may perhaps have been brought into Western Europe by the Slavs in the sixth or seventh centuries. Its introduction into the West opened up vast areas of rich, heavy soil in which the older scratch plow was ineffective, and accentuated the tendency toward dividing fields into long strips cultivated by the eight-ox teams that the heavy plow required. Peasants now pooled their oxen and their labor in order to exploit the new plow; in so doing they laid the foundation for the cooperative agricultural communities of medieval Europe with strong village councils to regulate the division of labor and resources.

The upsurge in productivity brought about by the introduction of the heavy compound plow made possible a fundamental change in the method of rotating crops. By the Carolingian age parts of Northern Europe were beginning to adopt the three-field system in place of the two-field system typical of Roman times. Formerly a farm had usually been divided into two fields, each of which in turn was planted one year and allowed to lie fallow the second year. But it was found that the rich northern soils, newly opened by the heavy plow, did not require a full year's rest between crops. Instead, they were often divided into three fields, each of which underwent a three-year cycle of autumn planting, spring planting, and fallow. The shift from two fields to three had an important impact on the European economy, for it increased food production significantly and brought a degree of prosperity to Northern Europe. It is possible that the heavy plow and the three-field system, which could not be employed efficiently in the light, dry soils of the Mediterranean South, contributed to the northward shift in the economic and cultural orientation of Carolingian Europe.

The Age of Charlemagne also profited from a trend toward mechanization. The water mill, which was used occasionally in antiquity for grinding grain, had now come into widespread use and was a typical feature of the Carolingian farm. During the centuries following Charlemagne's death the water mill was put to new uses—to power the rising textile industry of the eleventh century and to drive triphammers in forges. Thus the technological progress of Merovingian and Carolingian times continued into the centuries that followed. By A.D. 1000 the development of the horseshoe and a new, efficient horse collar, both apparently imported from Siberia or Central Asia, made possible the very gradual replacement of the ox by the more energetic horse as the chief draught animal on the farms of Northwestern Europe. And in the twelfth century the windmill made its debut in the European countryside. These new advances resulted in still greater productivity and underlay the rich and prosperous civilization of Northern Europe in the High Middle Ages (*c.* 1050–1300). Slowly one of the chief economic bases of human slavery was being eroded as human power gave way more and more to animal and machine power.

Carolingian Europe gained much from the earlier phase of this drawn-out revolution in agrarian technology, but even so the peasants of the Carolingian age remained near the level of subsistence. A single bad year could ruin them. During a great famine of 791, for example, the peasants were driven to cannibalism and were even reported to have eaten members of their own family. Conditions may have been improving, but only very gradually.

THE RISE OF THE CAROLINGIANS

The dynasty of Clovis, the Merovingians, had declined over the centuries from bloodthirsty autocrats to crowned fools. By the later 600s all real power had passed to the aristocracy. Meanwhile, as a consequence of the Merovingian policy of dividing royal authority and crown lands among the sons of a deceased king, Frankland had split into several distinct districts, the most important of which were Neustria (Paris and northwestern France), Austrasia (the heavily Germanized northeast including the Rhinelands), and Burgundy in the southeast.*

During the seventh century a great aristocratic family, known to historians as the Carolingians, rose to power in Austrasia. The Carolingians became "mayors of the palace"; that is, they held the chief administrative post in the Austrasian royal household and made it hereditary. As the Merovingians grew increasingly feeble and inept the Carolingians became the real masters of Austrasia. The Carolingian mayor of the palace increased his power by gathering around him a considerable number of trained warriors somewhat

* See map, p. 84.

luminations from the Flemish *Hours of the Virgin* (*c.* 1515): on the left, the month
July; on the right, the month of September. Note two examples of medieval
chnological achievement: the windmill and the compound plow with moldboard.

in the tradition of the old Germanic comitatus.† These men became
his vassals, placing themselves under his protection and maintenance
and swearing fealty to him. Other aristocrats also had their private
vassalic armies. But the Carolingians, with far the greatest number
of followers, dominated the scene. In 687 a Carolingian mayor
named Pepin of Heristal led his Austrasian army to a decisive
victory over the Neustrians at Tertry, and the Carolingians thenceforth were the leading family in all Frankland. Once Neustria was
under their control they established their influence over Burgundy.
Thus when the Moslems moved into Gaul in the early 730s they
faced a united Frankish people under the able leadership of Pepin
of Heristal's son, the vigorous Carolingian mayor, Charles Martel
("The Hammer," 714–741).

† See p. 19.

73

CHARLES MARTEL

This brilliant, ruthless warrior not only turned back the Moslems at the battle of Tours (733), he also won victory after victory over Moslems and Christians alike, consolidating his power over the Franks and extending the boundaries of the Frankish state. Like the Adams family in American history, the Carolingians of the seventh and eighth centuries had the good fortune to produce exceedingly able representatives over several generations. Martel's father, Pepin of Heristal, had conquered Neustria; Martel himself defeated the Moslems and, indeed, almost everybody he faced. His son, Pepin the Short, gained the Frankish crown, and his grandson, Charlemagne, won an empire.

Surprisingly, the Carolingians followed the same policy of divided succession among male heirs which had so weakened the Merovingians. But here too Carolingian luck played a crucial role in history. For as it happened, the Carolingian mayors and later kings, over several generations, had only one long-surviving heir. Frankish unity was maintained not by policy but in spite of it. When Charles Martel died in 741 his lands and authority were divided among his two sons, Carloman and Pepin the Short. But Carloman ruled only six years, retiring to a Benedictine monastery in 747—leaving the field to his brother Pepin. Carloman represented a new kind of barbarian ruler, deeply affected by the spiritual currents of his age, whose piety foreshadowed that of numerous saint-kings of later centuries. Christian culture and Germanic political leadership were beginning to draw together.

MISSIONS FROM NORTHUMBRIA

The fusion of these two worlds was carried still further by Pepin the Short (741–768) who supported a Benedictine Christian revival in Frankland and consummated an alliance of far-reaching consequences between the Frankish monarchy and the papacy. By the time of Charles Martel's death in 741, English Benedictine monks had long been engaged in evangelical work among the heathen Germanic peoples east of the Rhine. The earliest of these missions were directed at the Frisians, a maritime people who were settled along the coast of the Netherlands. The first of the Benedictine evangelists were monks from Northumbria who brought to the Continent not only the strict organizational discipline and devotion to the papacy that had been characteristic of the Northumbrian Benedictines but also the peripatetic missionary fervor that the Celtic monks had contributed to the Northumbrian revival. So it was that Benedictine monks such as Wilfrid of Ripon and Willibrord left their Northumbrian homeland during the later 600s to evangelize the heathen Frisians. The transference to Frankland and Germany of the vital force of Northumbrian Christianity, with its high culture, its Roman-Benedictine discipline, and its profound spiritual commitment was of immense significance in the development of Western civilization. Wilfrid of Ripon, Willibrord, and their devoted followers represent the first wave of a movement that was ultimately to infuse the Frankish empire of Charlemagne with the vibrant spiritual life that had developed in Anglo-Saxon England during the century following St. Augustine's mission. The dynamic thrust of Roman-Benedictine Christianity, having leapt from Rome to Kent and thence to remote Northumbria, was returning to the Continent at last.

SAINT BONIFACE IN GERMANY

The key figure in this crucial cultural movement was St. Boniface, an English Benedictine from Wessex. Reared in Benedictine monasteries in southern England, Boniface left Wessex in 716 to do missionary work among the Frisians. From that time until his death in 754 he devoted himself above all other tasks to the tremendous challenge of Christianizing the heathen Germanic peoples. Boniface was a man of boundless energy and considerable learning, a wise and charismatic leader of men. He worked in close cooperation with both the papacy and the Anglo-Saxon Church; a great number of his letters survive, many of which request support from his compatriots in Wessex and advice from Rome. On three occasions he visited Rome to confer with the pope, and from the beginning his work among the heathens was performed under papal commission. In 732 the papacy appointed him archbishop in Germany. Some years later he was given the episcopal see at Mainz as his headquarters. Throughout his career he was a devoted representative of the Anglo-Saxon Church, the Benedictine Rule, and the papacy. As he put it, he strove "to hold fast the Catholic faith and Unity, and to yield submission to the Church of Rome as long as life shall last for us."

Boniface also worked with the backing of the Frankish mayors—Charles Martel, Carloman, and Pepin the Short. Armed with the Christian faith and the Benedictine Rule, and supported by England, Frankland, and Rome, Boniface labored among the Germanic tribes in Frisia, Thuringia, Hesse, and Bavaria. There he won converts, founded new Benedictine monasteries in the German wilderness, and erected the organizational framework of a disciplined German Church. He had moments of discouragement, as when he wrote to an English abbot, "Have pity upon an old man tried and tossed on all sides by the waves of a German sea." Yet Boniface accomplished much, and the monasteries that he established—particularly the great house of Fulda in Hesse—were to become centers of learning and evangelism which played a great role in converting and civilizing the peoples of Germany.

REFORM OF THE FRANKISH CHURCH

During the decade following Charles Martel's death in 741 Boniface devoted much of his energy to Frankland itself, for the Frankish Church of the early eighth century stood in desperate need of reform. On the whole it was corrupt, disorganized, and ignorant—the product of several centuries of Merovingian misrule. Many areas of Frankland had no priests at all; numerous Frankish peasants were scarcely removed from heathenism. Priests themselves are reported to have sacrificed animals to the gods and shared their homes with concubines. Charles Martel, although willing enough to support Boniface's missionary endeavors among the Germanic heathens, had no taste for ecclesiastical reforms within his own Frankish Church. Indeed, he weakened the Church by confiscating a considerable amount of ecclesiastical property and granting it to his military vassals. Carloman and Pepin, however, encouraged Boniface to work toward the reform of the Frankish Church, and beginning in 742 he held a series of synods for that purpose. Working in close collaboration with the papacy, Boniface remodeled the Frankish ecclesiastical organization on the disciplined pattern of Anglo-Saxon England and papal Rome. He reformed Frankish monasteries along the lines of the Benedictine Rule, saw to the establishment of monastic schools, encouraged the appointment of dedicated prelates, and worked toward the development of an adequate parish system to bring the Gospel to the country folk. This great missionary and ecclesiastical statesman laid the groundwork for both the new Church in Germany and the reformed Church in Frankland. In doing so, he served as one of the chief architects of the Carolingian cultural revival.

THE FRANCO-PAPAL ALLIANCE

Boniface's introduction of Roman discipline and organization into the Frankish Church was followed almost immediately by the consummation of a fateful political alliance between Rome and Frankland. It may well have been at Boniface's prompting that Pepin the Short, mayor of the palace, sought papal support for his seizure of the Frankish crown. Although their family retained the enormous prestige always enjoyed by a Germanic royal dynasty, the Merovingians had long been shadowy, do-nothing kings. Even so, if the Carolingians hoped to replace the Merovingians on the Frankish throne, they would have to call upon the most potent spiritual sanction available to their age: papal consecration. In supporting Boniface and his fellow Benedictines the Carolingian mayors had fostered a notable upsurge of papal influence in the Frankish Church. Now, seeking papal support for a dynastic revolution, Pepin the Short could reasonably expect a favorable response in Rome.

For their part, the popes had been seeking a strong and loyal ally against the untrustworthy Byzantines and the aggressive Lombards who had long been contending for political supremacy in Italy. The Carolingians, with their policy of aid to the Benedictine missionaries and their support of Boniface's reform measures, must have seemed strong candidates for the role of papal champion. And by the mid-eighth century a papal champion was badly needed. Traditionally the papacy had followed the policy of turning to Byzantium for protection against the fierce Lombards who, although they had by now adopted trinitarian Christianity, remained an ominous threat to papal independence. By 750 the popes could no longer depend upon Byzantine protection for two reasons: (1) the Byzantine emperors had recently embraced a doctrine known as *iconoclasm*, which the papacy regarded as heretical; (2) Lombard aggression was rapidly becoming so intense that the Byzantine army could no longer be counted on to defend the papacy.

The iconoclastic controversy was the chief religious dispute of the Christian world in the eighth century. It was a conflict over the use in Christian worship of statues and pictures of Christ and the saints. These icons—statues and pictures—had gradually come to assume an important role in Christian worship. Strictly speaking, Christians might venerate them as symbols of the holy persons whom they represented, but in fact there was a strong tendency among the uneducated to worship the objects themselves. A line of reform emperors in Constantinople, beginning with Leo the Isaurian (717–741), sought to end the superstitious practice of worshiping images—vigorously fostered by the numerous itinerant monks of the Eastern Empire—by banning icons altogether. Such a radical decree was offensive to a great many Byzantines, image worshipers and intelligent traditionalists alike. In the West little or no support was to be found for the policy of iconoclasm; the papacy in particular opposed it as heretical and contrary to the Christian tradition. Although it ultimately failed in the Byzantine Church, iconoclasm in the 750s was a vital issue and a storm center of controversy which aroused intense enmity between Rome and Constantinople.* The papacy was deeply apprehensive of depending on the troops of an heretical emperor for its defense.

Even without the iconoclastic controversy it was becoming increasingly doubtful that the papacy could count on the military power of Byzantium in Italy. For by 750 the Lombards were on the rampage once again, threatening not only Byzantine holdings but also the territories of the pope himself. In 751 the Lombards captured Ravenna, which had long served as the Byzantines' Italian capital, and the papal position in Italy became more precarious than ever. If Pepin the Short needed the support of the papacy, the papacy needed Pepin's support even more.

Accordingly the alliance was struck. Pepin sent messengers to Rome with the far from theoretical question, "Is it right that a powerless ruler should continue to bear the title of king?" The pope

---

* That is, it failed in its extreme form. Eventually a compromise was reached which permitted flat representations of holy persons but not their representation in the round.

answered that by the authority of the Apostle Peter, Pepin was king of the Franks, and ordered that he should be anointed into his royal office at Soissons by a papal representative. The anointing ceremony was duly performed in 751. It had the purpose of buttressing the new Carolingian dynasty with the strongest of spiritual sanctions. Not by mere force, but by the supernatural potency of the royal anointing was the new dynasty established on the Frankish throne. Appropriately, this ceremony—the symbolic junction of the power of Rome and Frankland—was performed by the aged Boniface.

With Pepin's coronation the last of the Merovingians were shorn of their long hair and packed off to a monastery. Three years thereafter Boniface, now nearing 80, returned to his missionary work in Frisia and met a martyr's death. In the same year, 754, the Pope himself traveled northward to Frankland where he personally anointed Pepin and his two sons at the royal monastery of Saint-Denis, thereby conferring every spiritual sanction at his disposal upon the upstart Carolingian monarchy. At the same time he sought Pepin's military support against the Lombards.

Pepin obliged, leading his armies into Italy, defeating the Lombards, and granting a large portion of central Italy to the papacy. This "Donation of Pepin" was of notable historical significance. It had the immediate effect of relieving the popes of the ominous Lombard pressure. In the long run, it became the nucleus of the Papal States which were to remain a characteristic feature of Italian politics until the later nineteenth century. For the moment, the papacy had been rescued from its peril. It remained to be seen whether the popes could prevent their new champion from becoming their master.

CHARLEMAGNE

Pepin the Short, like all successful monarchs of the Early Middle Ages, was an able general. As the first Carolingian king he followed in the warlike traditions of his father. Besides defeating the Lombards in Italy he drove the Moslems from Aquitaine and left Frankland larger and better organized than he had found it. Pepin was a great monarch, but he was overshadowed by his even greater son. Charlemagne (768–814) was a phenomenally successful military commander, a statesman of rare ability, a friend of learning, and a monarch possessed of a deep sense of responsibility for the welfare of the society over which he ruled. In this last respect he represents a tremendous advance over his Merovingian predecessors whose relationship to their state was that of a leech to his host.

Charlemagne towered over his contemporaries both figuratively and literally. He was 6'3½" tall, thick-necked and pot-bellied, yet imposing in appearance for all that. Thanks to his able biographer, Einhard, whose *Life of Charlemagne* was written a few years after the Emperor's death, Charlemagne has come down to posterity as a remarkably three-dimensional figure. Einhard used the Roman historian Suetonius as his model, lifting whole passages from the *Lives of the Twelve Caesars* and adapting many others to his own purposes; yet there is much in Einhard's *Life* that represents his own appraisal of Charlemagne's deeds and character. Reared at the monastery of Fulda, Einhard served for many years in Charlemagne's court and so gained an intimate knowledge of the Emperor. Einhard's warm admiration for Charlemagne emerges clearly from the biography, yet the author was able to see Charlemagne's faults and foibles as well as his virtues:

> Charles was temperate in eating and particularly so in drinking, for he hated drunkenness in anybody, particularly in himself and those of his household. But he found it difficult to abstain from food, and often complained that fasts injured his health . . . . His meals usually consisted of four courses not counting the roast, which his huntsmen used to bring in on the spit. He was fonder of this than of any other dish. While at the table he listened to reading or music. The readings were stories and deeds of olden times; he was also fond of St. Augustine's books, and especially of the one entitled *The City of God*. So moderate was he in the use of wine and all sorts of drink that he rarely allowed himself more than three cups in the course of a meal.

Einhard provides full accounts of Charlemagne's military and political career; but the most fascinating passages in the biography deal with the Emperor's way of life and personal idiosyncrasies which reveal him as a human being rather than a shadowy hero of legend:

While he was dressing and putting on his shoes, he not only gave audience to his friends, but if the count of the palace told him of any suit in which his judgment was necessary, he had the parties brought before him forthwith, considered the case, and gave his decision, just as if he were sitting on the judgment seat.

Einhard was also at pains to show Charlemagne's thirst for learning. He portrays the Emperor as a fluent master of Latin, a student of Greek, a speaker of such skill that he might have passed for a teacher of eloquence, a devotee of the liberal arts, and in particular a student of astronomy who learned to calculate the motions of the heavenly bodies. Einhard concludes this impressive discussion of Charlemagne's scholarship with a final tribute which unwittingly discloses the Emperor's severe scholastic limitations:

He also tried to write, and used to keep tablets and blanks in bed under his pillow so that in his leisure hours he might accustom his hand to form the letters; but as he did not begin his efforts at an early age but late in life, they met with poor success.

Charlemagne could be warm and talkative, but he could also be hard, cruel, and violent, and his subjects came to regard him with both admiration and fear. He was possessed of a strong, if superficial, piety which prompted him to build churches, collect relics, and struggle heroically for a Christian cultural revival in Frankland. But it did not prevent him from filling his court with concubines and other disreputable characters. In short Charlemagne, despite his military and political genius, was a man of his age, in tune with its most progressive forces yet by no means removed from its barbaric past.

THE EXPANSION OF THE EMPIRE

Above all else Charlemagne was a warrior-king. He led his armies on yearly campaigns as a matter of course. When his magnates and their retainers assembled around him annually on the May Field, the question was not whether to go to war but where to fight. Traditionally the Franks had fought on foot; but the epoch of Charles

ETSYRIAM SOBAL · ETCONUERTIT
IOAB · ET PERCUSSIT EDOM INUAL
LESALINARUM · XII MILIA ·

This contemporary illustration, from the *Golden Psalter of St. Gall*, shows how the stirrup was used by Carolingian warriors.

Martel and Pepin the Short had witnessed the rise of cavalry as the elite force in the Frankish army. This momentous shift, which amounted in effect to the birth of medieval knighthood, was perhaps associated with the coming of the stirrup to Frankland in the earlier 700s. For the stirrup gave stability to the mounted warrior and made possible the charge of cavalrymen with lances braced against their arms which was such an effective feature of later feudal warfare. In any case, the conquering armies of Charlemagne were built around a nucleus of highly trained horsemen. Such warriors were still something of a novelty in the Age of Charlemagne, and under his masterful leadership they struck fear in their foes and acquired a reputation for invincibility.

It was only gradually, however, that Charlemagne developed a coherent scheme of conquest built on a notion of Christian mission and addressed to the goal of unifying and systematically expanding the Christian West. At the behest of the papacy Charlemagne followed his father's footsteps into Italy. There he conquered the Lombards completely in 774, incorporated them into his growing state, and assumed for himself the Lombard crown. Thenceforth he employed the title, "King of the Franks and the Lombards."

Between 778 and 801 Charlemagne conducted a series of campaigns against the Spanish Moslems which met with only limited success. He did succeed in establishing a frontier district, the "Spanish March," on the Spanish side of the Pyrenees. In later generations the southern portion of Charlemagne's Spanish March evolved into the county of Barcelona which remained more receptive to the influence of French institutions and customs than any other district in Spain. A relatively minor military episode in Charlemagne's Spanish campaign of 778—an attack by a band of Christian Basques against the rearguard of Charlemagne's army as it was withdrawing across the Pyrenees into Frankland—became the inspiration for one of the great epic poems of the eleventh century: the *Song of Roland*. The unknown author or authors of the poem transformed the Basques into Moslems and made the battle an heroic struggle between the rival faiths. Charlemagne was portrayed as a godlike conqueror, phenomenally aged, and Roland, the warden of the Breton March and commander of the rearguard, acquired a fame in literature far out of proportion to his actual historical importance.

Charlemagne devoted much of his strength to the expansion of his eastern frontier. In 787 he conquered and absorbed Bavaria, organizing its easternmost district into a forward defensive barrier against the Slavs. This East March or *Ostmark* became the nucleus of a new state later to be called Austria. In the 790s Charlemagne pushed still farther to the southeast, destroying the rich and predatory Avar state which had long tormented Eastern Europe. For many generations the Avars had been enriching themselves on the plunder of their victims and on heavy tribute payments from Byzantium and elsewhere. Charlemagne had the good fortune to seize

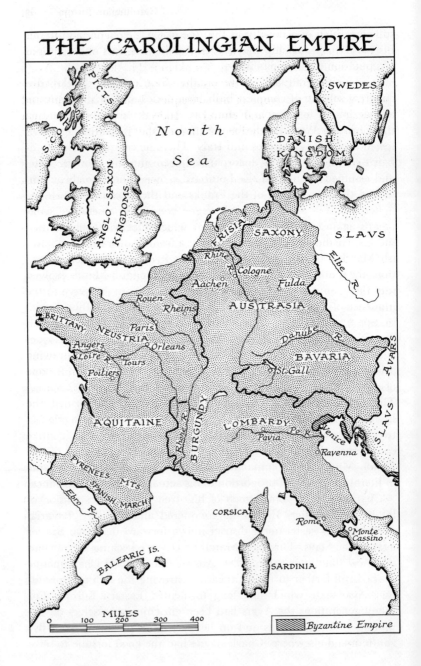

THE CAROLINGIAN EMPIRE

PICTS

SCO

SWEDES

North

DANISH
KINGDOM

Sea

ANGLO-SAXON
KINGDOMS

SLAVS

FRISIA

SAXONY

Rhine R.

Cologne

Elbe R.

BRITTANY

Aachen

Fulda

Rouen

Rheims

AUSTRASIA

NEUSTRIA

Paris

Danube R.

Angers

Orleans

BAVARIA

AVARS

Loire R.

Tours

St.Gall

Poitiers

AQUITAINE

Rhine R.

BURGUNDY

LOMBARDY

Po R.

Venice

SLAVS

Pavia

Ravenna

PYRENEES MTS.

SPANISH MARCH

CORSICA

Rome

Monte
Cassino

Ebro R.

BALEARIC IS.

SARDINIA

MILES

0   100   200   300   400

Byzantine Empire

84

a substantial portion of the Avar treasure; it is reported that 15 four-ox wagons were required to transport the hoard of gold, silver, and precious garments back to Frankland. The loot of the Avars contributed significantly to the resources of Charlemagne's treasury and broadened the scope of his subsequent building program and patronage to scholars and churches. Indeed, it placed him on a financial footing comparable to that of the Byzantine emperors themselves.

Charlemagne's greatest and most prolonged military effort was directed against the heathen Saxons of northern Germany. With the twin goals of protecting the Frankish Rhinelands and bringing new souls into the Church, he campaigned for some thirty years (772–804), conquering the Saxons repeatedly and baptizing them by force, only to have them rebel when his armies withdrew. In a fit of savage exasperation he ordered the execution of 4500 unfaithful Saxons in a single bloody day in 782. At length, however, Saxony submitted to the remorseless pressure of Charlemagne's soldiers and the Benedictine monks who followed in their wake. By about 800, Frankish control of Saxony was well established, and in subsequent decades Christianity seeped gradually into the Saxon soul. A century and a half later, Christian Saxons were governing the most powerful state in Europe and were fostering a significant artistic and intellectual revival that was to enrich the culture of tenth-century Christendom.

THE IMPERIAL CORONATION

Charlemagne's armies, by incorporating large areas of central Germany into the new civilization, had succeeded where the legions of Augustus and his successors had failed. No longer a mere Frankish king, Charlemagne, by 800, was the master of the West. A few small Christian states such as the principalities of southern Italy and the kingdoms of Anglo-Saxon England remained outside his jurisdiction, but with these relatively minor exceptions Charlemagne's political sway extended throughout Western Christendom. He was, in truth, an emperor, and on Christmas Day, 800, his immense accomplishment was given formal recognition when Pope Leo III placed the imperial crown upon his head and acclaimed him "Emperor of the Romans." From the standpoint of legal theory this dramatic and epoch-making act reconstituted the Roman Empire in the West after an interregnum of 324 years. In another sense it was the ultimate consummation of the Franco-Papal Alliance of 751.

The imperial coronation of Charlemagne is difficult to interpret and has evoked heated controversy among historians. According to Einhard, Pope Leo III took Charlemagne by surprise and bestowed upon him an unwanted dignity. Charlemagne had such an aversion to the titles of Emperor and Augustus, so Einhard reports,

> that he declared he would not have set foot in the Church the day that they were conferred, although it was a great feast day, if he could have forseen the design of the pope.

Modern historians have tended to be skeptical of this assertion. It has been argued that Charlemagne was much too powerful—much too firmly in control of events—to permit a coronation that he did not wish. More likely the imperial coronation of 800, like the royal coronation of Pepin the Short in 751, represents a coalescence of papal and Carolingian interests. For some years Charlemagne had been attempting to attain a status comparable to that of the Byzantine emperors. In 794 he had abandoned the practice, traditional among Germanic kings, of traveling constantly with his court from estate to estate and had established his permanent capital at Aachen in Austrasia. Here he sought, vainly, to create a Constantinople of his own. Aachen was called "New Rome," and an impressive palace church was built in the Byzantine style—almost literally a poor man's Sancta Sophia. Even though Charlemagne's "Mary Church" at Aachen was a far cry from Justinian's masterpiece, it was a marvel for its time and place and made a deep impression on contemporaries. Einhard describes it as a beautiful basilica adorned with gold and silver lamps, with rails and doors of solid brass, and with columns and marbles from Rome and Ravenna. It was evidently the product of a major effort on Charlemagne's part—an effort not only to create a beautiful church but also to ape the Byzantines. The coronation of 800 may well have been an expression of this same imitative policy.

EMPIRE AND CHURCH

The papacy, on the other hand, must have regarded the coronation as a priceless opportunity to regain some of the initiative it

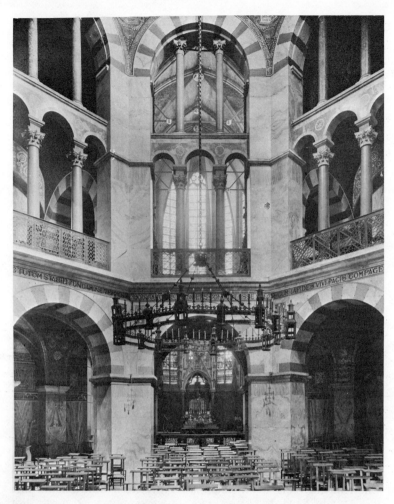

Interior of the "Mary Church" in Aachen (796–804). The Byzantine arches and the structural formation are very similar to Justinian's basilica of San Vitale in Ravenna.

had lost to the all-powerful Charlemagne. To be sure, the Carolingians had been promoted from kings to emperors; but their empire thenceforth bore the stamp, "Made in Rome." In later years the popes would insist that what they gave they could also take away. If the papacy could make emperors it could also depose them. Indeed, it was only shortly before this that the papal chancery had

87

produced a famous forged document called the "Donation of Constantine"* in which the first Christian emperor allegedly resigned all his authority to the pope and received it back as a kind of papal commission. The popes believed that the emperors ought to be papal stewards, wielding their secular political authority in the interests of the Roman Church. So convincing was this theory of papal supremacy in the eyes of the papacy that it justified the use of any documentation to support its case. The "Donation of Constantine," therefore, was not an effort to rewrite history but an attempt to buttress what the papacy regarded as historical truth.

Although Charlemagne always respected the papacy, he was unwilling to cast himself in the subordinate role that papal theory demanded of him. He was careful to retain the title, "King of the Franks and the Lombards," alongside his new title of "Emperor"; when the time came to crown his son emperor, Charlemagne excluded the pope from the ceremony and did the honors himself. In these maneuvers we are witnessing the prologue to a long, bitter struggle over the correct relationship between empire and papacy which reached its crescendo in the eleventh, twelfth, and thirteenth centuries. At stake was the ultimate mastery of Western Christendom.

But during the reign of Charlemagne the struggle remained latent for the most part. Charlemagne's power was unrivaled, and the popes were much too weak to oppose him seriously. Indeed, the warm Carolingian-papal relations of Pepin's day continued, and the papacy was nearly smothered in Charlemagne's affectionate embrace.

At no time since has Europe been so nearly united as under Charlemagne. And never again would Western Christendom flirt so seriously with theocracy. The papal anointing of Pepin and Charlemagne gave the Carolingian monarchy a sacred, almost priestly quality, and Charlemagne was able to use his vast authority to govern not only the body politic but the imperial Church as well. The laws and regulations of his reign, which are known as *capitularies*, dealt with both ecclesiastical and secular matters. Although he did not claim to legislate on Church doctrine, he felt a deep sense of responsibility for purifying and systematizing ecclesiastical discipline. He was a far greater force in the Carolingian

---

* Probably sometime in the 740s.

Church than was the pope. He summoned a number of ecclesiastical synods and even presided over one of them. Indeed, the significant intellectual revival known as the "Carolingian Renaissance" was mostly a product of Charlemagne's concern for the welfare of the Church and the perpetuation of ecclesiastical culture.

THE CAROLINGIAN RENAISSANCE

The term "Carolingian Renaissance" is dangerously misleading. Charlemagne's age produced no lofty abstract thought, no original philosophical or theological system, no Leonardo da Vinci. If we look for a "Renaissance" we are bound to be disappointed. The intellectual task of the Carolingian age was far less exalted, far more rudimentary: to rescue continental culture from the pit of ignorance into which it was sinking.

As with so many other aspects of the era, the Carolingian Renaissance bears the stamp of Charlemagne's will and initiative. It was he who saw the desperate need for schools in his kingdom and sought to provide them. There could be no question of establishing institutions of higher learning. None existed north of the Alps, and none would emerge until the High Middle Ages. It was for the Carolingians to build a system of primary and secondary education, and even this was an immensely difficult task. Frankland had no professional class of teachers either lay or clerical. The only hope for pedagogical reform lay with the Church, which had an almost exclusive monopoly on literacy. Accordingly, Charlemagne endeavored to force the cathedrals and monasteries of his realm to operate schools which would preserve and disseminate the rudiments of classical-Christian culture. A capitulary of 789 commands that

> In every episcopal See and in every monastery, instruction shall be given in the psalms, musical notation, chant, the computation of years and seasons, and grammar, and all books used shall be carefully corrected.

A curriculum of the sort described in this capitulary can hardly be described as intellectually sophisticated or demanding, yet it is clear enough that many Carolingian monasteries and cathedrals fell considerably short of the standards that it sought to establish.

Still, Charlemagne succeeded in improving vastly the quantity and quality of schooling in his empire. There was even an attempt to make village priests provide free instruction in reading and writing. Only a minute fraction of Charlemagne's subjects acquired literacy. But those few provided an all-important learned nucleus which kept knowledge alive and transmitted it to future generations. It was above all in the monastic schools that learning flourished—in houses such as Fulda, Tours, and Reichenau. During the turbulent generations following Charlemagne's death many of these monastic schools survived to become seedbeds of the far greater intellectual awakening of the eleventh and twelfth centuries. In sum, Charlemagne's pedagogical reforms insured that learning in Europe would never again descend to the pre-Carolingian level.

As an integral part of his effort to raise the intellectual standards of his realm and sustain Christian culture, Charlemagne assembled scholars at his court from all over Europe. One such scholar was the Emperor's biographer, Einhard, from eastern Frankland. Another was the poet-historian, Paul the Deacon, from the great Italian Benedictine house of Monte Cassino. Paul the Deacon's *History of the Lombards* provides an invaluable account of that Germanic tribe and its settlement in Italy. From Spain came Theodulf, later bishop of Orleans and abbot of Fleury, a tireless supporter of Charlemagne's pedagogical reforms as well as a poet of considerable talent. The most important of these Carolingian scholars was the Northumbrian Alcuin of York, a student of a student of Bede's and the last important mind to be produced by the Northumbrian Renaissance. Alcuin, along with his fellow countrymen of an earlier generation—Wilfrid of Ripon, Willibrord, and Boniface—represents the vital connecting link between the vigorous Christian cultural life of seventh- and eighth-century England and the intellectual upsurge of Carolingian Frankland.

Alcuin performed the essential task of preparing an accurate new edition of the Bible purged of the scribal errors that had crept into it over the centuries, thereby saving Christian culture from the hopeless confusion arising from the corruption of its most fundamental text. For many years the chief scholar in Charlemagne's court school, Alcuin spent his final years as abbot of St. Martin of Tours. He was extraordinarily well educated for his period, and his approach to learning typified the whole philosophy of the Carolingian Renaissance: to produce accurate copies of important traditional texts, to encourage the establishment of schools, and in every way possible to cherish and transmit the classical-Christian cultural tradition (without, however, adding to it in any significant way). Alcuin and his fellow scholars were neither intellectual innovators nor men of conspicuous holiness. Drawn by Charlemagne's wealth and power and enriched by his patronage, they struggled to improve the scholarly level of the Carolingian Church; but they showed little concern for deepening its spiritual life or exploring uncharted regions of speculative thought. They had the talents and inclinations—and the limitations—of the schoolmaster. At best they were scholars and humanists; in no sense could they be described as philosophers or mystics.

Accordingly, Alcuin, Theodulf, Einhard, Paul the Deacon, and others like them purified and regularized the liturgy of the Church and encouraged the preaching of sermons. They carried on some of the monastic reforms begun by Boniface and saw to it that every important monastery had a school. It was a question not of producing new Aristotles and Augustines but of preserving literacy itself. A new, standardized script was developed—the Carolingian minuscule—which derived in part from the Irish and Northumbrian scripts of the previous century. From then on the Carolingian minuscule superseded the heterogeneous and often illegible scripts earlier employed on the Continent. Throughout the realm monks set about copying manuscripts on an unprecedented scale. If classical-Christian culture was advanced very little by these activities it was at least preserved. Above all, its base was broadened. In the task they set for themselves, these Carolingian scholars were eminently successful.

THE RENAISSANCE AFTER CHARLEMAGNE

It is characteristic of the powerful theocratic tendencies of the age that this significant cultural-pedagogical achievement was accomplished through royal rather than papal initiative. Germanic monarchy and classical-Christian culture had joined hands at last. With the breakdown of European unity after Charlemagne's death the momentary fusion of political and cultural energies dissolved; yet the intellectual revival continued. A deeply spiritual movement of monastic reform and moral regeneration began in Aquitaine under the leadership of the ardent and saintly Benedict of Aniane. Soon the influence of this movement took hold at the court of Charlemagne's son and successor, Louis the Pious. Louis gave St. Benedict of Aniane the privilege of visiting any monastery in the Empire and tightening its discipline in whatever way he chose. And in 817 a significantly elaborated and modified version of the old Benedictine Rule, based on the strict monastic regulations of Benedict of Aniane, was promulgated for all the monasteries of the Empire and given the weight of imperial law. Benedict of Aniane's reform represents a marked shift from the spiritually superficial monastic regulations of Charlemagne's day to a deep concern for the Christ-centered life. The elaborated Benedictine Rule of 817 lost its status as imperial law upon Louis the Pious' death in 840, but it remained an inspiration to subsequent monastic reform movements in the centuries that followed. Thenceforth the Benedictine life *par excellence* was based on Benedict of Aniane's modification of the original Rule.

While Carolingian spiritual life was deepening in the years after Charlemagne's death, Carolingian scholarship continued to flourish in the cathedral and monastic schools. A vigorous controversy over the question of free will and predestination testifies to the vitality of Carolingian thought in the early and middle decades of the ninth century. And in keeping with the Carolingian intellectual program of preserving the classical-Christian tradition, learned churchmen of the Carolingian Renaissance's "second generation" devoted themselves to the preparation of encyclopedic compilations of received knowledge, unoriginal but important none the less in the significant process of cultural transmission. For example, Raban Maur (d. 856), abbot of the great monastery of Fulda, provided an elaborate encyclopedia on the pattern of Isidore of Seville's *Etymologies*, entitled *De Universo*. He also carried forward the Carolingian pedagogical tradition by writing a handbook on the instruction of the clergy—*De Clericorum Institutione*—which had a significant influence on the operation of monastic schools.

The most interesting scholar in this "second generation" was the Irishman, John Scotus Erigena, who stands as the one original thinker of the whole Carolingian age. John Scotus or John the Scot (the "Scots" in his day were inhabitants of Ireland rather than Scotland) served for years in the court of Charlemagne's grandson,

Charles the Bald. Not only a brilliant speculative thinker, he was also a rather precocious wit, at least if we can give credence to the later legend of a dinner-table conversation between John the Scot and King Charles the Bald. The King, intending to needle his court scholar, asked the rhetorical question, "What is there that separates a Scot from a sot," to which John is alleged to have replied, "Only the dinner table."

John Scotus was a profound student of Neoplatonism and the only Western European scholar of his age who was a master of the Greek tongue. He translated into Latin a crucially important Greek philosophical treatise, *On the Celestial Hierarchy*, written by an anonymous late-fifth-century Christian Neoplatonist known as the Pseudo-Dionysius. This author was incorrectly identified in the Middle Ages as Dionysius the Areopagite, the first-century Athenian philosopher who is described in the *Acts of the Apostles* as being converted to Christianity by St. Paul. Accordingly, the writings of the Pseudo-Dionysius, even though tinged with pantheism, passed into the Middle Ages with the powerful credentials of an early Christian author who was a Pauline convert. In reality, the importance of the Pseudo-Dionysius lay in his providing a Christian dimension to the philosophical scheme of Plotinus and other pagan Neoplatonists. The unknowable and indescribable Neoplatonic god—the center and source of the concentric circles of reality—was identified with the God of the Christians. Such a god could not be approached intellectually but only by means of a mystical experience; hence the Pseudo-Dionysius became an important source of inspiration to later Christian mystics.

Stimulated by the work of the Pseudo-Dionysius which he translated, John Scotus went on to write a highly original Neoplatonic treatise of his own, *On the Divisions of Nature*, which, in its merely shaded distinction between God and the created world, reflected the Neoplatonic tendency toward pantheism. The work was condemned as heretical in the thirteenth century, but it made little impact on contemporaries who lacked both the interest and the background to understand it. John Scotus is a lonely figure in intellectual history, without any immediate predecessors or successors. He founded no schools of thought and carried on no real philosophical dialogue with his contemporaries who were scholars, poets, and pedants rather than abstract thinkers. He figures as the supreme intellect in the West between St. Augustine and the philosophers of the High Middle Ages, yet being neither the direct product of earlier intellectual currents nor the cause of subsequent ones, he played a surprisingly minor role in the evolution of thought. He remains, nevertheless, the one interesting philosopher of the Carolingian epoch.

The intellectual revival instigated by Charlemagne reverberated down through subsequent generations. John Scotus' Neoplatonism may have been generally ignored and quickly forgotten. Yet in the monasteries and cathedrals of the ninth and tenth centuries, particularly in the German districts of Charlemagne's old empire, documents continued to be copied, schools continued to operate, and commentaries and epitomes of ancient texts continued to appear. By the eleventh century Europe was ready to build soaring and original intellectual edifices on her sturdy Carolingian foundations.

THE CAROLINGIAN STATE

Charlemagne's empire was an ephemeral thing, arising from a chaotic past and disintegrating in the turbulent age that followed. It is far easier to understand why the empire broke up than to explain how such a vast, primitive, amorphous state was able to coalesce even briefly. The answer to this puzzle is to be found above all in the person of Charlemagne himself. It was Charlemagne who held his immense empire together, and he did so by the quality of his leadership and the strength of his personality. In an era of primitive roads and wretched communications, he was obliged to depend heavily on the competence and loyalty of the counts, dukes, and margraves who administered his provinces. He kept some control over these great lords by sending pairs of inspectors known as *missi dominici* (envoys of the lord) from his court into the provinces to insure the implementation of his will. These *missi dominici*, consisting normally of one churchman and one layman, typified the theocratic trend of Charlemagne's age. They seem to have been moderately effective in binding the empire together but only because they were received respectfully in the provinces as representatives of a mighty, fear-inspiring monarch. The allegiance of Charlemagne's counts and dukes was mostly a product of their respect for Charlemagne himself. They obeyed his commands and submitted to his capitularies not out of patriotism to his state but because of their devotion to his person. In sum, the administrative institutions of the Carolingian Empire were grossly inadequate to the needs of a great state. Beneath the imposing military and cultural veneer Carolingian Europe was still semibarbaric. Alcuin was yielding to illusion when he told Charlemagne,

> If your intentions are carried out, it may be that a new Athens will arise in Frankland, and an Athens fairer than of old, for our Athens, ennobled by the teachings of Christ, will surpass the wisdom of the Academy.

Alcuin's vision was a pathetic mirage; the Carolingian state remained a land of rude, untutored warriors and peasants just emerging from barbarism.

Charlemagne's "Roman Empire" was an almost ludicrous parody of that of Augustus, yet one can only admire this dogged Carolingian who could do so much with so little; who could make such an effort to transcend his own barbaric past; who as an adult struggled vainly to learn how to write; who sought bravely but hopelessly to master the lofty subtleties of Augustine's *City of God*. The historian Christopher Dawson caught the spirit of Charlemagne's achievement perfectly when he wrote,

> The unwieldly empire of Charles the Great did not long survive the death of its founder, and it never really attained the economic and social organization of a civilized state. But, for all that, it marks the first emergence of the European culture from the twilight of prenatal existence into the consciousness of active life.*

* C. Dawson, *The Making of Europe*, Meridian Books, 1957, p. 187.

7

The New Invasions

Tentative though it was, the economic and cultural revival under Charlemagne might in time have produced a prosperous and sophisticated civilization had it not been for the new invasions that followed Charlemagne's death in 814. Until then the Carolingian realm had enjoyed relative peace. Intellectual life, although still rudimentary, was in the process of reawakening, and with the stimulus of the sound silver coinage which Charlemagne issued, commerce quickened. One historian has recently gone so far as to suggest that under the bracing influence of Charlemagne's economic policy towns were beginning to grow and flourish once again. But these hopeful signs proved to be a false dawn. For during the ninth and tenth centuries Europe was obliged to fight for its life against the thrust of three alien invaders—the semi-nomadic Hungarians from the East, the piratical Saracens (Moslems) from the South, and the wide-ranging Vikings from the North. As a result, the maturing of a higher civilization was delayed in Europe for another two centuries.

THE LATER CAROLINGIANS

It would be wrong to ascribe the political fragmentation of the Carolingian Empire entirely to these outside pressures. Charlemagne himself, in keeping with Frankish tradition, planned to divide his state among his several sons. As it happened, however,

96

Charlemagne outlived all but one of them. The luck of the Carolingians was still running, and when the great conqueror died in 814 his realm passed intact to his remaining heir, Louis the Pious (814–840).

Although Louis was by no means incompetent, his military and political talents were distinctly inferior to those of his father Charlemagne, his grandfather Pepin the Short, and his great-grandfather Charles Martel. Carolingian unity continued but Carolingian leadership showed signs of faltering. Louis the Pious was well named. He ran Charlemagne's minstrels and concubines out of the imperial court and replaced them with priests and monks. Far more than his hard-headed father, Louis committed himself to the dream of a unified Christian Empire—a City of God brought down to earth. Yet he was far less suited than Charlemagne to the Herculean task of maintaining unity and cohesion in the immense, heterogeneous empire which the Carolingians had won. He was the first of his line to conceive the notion of bequeathing supreme political authority to his eldest son and thereby making the unity of the kingdom a matter of policy rather than chance. Ironically, he turned out to be the last Carolingian to rule an undivided Frankish realm. His bold plan for a single succession was foiled by the ambitions of his younger sons who rebelled openly against him and plunged the Empire into civil war.

When Louis the Pious' unhappy reign ended in 840, his three surviving sons struggled bitterly for the spoils. The eldest of the three, Lothar, claimed the indivisible imperial title and hegemony over the entire realm. The other two sons, Louis the German and Charles the Bald, struggled to win independent royal authority in East and West Frankland respectively. In the end, Lothar was obliged to yield to the combined might of his younger brothers. The controversy was settled by the momentous Treaty of Verdun in 843 which permanently divided the Empire and foreshadowed the political structure of modern Europe. Lothar was permitted to keep the imperial title, but was denied any sort of superior jurisdiction over the realms of Louis the German and Charles the Bald. Louis ruled East Frankland, which became the nucleus of the modern German state. In a very real sense, he was Germany's first king. Charles the Bald became king of West Frankland, which evolved into modern France. The Emperor Lothar retained a long, narrow, heterogeneous strip

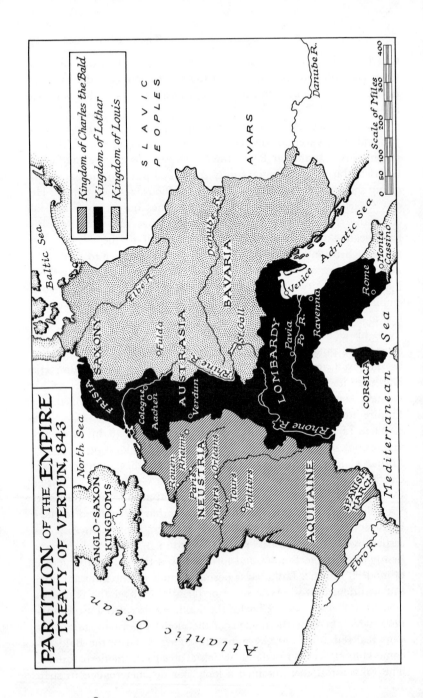

PARTITION OF THE EMPIRE
TREATY OF VERDUN, 843

Kingdom of Charles the Bald
Kingdom of Lothar
Kingdom of Louis

Scale of Miles
0 50 100 200 300 400

North Sea

Baltic Sea

SLAVIC PEOPLES

AVARS

ANGLO-SAXON KINGDOMS

Atlantic Ocean

FRISIA

SAXONY

Elbe R.

Fulda

AUSTRASIA

Cologne
Aachen
Verdun

Rhine R.

St. Gall

Danube R.

Danube R.

BAVARIA

Adriatic Sea

Venice

Ravenna

Po R.

Pavia

LOMBARDY

Rome

Monte
Cassino

CORSICA

Rhone R.

NEUSTRIA

Rouen
Paris
Rheims
Angers
Orleans
Tours
Poitiers

AQUITAINE

SPANISH MARCH

Ebro R.

Mediterranean Sea

98

of territory which stretched for some thousand miles northward from Italy through Burgundy, Alsace, Lorraine, and the Netherlands, embracing considerable portions of western Germany and eastern France. This Middle Kingdom included the two "imperial capitals"—Rome and Aachen—but its long exposed frontiers were virtually impossible to defend, and it was utterly lacking in unity. At Lothar's death in 855 it was subdivided among his three sons, one of whom inherited Carolingian Italy and the increasingly insig-

---

CAROLINGIAN CHRONOLOGY

687: Pepin of Heristal, Carolingian mayor of Austrasia, defeats Neustria; Carolingian hegemony established.
714–741: Rule of Charles Martel.
733: Arabs defeated at Tours.
741–768: Rule of Pepin the Short.
751: Pepin crowned king of the Franks. Merovingian Dynasty ends.
754: Death of St. Boniface.
768–814: Reign of Charlemagne.
772–804: Charlemagne's Saxon Wars.
800: Charlemagne crowned Roman Emperor.
814–840: Reign of Louis the Pious.
843: Treaty of Verdun.

---

nificant imperial title. From the ninth century to the twentieth, fragments of Lothar's middle kingdom have been the source of endless bitter territorial disputes between Germany and France.

The struggles among Charlemagne's grandsons occurred against a background of Viking, Hungarian, and Saracen invasions which accelerated and vastly increased the tendency toward political fragmentation brought about by internal weaknesses. But even without the invasions, and without the Frankish tradition of divided succession, it was unlikely that Charlemagne's huge, unwieldy empire could have long remained intact once his iron hand had been removed from control. As it turned out, even the more modest political units arising from the Treaty of Verdun were too large—

too far removed from the desperate realities of the countryside—to cope successfully with the lightning raids of Viking shipmen or Hungarian horsemen. During the ninth and tenth centuries Carolingian leadership was visibly failing. The incapacity of the later Carolingians was nowhere better illustrated than in their names: Charles the Fat, Charles the Simple, Louis the Child, Louis the Blind.

THE IMPACT OF THE INVASIONS

The Saracens, Hungarians, and Vikings, who plundered the declining Carolingian state, were in part drawn by the growing political vacuum, and in part impelled by forces operating in their own homelands. Europe suffered grievously from their marauding, yet it was strong enough in the end to survive the invasions and absorb the invaders. And they were the last that Western Christendom was destined to endure. From about A.D. 1000 to the present the West has had the unique opportunity of developing on its own, sheltered from alien attacks that have so disrupted other civilizations over the past millennium. As the historian Marc Bloch has said,

> It is surely not unreasonable to think that this extraordinary immunity, of which we have shared the privilege with scarcely any people but the Japanese, was one of the fundamental factors of European civilization . . . .*

Yet in the ninth and tenth centuries Europe's hard-pressed peoples had no way of knowing that the invasions would one day end. A Frankish historian of the mid-ninth century wrote in a tone of anguish: "The number of ships grows larger and larger; the great host of Northmen continually increases; on every hand Christians are the victims of massacres, looting, and incendiarism—clear proof of which will remain as long as the world itself endures. The Northmen capture every city they pass through, and none can withstand them." In southern Gaul people prayed for divine protection against the Saracens: "Eternal Trinity . . . deliver thy Christian people from the oppression of the pagans." To the north they prayed, "From the savage nation of the Northmen, which lays waste our realms, deliver

* Marc Bloch, *Feudal Society*, translator L. A. Manyon, Chicago, 1961, p. 56.

us, O God." And in northern Italy: "Against the arrows of the Hungarians be thou our protector."

THE SARACENS

The Saracens of the ninth and tenth centuries, unlike their predecessors in the seventh and early eighth, came as brigands rather than conquerors and settlers. From their pirate nests in Africa, Spain, and the Mediterranean islands they preyed on shipping, plundered coastal cities, and sailed up rivers to carry their devastation far inland. Saracen bandit lairs were established on the southern coast of Gaul from which the marauders conducted raids far and wide through the countryside and kidnapped pilgrims crossing the Alpine passes. Charlemagne had never possessed much of a navy, and his successors found themselves helpless to defend their coasts. In 846 Saracen brigands raided Rome itself, profaning its churches and stealing its treasures. As late as 982 a German king was severely defeated by Saracen bandits in southern Italy; but by then the raids were tapering off. Southern Europe, now bristling with fortifications, had learned to defend itself and was even beginning to challenge Saracen domination of the western Mediterranean.

THE HUNGARIANS AND VIKINGS

The Hungarians or Magyars, fierce nomadic horsemen from the Asiatic steppes, settled in the land now known as Hungary. From the late 800s to 955 they terrorized Germany, northern Italy, and eastern Gaul. Hungarian raiding parties ranged far and wide seeking defense-less settlements to plunder, avoiding fortified towns, outriding and outmaneuvering the armies sent against them. In time, however, they became more sedentary, gave more attention to their farms, and consequently lost much of their nomadic savagery. In 955 King Otto the Great of Germany crushed a large Hungarian army at the battle of Lechfeld and brought the raids to an end at last. Within another half century, the Hungarians had adopted Christianity and were becoming integrated into the community of Christian Europe.

The Vikings, or Norsemen, were the most fearsome invaders of all. These redoubtable warrior-seafarers came from Scandinavia, the very land that had, centuries before, disgorged many of the Germanic barbarians into Europe. Thus the ninth-century Vikings and the Germanic invaders of Roman times had similar ethnic backgrounds. But to the ninth-century European—the product of countless Germanic-Celtic-Roman intermarriages, tamed by the Church and by centuries of settled life—the Vikings seemed a hostile and alien people.

Then, as now, the Scandinavians were divided roughly into three groups: Danes, Swedes, and Norwegians. During the great age of Viking expansion in the ninth and tenth centuries, the Danes, who were brought cheek to jowl with the Carolingian Empire by Charlemagne's conquest of Saxony, focused their attention on Frankland and England. The Norwegians raided and settled in Scotland, Ireland, and the North Atlantic. The Swedes concentrated on the East—the Baltic shores, Russia, and the Byzantine Empire. Yet the three Norse peoples had much in common, and the distinctions between them were by no means sharp. It is therefore proper to regard their raids, their astonishing explorations, and their far-flung commercial enterprises as a single great international movement.

Although the breakdown of Carolingian leadership doubtless acted as a magnet to Viking marauders, their raids on the West began as early as Charlemagne's reign. The basic causes for their great outward thrust must be sought in Scandinavia itself. Since pre-tenth-century Scandinavia is almost a closed book to historians, explanations for the Viking outburst are little more than educated guesses. It is likely, however, that the Scandinavian population, once sharply reduced by the outward migrations of Roman times, had increased by the later 700s to a level that the primitive Norse agriculture was scarcely able to support. The pressure of overpopulation was probably aggravated by growing centralized royal power which cramped the more restless spirits and drove them to seek adventures and opportunities abroad. A third factor was the development of improved Viking ships, eminently seaworthy, propelled by both sail and oars, and capable of carrying crews of 40 to 100 warriors at speeds up to ten knots. In these long ships the tall, muscular, reddish-haired Viking warriors struck the ports of Northern Europe. They sailed up rivers far into the interior, plundering the towns and monasteries of Frankland and England, sometimes stealing horses and riding across the countryside to spread their devastation still further.

ATTACKS AGAINST ENGLAND

England was the first to suffer from Viking attacks. About 789 three long ships touched the Channel coast in Dorset and Vikings poured out of them to loot and sack a nearby town. From then on the Anglo-Saxon kingdoms were tormented by incessant Viking raids. In 794 Norse brigands annihilated the Northumbrian monastery of Jarrow, where Bede had lived and died. Other great monastic cultural centers of Northumbria suffered a like fate.

In 842 the Danes plundered London, and a few years thereafter they began to establish permanent winter bases in England which freed them from the necessity of returning to Scandinavia after the raiding season. By the later 800s they had turned from simple piracy to large-scale occupation and permanent settlement. One after another the Anglo-Saxon kingdoms were overrun until at length, in the 870s, only the southern kingdom of Wessex remained free of Danish control—and even Wessex came within a hair of falling before the Danish onslaught.

ATTACKS AGAINST THE CONTINENT

To mariners such as the Vikings the English Channel was a boulevard rather than a barrier, and their raiding parties attacked the English and Frankish shores indiscriminately. They established permanent bases at the mouths of great rivers, and sailed up them to plunder defenseless monasteries and sack towns. Antwerp was ravaged in 837, Rouen in 841, Hamburg and Paris in 845, and Charlemagne's old capital at Aachen in 881. Europe was truly under siege.

But if some Europeans were driven to helpless resignation, others fought doggedly to protect their lands and their heritage. King Alfred the Great of Wessex saved his kingdom from Danish conquest in the late 870s and began the arduous task of rolling back the Danish armies in England. King Arnulf of East Frankland won a decisive victory over the Norsemen in 891 at the battle of the Dyle and thereby vastly decreased the Viking pressure on Germany—although it was at this very moment that the Hungarian raids were beginning. West Frankland continued to suffer for a time, but in about 911 the Frankish King Charles the Simple created a friendly Viking buffer state in northern France by concluding an epoch-making treaty with a Norse chieftain named Rollo. The Vikings in Rollo's band had been conducting raids from their settlement at the mouth of the Seine River. Charles, less simple than his name would imply, believed that if he could make Rollo his ally the Seine settlement might prove an effective barrier against further raids. Rollo became a Christian, married Charles the Simple's daughter, and recognized at least in some sense the superiority of the West Frankish monarchy. Thus his state acquired legitimacy in the eyes of Western Christendom. Expanding gradually under Rollo and his successors it became known as the land of the Northmen or "Normandy." Over the next century and a half the Normans became as good Christians as the Franks. They adopted French culture and the French language, yet retained much of their old energy. In the eleventh century Normandy was producing some of Europe's most vigorous warriors, Crusaders, administrators, and monks.

IRELAND, GREENLAND, NORTH AMERICA

France, England, and Germany formed only a part of the vast Viking world of the ninth and tenth centuries. By the mid-800s Norwegians and Danes had conquered the greater part of Ireland, and between 875 and 930 they settled remote Iceland. There a distinctive Norse culture arose which for several centuries remained only slightly affected by the main currents of Western civilization. In Iceland the magnificent oral tradition of the Norse saga flourished and was eventually committed to writing. The Icelandic Norsemen were perhaps the greatest sailors of all. They settled on the coast of Greenland in the late 900s, and established temporary settlements on the northern coasts of North America itself in the eleventh century, thereby anticipating Columbus by half a millennium.

RUSSIA

To the east, Swedish Vikings overran Finland and penetrated far southward across European Russia to trade with Constantinople and Baghdad. The Byzantine emperors took inordinate pride in the tall Norse mercenaries who served in their imperial guard. In Russia a Swedish dynasty established itself at Novgorod in the later ninth

THE VIKING, HUNGARIAN AND MOSLEM INVASIONS

ICELAND

Atlantic Ocean

VIKINGS

NORWAY

SWEDEN

DENMARK

SCOTLAND

IRELAND

ENGLAND

Dnieper R.

Kiev

Aachen

Rhine R.

Rouen

Paris

Seine

Loire

Tours

Danube R.

HUNGARIANS

LOMBARDY

PROVENCE

Marseilles

Danube R.

Black Sea

CORSICA

Rome

Monte Cassino

Naples

Constantinople

SARDINIA

BALEARIC IS.

SICILY

MOSLEMS

Mediterranean Sea

→→→	Vikings
‑‑‑→	Moslems
▪▪▪▪→	Hungarians

MILES

0   200   400   600   800

century, ruling over the indigenous Slavic population. In the tenth century a Norse ruler at Novgorod captured the strategic Russian city of Kiev which became the nucleus of a powerful, well-organized Russian state. Deeply influenced by the culture of its subjects, the dynasty at Kiev became far more Slavic than Scandinavian. It adopted Byzantine Christianity around the turn of the millennium, and looked to Constantinople rather than to the West for its religious and cultural inspiration. In Russia, as elsewhere, the Norsemen showed that they could build kingdoms as well as destroy them.

TWILIGHT OF THE VIKING AGE

The development of centralized monarchies in Denmark, Norway, and Sweden ultimately resulted in taming the Viking spirit. As Scandinavia became increasingly civilized its kings discouraged the activities of roaming independent warrior bands, and its social environment gave rise to a somewhat more humdrum, sedentary life. Far into the eleventh century England continued to face the attacks of Norsemen, but these invaders were no longer pirate bands; rather, they were royal armies led by Scandinavian kings. The nature of the Scandinavian threat had changed profoundly; by the late eleventh century the threat had ceased altogether. Around the year 1000 Christianity was winning converts all across the Scandinavian world. In Iceland, in Russia—even in the kingdoms of Scandinavia itself—the ferocious Northmen were adopting the religion of the monks who had once so feared them. Scandinavia was becoming a part of Western European culture.

Even at the height of the invasions the Norsemen were by no means pure barbarians. They excelled at commerce as well as piracy. They were the greatest seafarers of the age. They introduced Europe to the art of ocean navigation and immeasurably enlarged the horizons of Western Christendom. In a word, they injected a spirit of enterprise and cosmopolitanism into the conservative, parochial outlook of Carolingian civilization.

8

Europe Survives the Siege

RESPONSE TO THE INVASIONS: ENGLAND

The invasions of the ninth and tenth centuries wrought significant changes in the political and social organization of Western Europe. Generally speaking, political authority tended to crumble into small local units as cumbersome royal armies failed to cope with the lightning raids. This was the case in France, but it was less true in Germany where the monarchy, after a period of relative weakness, underwent a spectacular recovery in the tenth century. In England, paradoxically, the hammer blows of the Danes had the ultimate result of unifying the several Anglo-Saxon states into a single kingdom.

In the later eighth century, on the eve of the Viking invasions, England was politically fragmented, just as it had been ever since the Anglo-Saxon conquests. But over the centuries the several smaller kingdoms had gradually passed under the control of three larger ones: Northumbria in the north, Mercia in the Midlands, and Wessex in the south. The Danish attacks of the ninth century, by destroying the power of Wessex's rivals, cleared the field for the Wessex monarchy and thereby hastened the trend toward consolidation that was already under way. But if the Danes were doing the Wessex monarchy a favor neither side was aware of it during the dark days of the later ninth century. England suffered grievous devastation, and for a time it appeared as though the Danes might conquer Wessex itself.

KING ALFRED

At the moment of crisis a leader rose to the Wessex throne who was perhaps the most remarkable king England has known: Alfred the Great (871–899). Alfred did everything in his power to save his kingdom from the Vikings. He fought ferocious battles against them. He even resorted to bribing them. In the winter of 878 the Danes, in a surprise attack, invaded Wessex and forced Alfred to take refuge, with a handful of companions, in a remote swamp on the isle of Athelney. As it turned out, Athelney was England's Valley Forge. In the following spring Alfred rallied his forces and smashed a Danish army at the battle of Edington. This victory turned the tide of the war; the Danish leader agreed to take up Christianity, to withdraw from the land, and to accept a "permanent" peace. Wessex was never again seriously threatened.

But other Danes under other leaders refused to honor the peace, and Alfred, in his later campaigns, conquered Kent and most of Mercia and captured London—even then England's greatest city. In the 880s a new peace treaty gave Wessex most of southern and southwestern England. The remainder of England—the "Danelaw" —remained hostile, but all non-Danish England was now united under King Alfred.

Like all successful leaders of the age Alfred was an exceedingly able warrior. But he was far more than that. He was a brilliant, imaginative organizer who systematized military recruitment and founded the English navy, seeing clearly that Christian Europe could not hope to drive back the Vikings without challenging them on the seas. He filled his land with fortresses which served both as defensive strongholds and as places of sanctuary for the agrarian population in time of war. And gradually, as the Danish tide was rolled back, new fortresses were built to secure the territories newly reconquered. Alfred clarified and rationalized the laws of his people, enforced them strictly, and ruled with an authority such as no Anglo-Saxon king had exercised before his time.

This remarkable monarch was also a scholar and a patron of learning. His intellectual environment was even less promising than Charlemagne's. The great days of Bede, Boniface, and Alcuin were far in the past, and by Alfred's time, Latin—the key to classical-Christian culture—was almost unknown in England. Like Charle-

ENGLAND ABOUT 885

Scale of Miles
0 20 40 60 80 100

SCOTS

Picts

Tay

Firth of Forth

ENGLISH NORTHUMBRIA

Picts

LINDISFARNE

North Sea

IRELAND

Irish Sea

Whitby

York

DANELAW

Trent R.

WALES

ENGLISH MERCIA

Severn R.

Ouse

EAST ANGLIA

Thames R.

London

Surrey

Kent

Canterbury

DEVON

WESSEX

SUSSEX

CORNWALL

English Channel

magne, Alfred gathered scholars from far and wide—England, Wales, the Continent—and set them to work teaching Latin and translating Latin classics into the Anglo-Saxon language. Alfred himself participated in the work of translation, rendering such works as Boethius' *Consolation of Philosophy*, Pope Gregory's *Pastoral Care*, and Bede's *Ecclesiastical History* into the native tongue. In his translation of Boethius, Alfred added a wistful comment of his own: "In those days one never heard tell of ships armed for war." And in his preface to the *Pastoral Care* he alluded with nostalgia to the days "before everything was ravaged and burned, when England's churches overflowed with treasures and books." Alfred's intellectual revival, even more than Charlemagne's, was a salvage operation rather than an outburst of originality. He was both modest and accurate when he described himself as one who wandered through a great forest collecting timber with which others could build.

Alfred's task of reconquest was carried on by his able successors in the first half of the tenth century. Midway through the century all England was in their hands, and the kings of Wessex had become the kings of England. Great numbers of Danish settlers still remained in northern and eastern England—the amalgamation of Danish and English customs required many generations—but the creative response of the Wessex kings to the Danish threat had transformed and united the Anglo-Saxon world. Out of the agony of the invasions the English monarchy was born.

THE RENEWAL OF THE DANISH ATTACK

For a generation after the conquest of the Danelaw, from about 955 to 980, England enjoyed relative peace and prosperity. English flotillas patrolled the shores, the old fortresses began to evolve into commercial centers, and dedicated churchmen addressed themselves to the task of monastic reform. But the Danish inhabitants of northern and eastern England remained only half committed to the new English monarchy, and with the accession of an incompetent child-king, Ethelred the Unready (978–1016), Danish invasions began anew.

The new invasions evolved into a campaign of conquest directed by the Danish monarchy. The English defense was characterized by incompetence, treason, and panic. In 991 Ethelred began paying a tribute to the Danes, known thereafter as "danegeld." In later years the danegeld evolved into a land tax which was exceedingly profitable to the English monarchy, but at the time it was a symbol of a profound humiliation. In 1016 Ethelred fled the country altogether, and in the following year King Canute of Denmark became the monarch of England (1017–1035).

Canute has been described as very nearly a dwarf and very nearly a genius. He conquered Norway as well as England, and, joining these lands to his kingdom of Denmark, he became the master of a vast, heterogeneous empire centering on the North Sea. A product of the new civilizing forces at work in eleventh-century Scandinavia, Canute was no bloodthirsty Viking. He issued law codes, practiced Christianity, and kept the peace. Devoting much of his time to England, he cast himself as an English king in the old Wessex tradition. He respected and upheld the ancient customs of the land and gave generously to the monasteries. Despite his Danish background, he was a far better English monarch than Ethelred. In a very real sense his reign was a continuation of the past, adding luster to the crown that Alfred's dynasty had forged. English religion and culture prospered as before: "Merry sang the monks of Ely as Canute the king rowed by."

Canute's immense Danish-Norwegian-English empire was hopelessly disunited and failed to survive his death in 1035. When the last of his sons died in 1042 the English realm fell peacefully to Edward the Confessor, a member of the old Wessex dynasty who had grown up in exile in Normandy.

THE AFTERMATH

Although a poor general and a mediocre administrator, Edward the Confessor was a man of piety who won the love of his people despite his political ineptitude. His insistence on his own virginity insured a disputed succession upon his death in 1066 and set the stage for the Norman Conquest. When William the Conqueror, duke of Normandy, invaded England and won its crown in 1066 he inherited a prosperous kingdom with strong and well-established political and legal traditions—a kingdom still divided by differences in custom but with a deep-seated respect for royal authority. Ethelred the Unready notwithstanding, the Wessex dynasty had done its work well. With the timber that Alfred collected his successors had built an ample and sturdy edifice.

RESPONSE TO THE INVASIONS: FRENCH FEUDALISM

In England the invasions stimulated the trend toward royal unification; in France they encouraged a shattering of political authority into small local units. This paradox can be explained in part by the fact that France, unlike England, was far too large for the Vikings to conquer. Although many of them settled in Normandy, the chief Norse threat to France came in the form of plundering expeditions rather than large conquering armies. Distances were too great, communications too primitive, and the national territorial army too unwieldy for the king to take the lead in defending his realm. Military responsibility descended to local lords who alone could hope to protect the countryside from the swift and terrible Viking assaults. The French Carolingians became increasingly powerless until at length, in 987, the crown passed to a new dynasty —the Capetians. During the twelfth and thirteenth centuries the Capetian family produced some of France's most illustrious kings, but for the time being the new dynasty was as powerless as the old one. After 987, as before, the nobles overshadowed the king. About all one can say of the French monarchy in these dark years is that it survived.

The Viking Age witnessed the birth of feudalism in France. In a very real sense feudalism was a product of France's response to the invasions. Yet in another sense the Franks had long been drifting in a feudal direction. The roots of feudalism ran deep: one root was the honorable bond of fidelity and service of a warrior to his lord, which characterized the lord-vassal relationship of late-Merovingian and early-Carolingian times, and the still earlier comitatus of the Germanic barbarians. Another root was the late-Roman and early-medieval concept of land-holding in return for certain services to the person who granted the land. An estate granted to a tenant in return for service was known as a *benefice*.

Charles Martel took an important step toward feudalism by joining the institutions of benefice and vassalage. He undertook heavy confiscations of Church property and granted the appropriated estates to his military vassals. There were several reasons for this step. For one thing money was in very short supply throughout the Early Middle Ages so that it was difficult for a ruler to support his soldiers with wages. Often the vassals of an important Frankish lord were fed and sheltered in his household. Indeed, the "household knight" persisted throughout the feudal age. But as their military importance grew these warrior-vassals exhibited an ever-increasing hunger for land. Their lords were therefore under considerable pressure to grant them estates—benefices—in return for their loyalty and service.

This tendency was associated with a profound revolution in Frankish military tactics which occurred around the 730s. Previously the Franks had been foot soldiers for the most part. Thereafter, cavalry became increasingly important; within a century and a half it had become all-important. The Frankish warrior *par excellence* was now the armored, mounted knight, far more effective than the infantryman, but also far more expensive to support or maintain. The knight needed a fine mount, heavy armor and weapons, several attendants, and many years of training. Hence the tendency for a lord to support his knightly vassals by granting them estates in return for their service. The knight did not, of course, labor on his own fields; rather he administered them and collected dues, chiefly in kind from his peasants.

The Carolingian military vassal was typically a knight. As knightly tactics came more and more to dominate warfare the custom of vassalage spread widely. The great Frankish magnates of Charlemagne's time pledged their allegiance to their emperor and thereby recognized that they were his vassals and he their lord. Moreover, these royal vassals had vassals of their own who owed primary allegiance to their immediate lords rather than to the emperor. Charlemagne himself approved of this practice and encouraged the free men of his realm to become vassals of his magnates. In time of war these vassals of vassals (or subvassals) were expected to join their lords' contingents in the royal army. The centrifugal tendencies implicit in such an arrangement are obvious. Yet Charlemagne, lacking a coherent civil service or adequate funds to hire a professional army of his own, was obliged to depend on this potentially unstable hierarchy of authority and allegiance.

With the removal of Charlemagne's commanding personality and under the pressure of the invasions, the rickety hierarchy began to crumble into its component parts. Charlemagne's old territorial officials, the dukes, counts, and margraves, backed by their own vassals, tended increasingly to usurp royal rights, revenues, and prerogatives. They administered justice and collected taxes without regard for the royal will. In time, they built castles and assumed all responsibility for the defense of their districts. Nominally these feudal magnates remained vassals of the kings of France, but they soon became much too powerful to be coerced by the crown. Their authority was limited chiefly by the independence of their own vassals who began to create subvassals or sub-subvassals of their own. At the height of the feudal age the lord-vassal relationship might run down through some ten or twenty levels; there was scarcely a vassal to be found who was not the lord of some still lower vassal.

The ultimate consequences of these developments have been described as "feudal anarchy." In a sense the term is well chosen, but it should not mislead us into thinking of feudalism simply as a "bad thing." Given the instability of the Carolingian Empire and the desperate plight of France in the Viking era, feudalism emerges as a realistic accommodation to the hard facts of the age. It should never be forgotten that whereas Roman Europe succumbed to barbarian invasions, Feudal Europe survived its invaders and ultimately absorbed them.

French feudalism reached its height in the tenth and eleventh centuries. Its key institution was the military benefice, the estate granted by a lord to his vassal in return for allegiance and service—primarily knightly military service. This military benefice was commonly known as a *fief* (rhyming with beef). It was a logical response to the desperate requirements of local defense, the perpetuation of at least some degree of political authority, and the scarcity of money which necessitated paying for service in land rather than wages. A great lord would grant an estate—a fief—to his vassal. The vassal might then grant a part of the estate—another fief—to a vassal of his own. And so on and on, down and down, the process of enfeoffment went. The result was a hierarchically organized landed knightly aristocracy. Each knight gave homage and fealty—that is, the pledge of his personal allegiance—to his immediate lord; each lived off the labor and dues of a dependent peasantry which tilled the fields that his fief embraced; each administered a court and dispensed justice to those below him.

Such were the essential ingredients of feudalism. The term is extremely difficult to define and has been frequently abused and misunderstood. If we wish to put the whole institution in a nutshell we can do no better than repeat the definition—or description—of medieval feudalism's greatest modern scholar, the French historian Marc Bloch:

> A subject peasantry; widespread use of the service tenement (that is, the fief) instead of a salary, which was out of the question; the supremacy of a class of specialized warriors; ties of obedience and protection which bind man to man and, within the warrior class, assume the distinctive form called vassalage; fragmentation of authority—leading inevitably to disorder; and in the midst of all this, the survival of other forms of association, family and state . . . —such then seem to be the fundamental features of European feudalism.*

With this description in mind it may be helpful to emphasize some of the things that feudalism was not. It was not, for one thing, a universal and symmetrical system. Born in northern France in the Viking age it took on many different forms as it spread across Europe. In northern France itself it varied widely from one region to another. It by no means encompassed all the land, for even at its height many landowners owed no feudal obligations and had no feudal ties. The feudal hierarchy or feudal "pyramid" was riddled with ambiguities: a single vassal might hold several fiefs from several lords; a lord might receive a fief from his own vassal, thereby putting himself in the extraordinary position of being his vassal's vassal. The degree of confusion possible in feudalism can best be appreciated by examining a typical document of the age:

> I, John of Toul, affirm that I am the vassal of the Lady Beatrice, countess of Troyes, and of her son Theobald, count of Champagne, against every creature living or dead, excepting my allegiance to Lord Enjourand of Coucy, Lord John of Arcis, and the count of Grandpré. If it should happen that the count of Grandpré should be at war with the countess and count of Champagne in his own quarrel, I will aid the count of Grandpré in my own person, and will aid the count

---

* Bloch, *op. cit.*, p. 446.

and countess of Champagne by sending them the knights whose services I owe them from the fief which I hold of them.

So much for feudal order.

Feudalism was not, in its heyday, associated with the romantic knight errant, the many-turreted castle, or the lady fair. The knight of the ninth, tenth, and eleventh centuries was a rough-hewn warrior. His armor was simple, his horse was tough, his castle was a crude wooden tower atop an earthen mound, and his lady fair was any available wench. Chivalry developed after a time, to be sure, but not until the foundations of the old feudal order were being eroded by the revival of commerce and a money economy, and by stronger monarchies. Only then did the knight seek to disguise his declining usefulness by turning to elaborate shining armor, lace and ruffles, courtly phrases, and wedding-cake castles.

Feudalism was not entirely military. The vassal owed his lord not only military service but a variety of additional obligations as well. Among these were the duty to join his lord's retinue on tours of the countryside; to serve, when summoned, in his lord's court of justice; to feed, house, and entertain his lord and his lord's retinue on their all-too-frequent visits; to give money to his lord on a variety of specified occasions; to contribute to his lord's ransom should he be captured in battle. Early in its history the fief became hereditary. The lord, however, retained the right to confiscate it should his vassal die without heirs, to supervise and exploit it during a minority, and to exercise a power of veto over the marriage of a female fief-holder. In return for such rights as these the lord was obliged to protect and uphold the interests of his vassals. The very essence of feudalism was the notion of reciprocal rights and obligations. Consequently the feudal outlook played a key role in steering medieval Europe away from autocracy.

Feudalism was both a military system and a political system. With military responsibility went political power. As the central government of West Frankland demonstrated an ever-increasing incapacity to cope with the invasions or keep peace in the countryside, sovereignty tended to descend to the level of the greater feudal lords. Although nominally royal vassals, these magnates were in effect powers unto themselves, ruling their own territories without royal interference and maintaining their own courts and administrative systems as well as their own armies. In the days of the Viking raids many of these magnates had extreme difficulty in controlling their own turbulent vassals; feudal tenants several steps down in the pyramid were often able to behave as though they had no real superiors. Subvassals with their own courts and armies were frequently in a position to defy their lords. It is difficult therefore to identify the real locus of political power in early feudal France. Sovereignty was spread up and down the aristocratic hierarchy, and a lord's real power depended upon his military prowess, his ambition, and the firmness of his leadership.

Specialists in medieval history are inclined to limit "feudalism" to the network of rights and obligations existing among members of the knightly aristocracy—the holders of fiefs. Although it rested on the labor of peasants the feudal structure itself encompassed only the warrior class of lords and vassals. There was, in other words, a world of difference between a vassal and a serf. Beneath the level of the feudal warrior class, 80 or 90 per cent of the population continued to labor on the land, producing the food that sustained society. Yet the peasantry was disdained by the nobility and largely ignored by the chroniclers of the age.

The feudal chaos of the ninth and tenth centuries, with its extreme fragmentation of sovereign power and its incessant private wars, gradually gave way to a somewhat more orderly regime. Great territorial magnates such as the counts of Anjou and Flanders and the dukes of Normandy extended their frontiers at the expense of weaker neighbors and tightened their control over their own vassals and subvassals. But it was not until the twelfth century that the French monarchs began to rise above the level of their great feudal magnates and assert real authority over the realm. Indeed, the high noon of feudalism was a period of virtual eclipse for the French crown.

RESPONSE TO THE INVASIONS: GERMANY

Different peoples responded differently to the invasions of the "new barbarians." In England the invasions brought royal unification; in France, feudal particularism. The response of Germany differed from those of both England and France, because of the special nature of the invasions that Germany faced and the unique conditions prevailing in Germany itself. Although the East Frankish kingdom—which evolved directly into the medieval German state —was subject to Viking attacks, the real threat came from the Hungarian horsemen of the East. The late Carolingian kings of Germany—the successors of Louis the German who was granted East Frankland by the Treaty of Verdun—proved incapable of coping with the Hungarian raids. As in France, real authority descended to the great magnates of the realm. But these magnates were not the dukes and counts of Carolingian officialdom. Most of Germany had remained outside Frankish control until the Carolingian conquests of the eighth century; consequently the Frankish system of local administration was but imperfectly established there. Moreover, the ancient tribal consciousness of Saxons, Bavarians, and Swabians was still strong. In the critical decades of the late ninth and early tenth centuries ambitious aristocrats exploited this tribal patriotism by grasping leadership over the old tribal districts. These men of the hour assumed the title of duke and the regions that they ruled came to be known as tribal duchies.* The "tribal" dukes sought to dominate the local ecclesiastical organizations, to seize the royal Carolingian estates in their duchies, and to usurp royal powers. It was they who stood up to the Hungarian thrust.

In the early tenth century there were five important tribal duchies: Saxony, Swabia, Bavaria, Franconia, and Lorraine. Saxony, Swabia, and Bavaria had been incorporated only superficially into the Carolingian state, whereas the western duchies of Franconia and Lorraine were much more strongly Frankish in outlook and organization.

The five "tribal" dukes might well have become the masters of Germany. Their ambitions were frustrated by two closely related factors: (1) their failure to curb the Hungarians, and (2) the reinvigoration of the German monarchy under an able new dynasty. The Carolingian line came to an end in Germany in 911 with the death of King Louis the Child. He was succeeded first by the duke of Franconia and then, in 919, by the duke of Saxony—the first of a remarkable and illustrious line of kings who based their royal power on their domination of the powerful Saxon duchy.

* Otherwise known as "stem duchies."

OTTO I

The Saxon kings struggled vigorously to assert their authority over the tribal duchies. With the duchy of Saxony under the authority of the monarchy the Saxon kings quickly won direct control over Franconia as well. But the semi-independent dukes of the two southern duchies, Swabia and Bavaria, presented problems. The real victory of the Saxon monarchy occurred in the reign of the second and greatest of the Saxon kings, Otto I (936–973).

Otto I, or Otto the Great as he is often called, devoted his considerable talents to achieving three goals: (1) the defense of Germany against the Hungarian invasions, (2) the establishment of royal power over the remaining tribal duchies, and (3) the extension of German royal control to the crumbling, unstable Middle Kingdom which the Treaty of Verdun had assigned to Emperor Lothar back in 843. We have already seen how this heterogeneous Middle Kingdom began to fall to pieces after Lothar's death. By the mid-tenth century it had become a confused political shambles. Parts of it had been taken over by Germany and France but its southern districts—Burgundy and Italy—retained a chaotic independence. The dukes of Swabia and Bavaria both had notions of seizing these territories. Otto the Great, in order to forestall the development of an unmanageable rival power to his south, led his armies into Italy in 951 and assumed the title "King of Italy."

From 951 onwards events developed rapidly. Otto the Great was obliged to leave Italy in haste to put down a major uprising in Germany. His victory over the rebels enabled him to establish his power there more strongly than ever. In 955 he won the crucial battle of the age when he crushed a large Hungarian army at Lechfeld. In this one blow he terminated forever the Hungarian menace. Lechfeld served as a vivid demonstration of royal power—a vindication of the monarch's claim that he, not the "tribal" dukes, was the true defender of Germany. With the Hungarians defeated Germany's eastern frontier now lay open to the gradual penetration of German-Christian culture. The day of the tribal duchies was over; the monarchy reigned supreme. Otto the Great now towered over his contemporaries as the greatest monarch of the West and the most powerful ruler since Charlemagne. The invasions of Germany, which had begun by uplifting the tribal duchies, ended by contributing to the revival of royal authority.

After Lechfeld there remained for Otto I one important piece of unfinished business. Since his departure from Italy a usurper had seized the Italian throne and was harassing the pope. In response to a papal appeal—which conveniently dovetailed with his own interests—Otto returned to Italy in force, conquered the usurper, and recovered the Italian crown. In 962 the pope hailed Otto as Roman Emperor and placed the imperial crown on his head. It is this momentous event, rather than the coronation of Charlemagne in 800, that marks the true genesis of the medieval institution known as the Holy Roman Empire. Although the events of 962 are reminiscent of those of 800, Otto's empire was vastly different from Charlemagne's. Above all, Otto and his imperial successors made no pretensions of universal jurisdiction over France or the remainder of Western Christendom. The medieval Holy Roman Empire had its roots deep in the soil of Germany, and most of the emperors subordinated imperial interests to those of the German monarchy. From its advent in 962 to its long-delayed demise in the early nineteenth century the Holy Roman Empire remained fundamentally a German phenomenon.

The German orientation of Otto's empire is illustrated dramatically by the fact that neither he nor the majority of his successors over the next two centuries made any real effort to establish tight control over Italy. Only when they marched south of the Alps could they count on the obedience of the Italians; when they returned to Germany they left behind them no real administrative structure but depended almost solely on the fickle allegiance of certain Italian magnates. The medieval German emperors were never really successful in straddling the Alps.

In Germany conditions were quite different. There the coming of feudalism was delayed for more than a century after Otto's imperial coronation. The great magnates, to be sure, became vassals of the king. But they normally had no vassals of their own. The chief tool which Otto and his successors employed in governing their state was the Church. In an era of a weak papacy the German kings dominated the Church within their realm and kept close control over important ecclesiastical appointments. Otto had successfully wrested control of the Church in the various tribal duchies

THE HOLY ROMAN EMPIRE IN 962

North Sea

Baltic Sea

K. OF DEN.

SLAVS

FRISIA

SAXONY

Rhine R.

LORRAINE

Elbe R.

FRANCONIA

BOHEMIA

FRANCE

SWABIA

Lechfeld

BAVARIA

Danube R.

KINGDOM OF BURGUNDY

CARINTHIA

HUNGARIANS

Rhone R.

KDM. OF ITALY

Venice

KDM. OF CROATIA

SERVIA

CORSICA

Rome

SARDINIA

BENEVENTO

APULIA

CALABRIA

SICILY

0   100   200   300 MILES

▨ The Holy Roman Empire
░ The Five Stem Duchies

from the defunct dukes, and in a very real sense the great bishops and abbots of Germany were the king's men. They made ideal royal lieutenants. They could not make their estates hereditary for when a bishop or abbot died his successor was hand-picked by the king. Thus the loyalty and political capacity of the churchly royal administrators was assured. After 962 the German monarchy was even moderately successful in appointing popes. There would come a time when churchmen would rebel at such high-handed treatment; but in Otto's reign the time was still far off.

Otto's lofty claims to proprietorship over the imperial Church were supported by both tradition and theory. Otto was regarded as far more than a mere secular monarch. He was *rex et sacerdos*, king and priest, sanctified by the holy anointing ceremony which accompanied his coronation. He was the vicar of God—the living symbol of Christ the king—the "natural" leader of the Church in his empire. In the closing years of his reign his actual political power over Church and state came close to matching his exalted pretensions.

THE OTTONIAN RENAISSANCE

Otto's remarkable reign provided the impulse for an impressive intellectual revival which reached its culmination under his two successors, Otto II (973–83) and Otto III (983–1002). This "Ottonian Renaissance" produced a series of able administrators and scholars, the greatest of whom was the brilliant churchman Gerbert of Aurillac—later Pope Sylvester II (d. 1003). Gerbert visited Spain and returned with a comprehensive knowledge of Islamic science. This event marked the beginning of the infiltration of the intellectual legacy of Arab civilization into Western Christendom. Gerbert had an encyclopedic, although unoriginal, mind. A master of classical literature, logic, mathematics, and science he astonished his contemporaries by teaching the Greco-Arab doctrine that the earth was spherical. There were widespread rumors that he was some kind of wizard in league with the Devil—rumors somewhat dampened by his elevation to the papacy. Rather than being a wizard Gerbert was the advance agent of a momentous intellectual awakening that Europe was about to undergo—a harbinger of the High Middle Ages.

CHRONOLOGY OF THE AGE OF SIEGE AND ITS AFTERMATH

England	France	Germany
c.787: First Danish raid	814–840: Louis the Pious	814–840: Louis the Pious
	840–877: Charles the Bald	840–876: Louis the German
871–899: Reign of Alfred	843: Treaty of Verdun	843: Treaty of Verdun
878: Battle of Edington	911: Normandy recognized	891: Vikings defeated by Arnulf
c.954: Reconquest of Danelaw completed		936–973: Reign of Otto the Great
		955: Otto defeats Hungarians at Lechfeld
		962: Otto crowned Roman Emperor
978–1016: Reign of Ethelred	987: Capetians replace Carolingians	973–983: Reign of Otto II
1017–1035: Reign of Canute		983–1002: Reign of Otto III
1042–1066: Reign of Edward the Confessor		1003: Gerbert of Aurillac dies
1066: Norman Conquest of England		1039–1056: Reign of Henry III

Although the successors of Otto the Great were no longer troubled by the tribal duchies or the Hungarians, they were obliged as all men are to cope with new problems and devise new solutions. In 1024 the Saxon dynasty died out and was replaced by a Franconian family known as the Salian dynasty (1024–1125). The "tribal" dukes gave way to a new, particularistic aristocracy whose impulse toward independence taxed the ingenuity of the emperors. Still, the early Salian kings were generally successful in maintaining their power. Working hand in glove with the German Church, the Salians improved and elaborated royal administration and ultimately came to exercise even greater authority than Otto I had known. In the mid-eleventh century the mightiest of the Salian emperors, Henry III (1039–1056), ruled unrivaled over Germany and appointed popes as effortlessly as he selected his own bishops. In 1050, at a time when France was still a medley of feudal principalities and England, under Edward the Confessor, was relatively small and more-or-less isolated, the German Emperor Henry III dominated Central Europe and held the papacy in his palm.

MANOR AND VILLAGE

During the centuries between the fall of the Roman Empire in the West and the great economic and cultural revival of the later eleventh century, the foundations were built on which Western civilization rose. Kingdoms were forming, distinctive customs and institutions were developing, and a classical-Christian intellectual tradition was gradually being absorbed, adapted, and broadened. And at the bottom of the social order, the peasant had become firmly attached to the soil, hedged about with various obligations, and trained from childhood in a variety of traditional techniques.

To discuss the typical medieval manor is as difficult as to discuss the typical American business. Medieval agrarian institutions were almost infinitely diverse; medieval agriculture exhibited countless variations. Nevertheless some features of agrarian life recur throughout much of the more fertile and more heavily populated portions of Northern Europe. Certain generalizations can be made about medieval agrarian institutions if we bear in mind that numerous exceptions to any of them can always be found.

Any discussion of medieval husbandry must begin by distinguishing between two fundamental institutions: the village and the manor. The village, the basic unit of the agrarian economy, consisted of a population nucleus ranging from about a dozen to several hundred peasant families living in a cluster. In some of the poorer or more isolated districts, peasant families lived in separate farms or hamlets; but village life was the norm in medieval agriculture.

The manor, on the other hand, was an artificial unit—a unit of jurisdiction and economic exploitation controlled by a single lord. The lord might be a king, a duke or count, a bishop or abbot, or a great baron. He might and commonly did have numerous manors under his control. Or he might be a simple knight, at the bottom of the feudal pyramid, with only one or two manors at his disposal. The manor—the unit of jurisdiction—was often coterminous with the village; but some manors embraced two or more villages and, on occasion, a village might be divided into two or more manors. In any case, the agrarian routine of plowing, planting, and harvesting was based on the village organization, whereas the peasants' dues, obligations, and legal and political subordination were based on the manor.

Let us discuss these two institutions—the village and the manor— in turn. The ordinary village consisted of a grouping of peasants' huts surrounded by open fields. There would normally be either two or three such fields. Two was the traditional number, but, as we have seen, the agrarian economy had been shifting in many districts of Northern Europe from a two-field to a three-field system of rotation. The peasants of a three-field village would plant one field in the spring for fall harvesting, plant one field in the fall for early summer harvesting, and let the third field lie fallow throughout the year. The next year the fields would be rotated and the process repeated.

The arable lands surrounding the village were known as *open fields* because they were unfenced. They were divided into strips of about 220 yards in length separated from one another by furrows. Each peasant possessed several strips scattered throughout the fields, but the peasant community labored collectively, pooling their plows, their draught animals, and their toil. Collective husbandry was necessary because plows were scarce and had to be shared and because no one peasant owned sufficient oxen or horses to make up a plow team of eight beasts which was necessary to draw the heavy plow. The details of this collective process were usually worked out in the village council and were guided by immemorial custom.

The shape, contour, and method of cultivation of the open fields was determined by the topography of the region and the fertility of the soil. It therefore varied enormously from place to place. The strips themselves were products of the heavy plow and the necessity of reversing the eight-ox team as infrequently as possible. The length of the strips was determined by the distance a team could draw the plow without rest. A group of four strips, the plowing of which constituted a normal day's work, became the basis of our modern acre.

The open fields were the fundamental element in the village

economy and, indeed, the entire agrarian economic system of the Middle Ages. But there was more to the village community than the cluster of peasants' huts and the encircling fields. Besides his scattered strips in the fields, a peasant ordinarily had a small garden adjacent to his hut where vegetables and fruits could be raised and fowl kept to provide variety to his diet. The village also included a pasture where the plow animals might graze, and a meadow from which hay was cut to sustain the precious beasts over the winter. Some village communities kept sheep on their pasture as a source of cheese, milk, and wool. Indeed, certain districts, particularly in Flanders and northern England, took up sheep raising on a scale so large as almost to exclude the growing of grains.

Attached to most village communities was a wooded area that served as a source of fuel and building materials. It also served as a forage for pigs, which provided most of the meat in the peasants' diet. There was commonly a stream or pond nearby which supplied the community with fish, a water mill for grinding grain, and a large oven which the community used for baking bread. By the eleventh century most village communities were organized as parishes. Each parish possessed a village church supervised by a priest who was drawn from the peasant class and who had land of his own scattered among the strips of the open fields.

The village community was something of a closed system, economically self-sufficient, capable of sustaining the material and spiritual needs of the villagers without much contact with the outside world. The economy of the Early Middle Ages, lacking a vigorous commercial life and a significant urban population, failed to provide villages with much incentive to produce beyond their immediate needs. There was only the most limited market for surplus grain. Therefore village life tended to be uneventful, tradition-bound, and circumscribed by the narrowest of horizons. On the other hand, gradual but profound changes were occurring in medieval civilization which eventually made a deep impact upon the village. The medieval innovations in agrarian technology already discussed significantly increased agricultural efficiency and productivity. Moreover the commercial and urban revival of the High Middle Ages provided an ever-expanding market for surplus grain. These developments in turn eroded village parochialism, freed the village economy from its self-sufficiency by incorporating it into a far vaster economic system, and provided enterprising peasants with a means of acquiring considerable money. They also encouraged a tremendous expansion of villages and fields through the clearing of forests and wilderness and the draining of marshes. Timeless though it might have seemed, the village economy was changing; its dynamic elements must never be overlooked.

In the foregoing summary of the village economy one essential element has been deliberately excluded: that of private lordship. Superimposed on the economic structure of the village was the political-juridical structure of the manor. The average peasant was bound to a manorial lord. Some agrarian laborers were outright slaves, although slavery was in decline throughout the Early Middle Ages and had practically disappeared by the end of the eleventh century. Some peasants, on the other hand, were of free status, owing rents to their lord but little or nothing more. A few were landless laborers working for a wage. But the great middle stratum of the medieval peasantry consisted of serfs—men of unfree status, bound to the land like the Roman *coloni* and possessed of strips of their own in the open fields. They owed various dues to their manorial lord, chiefly in kind, and were normally expected to labor for a certain number of days per week—often three—on the lord's fields.

The lord drew his sustenance from the dues of his peasants and from the produce of his own fields. The lord's fields were strips scattered among the strips of the peasants, and were known collectively as the lord's demesne. Theoretically, then, the fields of the manor were divided into two categories: the lord's demesne (perhaps one-fourth to one-third of the total area) and the peasants' holdings —known as tenements. But in fact the demesne strips and the peasants' strips were intermixed. The demesne was worked by the peasants who also paid their lord a percentage of the produce of their own fields and rendered him fees for the use of the pasture, the woods, and the lord's mill and oven. Such were some of the more common and more important peasant obligations on many manors.

The lord also enjoyed significant political authority over his peasants—an authority that flourished and grew in proportion to the disintegration of sovereign power which occurred in late Carolingian times. The administrative nexus of the manor was the manorial court, usually held in the lord's castle or manor house. Here a rough, custom-based justice was meted out, disputes settled, mis-

deeds punished, and obligations enforced. Since most lords possessed more than one manor, authority over individual manors was
commonly exercised by an agent of the lord known as a bailiff or
steward. It was he who supervised the manorial court, oversaw the
farming of the demesne, and collected the peasants' dues. In addition to the peasants' agrarian obligations, the lord was also entitled
to certain payments deriving from his political and personal authority over his tenants. He might levy a tallage—an arbitrary
manorial tax that was theoretically unlimited in frequency and
amount but was in fact circumscribed by custom. He was normally
entitled to payments when a peasant's son inherited the holdings
of his father, and when a peasant's daughter married outside the
manor.

In general the serfs had no standing before the law. The lord was
prevented from exploiting them arbitrarily only by the force of
custom. But custom was exceedingly strong in the Middle Ages and
protected the serf in many different ways. He was by no means a
chattel slave. He could not be sold, nor could his own hereditary
fields be taken from him. After paying his manorial dues he was
entitled to keep the produce of his own fields. Hardly enviable, his
situation could have been worse.

Although drawing from Roman and Germanic traditions the
manor and the village were typically medieval. They showed endless variations—evolving in time and differing significantly from
place to place. In the eleventh century the manorial regime was
only incompletely established in England and was scarcely evident
at all in Scandinavia and in parts of northern Germany and southern
France. Although the two-field system was common in Southern
Europe and the three-field system in the north, many northern
villages had only two fields. Others had four or five or even more,
all subjected to complex rotation arrangements. Vital, diverse, and
on the whole healthy, medieval agriculture proved itself capable
of expanding sufficiently to support the soaring new economy and
the rich civilization of the High Middle Ages.

THE CHURCH

The existence of parish churches in the villages of the eleventh
century illustrates the deeply significant fact that the process of

Model of the Abbey Church at Cluny showing Romanesque apse.

Christianizing Europe was reaching the point of successful completion. Whatever were the intellectual and moral shortcomings of the village priests, they were at least representatives of the international Church operating at the most immediate local levels throughout the European countryside. At a rather more elevated level was the work and influence of the Benedictines. They offered prayers to God, copied manuscripts, taught in their schools, supplied knights to secular armies, and served as prelates and counsellors under counts, dukes, and kings. While continuing their traditional spiritual activities they played an ever-growing role in lay political life.

The greatest Benedictine house of the later tenth and earlier eleventh centuries was Cluny in Burgundy. Founded in 910 by the duke of Aquitaine, Cluny was free of local episcopal jurisdiction, subject to the pope alone, and blessed with a series of remarkably able and long-lived abbots. Cluny followed Benedict of Aniane's modifications of the original Benedictine Rule. Its monks, shunning field work, devoted themselves to an unusually elaborate and magnificent sequence of daily prayers and liturgical services, and a strict, godly life. This strictness was relative, falling far short of the austere regimes of several of the more ascetic orders of the High

Middle Ages. Yet the Cluniacs were successful in avoiding the abuses and corruption that flourished in many monasteries of their day. Richly endowed, holy, and seemingly incorruptible, Cluny became famous and widely admired. In time it began to acquire daughter houses. Gradually it became the nucleus of a great congregation of reform monasteries extending throughout Europe—all of them obedient to the abbot of Cluny. In the mid-eleventh century the Congregation of Cluny was both powerful and wealthy. Its high ideals were tempered by a sense of dignity—and perhaps also by a comfortable feeling of spiritual success and social acceptance. Enriched and supported by the lay aristocracy, it was by no means in radical opposition to secular society; rather it tended on the whole to accept and uphold the social system of its day and to worship the Lord God without disparaging the lords of men.

Cluny's attitude typified that of the entire Church in the earlier eleventh century. As the lay world became more and more exposed to Christianity, as pious kings such as Edward the Confessor in England and Henry III in Germany demonstrated their concern for the welfare of their churches, the Church itself tended increasingly to come to terms with lay society. Through the ceremony of anointing, kings became virtual priest-kings. Indeed, contemporary political theory taught that the Church and the world were one—a single, God-oriented organism in which churchmen and lay lords each had appropriate roles to play.

Apart from Cluny, the monasteries and bishoprics of eleventh-century Europe tended to be under lay control. They were dependent on lay patronage and were often subsumed under the feudal system. Their prelates were appointed by lay lords in much the same way that village priests were chosen and controlled by manorial lords. Although not free, the Church was wealthy, respected, and comfortable, and few churchmen were inclined to challenge the situation. Those few, however, were to undertake in the later eleventh century a political-spiritual revolution which severely undermined the long established Church-state entente.

EUROPE ON THE EVE OF THE HIGH MIDDLE AGES

By 1050 both England and Germany were comparatively stable, well-organized kingdoms. The French monarchy was still weak, but within another century it would be on its way toward dominating France. Meanwhile feudal principalities such as Normandy, Flanders, and Anjou were well on the road to political coherence. Warfare was still endemic, but it was beginning to lessen as Europe moved toward political stability. Above all, the invasions were over —the siege had ended. Hungary, Poland, and the Scandinavian world were being absorbed into Christendom, and Islam was by now on the defensive. The return of prosperity, the increase in food production, the rise in population, the quickening of commerce, the intensification of intellectual activity, all betokened the coming of a new era. Western civilization was on the threshold of an immense creative upsurge which was destined ultimately to transform the world.

Suggested Readings

The asterisk indicates a paperback edition.

GENERAL HISTORIES OF THE EARLY MIDDLE AGES

Margaret Deanesly, *A History of Early Medieval Europe, 476–911* (2nd ed., Methuen). An excellent, accurate, and highly detailed text.

H. St. L. B. Moss, *The Birth of the Middle Ages* (*Oxford). A brief, thoughtful survey running from the Principate through Charlemagne.

J. M. Wallace-Hadrill, *The Barbarian West* (*Harper). Still more condensed; the discussion of the Carolingian Renaissance is especially illuminating.

William C. Bark, *Origins of the Medieval World* (*Anchor). A provocative interpretive study.

Robert Latouche, *The Birth of Western Economy* (Methuen). A splendid, up-to-date account of early medieval economic trends.

M. L. W. Laistner, *Thought and Letters in Western Europe, A.D. 500 to 900* (rev. ed., Methuen). The best intellectual history of the period.

Christopher Dawson, *The Making of Europe* (*Meridian). A brilliant analysis of early medieval culture by a distinguished Catholic scholar.

THE MYSTERY RELIGIONS AND CHRISTIANITY

F. Cumont, *The Mysteries of Mithra* (*Dover), and *Oriental Religions in Roman Paganism* (*Dover). Two fundamental studies by a great scholar, outdated in details but still useful.

R. Bultmann, *Primitive Christianity in its Contemporary Setting* (*Meridian). Readable and authoritative.

Michael Gough, *The Early Christians* (Praeger). A good popular account with fine illustrations.

E. R. Goodenough, *The Church in the Roman Empire* (*Henry Holt). A brief, lucid survey.

V. Latourette, *History of Christianity* (Harper). One of the best short histories of the Christian Church.

H. O. Taylor, *The Emergence of Christian Culture in the West* (*Harper). An ageless study by one of the masters of medieval intellectual history.

C. N. Cochrane, *Christianity and Classical Culture* (*Oxford Galaxy). An intellectual tour de force, sympathetic to the rise of the mystical point of view.

132

THE LATER EMPIRE AND THE GERMANIC INVASIONS

J. B. Bury, *History of the Later Roman Empire* (*2 vols., Dover). The standard account, full and authoritative, by one of the distinguished historians of this century.

F. Lot, *The End of the Ancient World and the Beginnings of the Middle Ages* (*Harper). A masterly study that places stress on the economic factors in the decline. A valuable introduction by Glanville Downey summarizes recent scholarship on the problem of "decline and fall."

Mortimer Chambers (Ed.), *The Fall of Rome* (*Holt, Rinehart, and Winston). Well-chosen excerpts from historical writings dealing with the decline of Rome provide a compact, illuminating survey of historical opinion on the subject.

Solomon Katz, *The Decline of Rome* (*Cornell). A brief, perceptive, well-written survey.

Samuel Dill, *Roman Society in the Last Century of the Western Empire* (*Meridian). A brilliant older work.

Edward Gibbon, *The Triumph of Christendom in the Roman Empire* (*Harper). Chapters XV–XX from Gibbon's masterpiece, *The Decline and Fall of the Roman Empire*. The entire work is available in a three-volume Modern Library edition.

BYZANTIUM

N. H. Baynes and H. St. L. B. Moss (Eds.), *Byzantium, An Introduction to East Roman Civilization* (*Oxford). An anthology of essays by scholarly specialists, organized topically.

Two short general accounts of Byzantine history and civilization, available in paperback, are highly recommended:

J. M. Hussey, *The Byzantine World* (*Harper).

Steven Runciman, *Byzantine Civilization* (*Meridian).

G. Ostrogorsky, *History of the Byzantine State* (Blackwell). Longer and more detailed than the above works, this is the best single-volume history of Byzantium.

THE WEST BEFORE THE CAROLINGIANS

J. M. Wallace-Hadrill, *The Long-Haired Kings* (Barnes and Noble). A collection of illuminating essays on the Merovingian period.

A. F. Havinghurst (Ed.), *The Pirenne Thesis—Analysis, Criticism, and Revision* (*Heath). An excellent approach to one of the central problems in early medieval history through excerpts from the writing of contending historians. For a fuller account of Pirenne's thesis see:

Henri Pirenne, *Mohammed and Charlemagne* (*Meridian).

ISLAM

G. E. von Grunebaum, *Medieval Islam* (2nd ed., University of Chicago Press). A learned and original work, the best on the subject.

P. K. Hitti, *History of the Arabs* (St. Martin's Press). Broad yet full; a monumental work. For a good introduction to Hitti's work, see:

P. K. Hitti, *The Arabs: A Short History* (*Gateway).

Two other useful surveys in paperback are

H. A. R. Gibb, *Mohammedanism: An Historical Survey* (*Mentor).

Bernard Lewis, *The Arabs in History* (*Arrow Books).

CAROLINGIAN AND POST-CAROLINGIAN EUROPE

H. Fichtenau, *The Carolingian Empire* (*Harper). The best English-language work on the subject.

P. H. Sawyer, *The Age of the Vikings* (St. Martin's Press). A highly significant reappraisal of the Viking age.

Marc Bloch, *Feudal Society* (*U. of Chicago Press). A masterly work, challengingly written and boldly original in its conclusions.

Lynn White, Jr., *Medieval Technology and Social Change* (*Oxford). An important and provocative pioneering work which defies categorization. Beautifully written and opulently annotated.

Geoffrey Barraclough, *The Origins of Modern Germany* (*Capricorn). Incorporates recent scholarship in medieval German constitutional history.

Sidney Painter, *French Chivalry* (*Cornell). Short, witty, and perceptive.

F. M. Stenton, *Anglo-Saxon England* (2nd ed., Oxford). A massive masterpiece.

H. R. Loyn, *Anglo-Saxon England and the Norman Conquest* (St. Martin's Press). An authoritative recent work emphasizing economic and social history.

F. L. Ganshof, *Feudalism* (*Harper). A short, authoritative and rather technical survey of medieval feudal institutions.

Carl Stephenson, *Medieval Feudalism* (*Cornell). A brief, lucid, well-organized account.

SOURCES

B. Davenport (Ed.), *The Portable Roman Reader* (*Viking). One of several good anthologies now available in paperback.

St. Augustine's *Confessions* has been published in several paperback editions. For the *City of God*, see Vernon J. Bourke (Ed.), *St. Augustine's City of God* (*Doubleday Image). An intelligent abridgment.

Gregory of Tours, *History of the Franks*, tr. O. M. Dalton (Oxford). Provides an interesting account of Clovis and the early Franks in Gaul.

Norman F. Cantor (Ed.), *The Medieval World* (*Macmillan). A good recent collection of medieval sources.

Einhard, *Life of Charlemagne*, tr. S. E. Turner (*Ann Arbor Paperbacks). A short, reasonably trustworthy biography by Charlemagne's secretary.

Bede, *A History of the English Church and People*, tr. Leo Sherley-Price (*Penguin).

Part 2

THE HIGH MIDDLE AGES:

The First Flowering of European Culture

9

Economic Revolution and New Frontiers

THE HIGH MIDDLE AGES: 1050-1300

History, it has often been said, is a seamless web. But the human mind can only cope with the flow of historical reality by dividing it into arbitrary chronological units—forcing it into compartments of the historian's own making. In this sense every historical "period" is a kind of falsehood—an affront to the continuity of human development. Yet unless we concoct historical epochs, unless we invent ages, unless we force the past into some relatively tidy chronological framework, we cannot make history intelligible to the human mind. Thus the historian speaks of "Classical Antiquity," "The Early Middle Ages," "The High Middle Ages," "The Renaissance," etc. These are all historical lies, to be sure, but they are necessary lies—white lies—without which the past would have little meaning. We cannot get along without "eras," but we should never forget that they are inventions of our own. We should never lose sight of their limitations.

The term *High Middle Ages* has been applied to the great cultural upsurge of the later eleventh, twelfth, and thirteenth centuries. Yet no spectacular event occurred in 1050 to signal the advent of the new era; no cataclysm occurred in 1300 to mark its end. The transition from Early Middle Ages to High Middle Ages was gradual and uneven. It might even be argued that the High Middle Ages came to Germany as early as the tenth century, under the Ottos, or that it was delayed in France until the twelfth century when the Capetian monarchy rose from its torpor. Ever since the waning of the Viking, Hungarian, and Saracen invasions—many decades before 1050— Europe had been pulsing with new creative energy. Broadly speaking, however, the scope and intensity of the revival did not become evident until the later eleventh century. By the century's end, Europe's lively commerce and bustling towns, her intellectual vigor and political inventiveness, her military expansion and her heightened religious enthusiasm left no doubt that vast new forces were at work—that Western Christendom had at last become a great creative civilization. As the historian would say, a new age had dawned.

The causes of an immense cultural awakening such as occurred in the High Middle Ages are far too complex to be identified precisely or listed in order of importance. One essential element was the ending of the invasions and the increasing political stability that followed. We know that in the eleventh century Europe's population was beginning to increase significantly and that her food production was rising. Whether increased productivity led to increased population or vice versa is difficult to say. But productivity could not have risen as it did without the revolutionary developments in agricultural technology: the three-field system which spread across much of northern Europe, the windmill, the water mill (by 1086 there were over 5000 water mills in England alone), the heavy, wheeled plow, the horseshoe and improved horse collar which transformed horses into efficient draught animals, and the tandem harness which made it possible to employ horses and oxen in large teams to draw plows or to pull heavy wagons. These and numerous related inventions came to the West gradually over the centuries, but they had a powerful cumulative influence on the great economic boom of the High Middle Ages.

TOWNS AND COMMERCE

The rise in productivity and population was accompanied by a great commercial revival and a general reawakening of urban life. In turn, the new towns became the foci of a brilliant, reinvigorated culture. The intimate human contacts arising from

town life stimulated European thought and art. The cathedral
and the university, perhaps the two greatest monuments of high
medieval culture, were both urban phenomena; the Franciscan
order, possibly the loftiest and most dynamic religious institution
that the new age produced, devoted itself primarily to evangelical
work among the new urban population. Yet the towns were also,
and above all, centers of commercial and industrial enterprise.
The European economy in the High Middle Ages remained fundamentally agrarian, but the towns were the great economic and
cultural catalysts of the era. In them, God and mammon stood
face to face and often worked hand in hand.

There had been towns in Europe ever since antiquity. The
administrative-military town of the Roman Empire gave way in
time to the far humbler cathedral town of the Early Middle Ages.
But both had one crucial thing in common: both were economic
parasites, living off the blood, labor, and taxes of the countryside;
both consumed more than they produced. The towns of the High
Middle Ages, on the other hand, represented something radically
new. With few exceptions they were true commercial entities that
earned their own way, living off the fruits of their merchant and
industrial activities. Small, foul, disease-ridden, and often torn
by internal conflict, they were nevertheless Western Europe's first
cities in the modern sense of the word.

These commercial towns arose in rhythm with the upsurge of
commerce. Often they began as suburbs of older cathedral towns
or as humble settlements outside the walls of some of the many
fortresses that had arisen in ninth- and tenth-century Europe.
These fortresses were generally known by some form of the Germanic word *burgh*, and in time the term came to apply to the
town itself rather than the fortress that spawned it. By the twelfth
century a *burgh* or *borough* was an urban commercial center, in-
habited by *burghers* or *burgesses*, who constituted a new class known
later as the bourgeoisie.

At the end of the eleventh century, towns were developing rapidly all over Europe. They were thickest in Flanders and northern
Italy, where the immense opportunities of international commerce
were first exploited. The greatest Italian city of the age was Venice,
long a Byzantine colony but now an independent republic, whose
merchants carried on a lucrative trade with Constantinople and

the East. Other Italian coastal towns—Genoa, Pisa, and Amalfi—soon followed Venice into the profitable markets of the eastern Mediterranean, and the ramifications of their far-flung trade brought vigorous new life to the towns of interior Italy, such as Milan and Florence. During the High Middle Ages the Moslems were virtually driven from the seas and Italian merchants dominated the Mediterranean.

Meanwhile, the towns of Flanders were growing wealthy from the commerce of the North—from trade with northern France and the British Isles, the Rhineland, and the shores of the Baltic Sea. Flanders itself was a great sheep-growing district; her towns became centers of woolen textile production. In time the towns were processing more wool than Flemish sheep could supply so that from the twelfth century onward Flemish merchants began to import wool on a huge scale from England. By then Flanders was the great industrial center of northern Europe, with the textile industry the supreme manufacturing enterprise of the age.

The rise of towns and commerce injected a vigorous new urban class into a society that had previously been almost exclusively agrarian. The merchant class was drawn from vagabonds, runaway serfs, avaricious minor noblemen, and, in general, the surplus of a mushrooming population. At an early date these ambitious traders began to form themselves into merchant guilds in order to protect themselves against confiscatory tolls and other exactions levied by a hostile landed aristocracy. A town was almost always situated on the territories of some lord—sometimes a duke or a king—and the merchants found that only by collective action could they win the privileges essential to their calling: personal freedom from serf-like status, freedom of movement, freedom from inordinate tolls at every bridge or feudal boundary, the rights to own property in the town, to be judged by a town court, to execute commercial contracts, and to buy and sell freely. By the twelfth century, a number of lords, recognizing the economic advantages of having flourishing commercial centers on their lands, were issuing town charters which guaranteed many of these rights. Indeed, some farsighted lords began founding and chartering new towns on their own initiative.

At first the urban charters differed greatly from one another, but in time it became customary to pattern them after certain well-known models. The charter granted by the king of England to Newcastle-on-Tyne, and that of the French king to the town of Lorris, were copied repeatedly throughout England and France. In effect, these charters transformed the commercial communities into semi-autonomous political and legal entities, each with its own local government, its own court, its own tax-collecting agencies, and its own customs. These urban communes paid well for their charters and continued to pay regular taxes to their lord. But—and this is all important—they did so as political units. Individual merchants were not normally subject to the harassments of their lords' agents. These townsmen enforced their own law in their own courts, collected their own taxes, and paid their dues to their lord in a lump sum. In short, they had won the invaluable privilege of handling their own affairs.

We should not conclude, however, that the medieval towns were even remotely democratic. It was the prosperous merchants and master craftsmen who profited chiefly from the charters, and it was they who normally came to control the town governments, ruling as narrow oligarchies over the towns' less exalted and less fortunate inhabitants. Some towns witnessed the beginning of a significant split between large-scale producers and wage-earning workers along the lines of modern capitalism. It can be said, in fact, that the medieval town was the birthplace of European capitalism. For as time passed, towns tended to become centers of industry as well as commerce. Manufacturing followed in the footsteps of trade. And although most industrial production took place in small shops rather than large factories, some enterprising businessmen employed considerable numbers of workers to produce goods—usually textiles—on a large scale. Normally these workers did not labor in a factory but rather in their own shops or homes. Since the entrepreneur sent his raw materials out to his workers, instead of bringing the workers to the materials, this mode of production has been called the "putting-out system." As a direct antecedent of the factory system, it was a crucial phase in the early history of capitalism.

The more typical medieval manufacturer worked for himself in his own shop, producing his own goods and selling them directly to the public. As early as the eleventh century these craftsmen were organizing themselves into craft guilds—as distinct from merchant guilds. In an effort to limit competition and protect their market, the craft guilds established strict admission requirements and stringent rules on prices, wages, standards of quality, and operating procedures. A young craftsman would learn his trade as an apprentice in the shop of a master craftsman. After a specified period, sometimes as long as seven years, he ended his apprenticeship. With good luck and rich parents he might then become a master himself. Normally, however, he had to work for some years as a day laborer— a journeyman—improving his skills and saving his money, until he was able to demonstrate sufficient craftsmanship to win guild membership and accumulate enough money to establish a shop of his own. Toward the end of the High Middle Ages, as prosperity began to wane and urban society became more crystallized, it became increasingly common for journeymen to spend their whole lives as wage earners, never becoming masters at all. Accordingly, the town became the scene of bitter class feelings which erupted from time to time into open conflict.

There were many who made their fortunes in commerce and manufacturing. Europe was astir with new life; for a clever, enterprising man the possibilities were vast. In the twelfth and thirteenth century, merchants were moving continuously along the roads and rivers of Europe. Italians crossed the Alps bringing spices and luxury goods from the Near East and the Orient to the aristocracy of France and Germany. French, Flemish, and German merchants carried goods far and wide across the Continent, "buying cheap and selling dear." A series of annual fairs along the overland trade routes provided the long-distance merchants with excellent opportunities to sell their goods. As large-scale commerce grew, credit and banking grew with it, and by the thirteenth century several banking families had amassed immense fortunes. It may seem paradoxical that the period which is often regarded as the supreme age of faith witnessed the rise of large-scale commerce and a money economy. Yet it was money that built the Gothic cathedrals and supported the Crusades, that financed the pious charities of St. Louis and gave zest to the magnificent religious culture of the thirteenth century—money, and, of course, an ardent faith. In time faith itself would fall victim to the acquisitive spirit which was evolving in the towns, but during the High Middle Ages the townsmen, by and large, exhibited a piety that was far more vibrant and intense than that of the peasantry and the aristocracy. Indeed, the powerful upsurge of lay piety among the European townsmen became a crucial factor in the evolution of medieval Christianity.

THE DECLINE OF FEUDALISM

Feudalism, based as it was on hereditary land tenure in return for service, was a characteristic product of a money-poor society which could not afford to pay wages to its warriors. With the rise of a money economy in Europe, the basic feudal relationship began to dissolve. The deep impact of feudal custom on the European mind is demonstrated by the various ingenious ways in which the aristocracy sought to adopt feudalism to the new economic realities. Indeed, during the eleventh and twelfth centuries the feudal system spread from France into England, Germany, and the Crusader States of the Holy Land. At the same time, however, kings and dukes were resorting increasingly to the hiring of mercenaries for warfare and professional judges and civil servants for the administration of their realms. As the twelfth century progressed, the feudal vassal was, oftener than not, asked to pay a tax in lieu of his personal service in the feudal army. With the income from this tax—which was sometimes called *scutage*—a monarch could hire professional warriors who were better trained, better disciplined, and much more obedient than the landed knights. The feudal aristocracy retained its lands and much of its power for centuries to come, and even continued to produce warriors. But the knights of the new age expected to be paid. They no longer served at their own expense in return for their fiefs. Once the paying of taxes had replaced personal service as the vassal's primary obligation—and this was the case almost everywhere by the thirteenth century—feudalism had lost its soul.

THE EVOLUTION OF AGRARIAN LIFE

The new social and economic conditions of the High Middle Ages wrought a profound transformation in the European countryside. Doubtless the most spectacular change was the immense expansion of arable land. The great primeval forest of northern Europe was reduced to isolated patches, swamps and marshes were drained, and vast new territories were opened to cultivation. This prodigious clearing operation was stimulated by the soaring population and the rising money economy. Agricultural surpluses could now be sold to townsmen and thereby converted into cash. Consequently, the peasant was strongly motivated to produce as far in excess of the consumption level as he possibly could. Every new field that could be put into operation was likely to bring a profit.

A second change, no less significant than the first, was the elevation of the peasant. Slavery, which was rare in Carolingian times, had virtually disappeared from Europe by the eleventh century. The tillers of the land were chiefly freemen and serfs. Often the freeman owned his own small farm, but the serf was generally to be found on a manor. Normally the manor included the peasants' fields and the lord's fields—his *demesne*—the produce of which went directly and entirely to the lord. Among the obligations that the serf normally owed his lord were a rent in kind from the serf's own fields and labor service for a stipulated number of days on the lord's demesne. In Carolingian times, manorial lords had augmented the part-time serf labor on their demesne fields by using slaves. As slavery gradually died out, the lords were faced with a severe labor shortage on their demesne.

As a result of this problem, and in keeping with the trend toward transforming service obligations into money payments, the lords tended to abandon demesne farming altogether. They leased out their demesne fields to peasants and, in return for a fixed money payment, released their serfs from the traditional obligation of working part-time on the demesne. At about the same time they translated the serf's rent-in-kind from his own fields into a money rent. By freeing the serf of his labor obligation they transformed him, in effect, into a tenant farmer, thereby improving his status immensely. The obligations of the serf, like those of the feudal vassal, were gradually being placed on a fiscal basis.

The abandonment of demesne farming was a slow and uneven trend which progressed much more rapidly in some areas than in others. In thirteenth-century England, a counter-trend developed whereby many lords successfully reclaimed and enlarged their demesnes. But on the Continent the demesne gradually disappeared and, in quite a literal sense, the peasant inherited the earth.

When the lords transformed the dues and services of their serfs into fixed money rents they failed to reckon with inflation. The booming economy of the High Middle Ages was accompanied by

an upward spiral of prices and a concomitant decline in the pur-
chasing power of money. Hence the real value of the peasants'
fixed rents steadily diminished, and many lords of the later Middle
Ages came to regret the bargains their ancestors had made. Inflation ruined more than one lord, but it was a godsend to the medieval
peasantry. The lords could do little to recoup their losses; they were
often obligated to improve the condition of their peasants still more
in order to keep them from fleeing to the towns or to the newly
cleared lands. The peasant was in great demand, and the enterprising land developers who were engaged in turning woods and
marshes into fields competed for his services. As a consequence, the
High Middle Ages witnessed the elevation of innumerable peasants
from servile status to freedom. Rural communes emerged—peasant
villages whose lords had granted them charters closely paralleling
those of townsmen. We should be careful not to idealize the lot of
the thirteenth-century peasant—it was still impoverished and
brutish by present standards—yet it was distinctly superior to
peasant life in the Roman Empire or the Early Middle Ages. The
terrifying peasants' rebellions of early Modern Europe were products of a later and different era when the expansion and prosperity
of the High Middle Ages had given way to an epoch of recession
and closed frontiers.

THE NEW FRONTIERS

The open, expanding frontier is one of the most characteristic
aspects of the High Middle Ages. The clearing of forests and draining of swamps represent the conquest of a great internal frontier.
They were paralleled by an external expansion all along the periphery of Western Christendom, which brought vast areas of the Arab,
Byzantine, and Slavic worlds within the ballooning boundaries of
European civilization and added wealth to the flourishing economy.

Western Europe had been expanding ever since Charles Martel
repelled the Arabs in 733. Charlemagne had introduced Frankish
government and Christianity into much of Germany and had
established a Spanish bridgehead around Barcelona. The stabilization and conversion of Hungary and Scandinavia around the
turn of the millennium pushed the limits of Western civilization
far northward and eastward from the original Carolingian core.

Now, in the eleventh, twelfth, and thirteenth centuries, the population boom produced multitudes of landless aristocratic younger sons who sought land and military glory on Christendom's frontiers. And the ever-proliferating European peasantry provided a potential labor force for the newly conquered lands. While the Christian warrior of the frontier was carving out new estates for himself, he was also storing up treasures in heaven, for as a result of his aggressive militancy Christendom was everywhere expanding at the expense of the heathen Slavs of eastern Europe and the infidel Moslems of Spain, Sicily, and Syria. Land, gold, and eternal salvation—these were the alluring rewards of the medieval frontier.

SPAIN

So it was that knightly adventurers from all over Christendom—and particularly from feudal France—flocked southwestward into Spain during the eleventh century to aid in the reconquest of the Iberian Peninsula from Islam. The powerful Moslem caliphate of Cordova had broken up after 1002 into a kaleidoscope of small, warring Moorish states, thereby providing the Christians with a superb opportunity. Unfortunately, the Christians were themselves divided into several kingdoms that consumed more energy fighting one another than fighting the Moors. Taking the lead in the reconquest, the Christian kingdom of Castile captured the great Moslem city of Toledo in 1085. In later years Toledo became a crucial point of contact between Islamic and Christian culture. Here numerous Arab scientific and philosophical works were translated into Latin and then disseminated throughout Europe to challenge and invigorate the Western mind.

Early in the twelfth century the Spanish Christian kingdom of Aragon contested the supremacy of Castile and undertook an offensive of its own against the Moors. In 1140 Aragon was greatly strengthened by its unification with Catalonia—the wealthy state whose center was Barcelona—the Spanish March of Charlemagne's time. During the greater part of the twelfth century, Aragon, Castile, and the smaller Christian kingdoms exhausted themselves in fighting one another and the reconquest momentarily stalled. But in 1212 the powerful Pope Innocent III proclaimed a crusade against the Spanish Moslems, and the king of Castile ad-

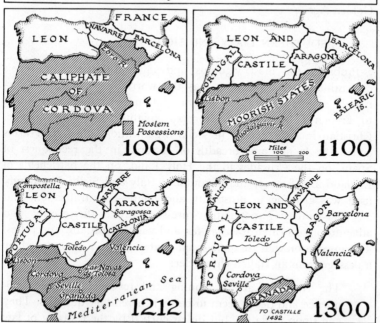

THE RECONQUEST OF SPAIN

1000
FRANCE
LEON
NAVARRE
BARCELONA
CALIPHATE OF CORDOVA
Moslem Possessions

1100
LEON AND CASTILE
PORTUGAL
NAVARRE
ARAGON
BARCELONA
Lisbon
MOORISH STATES
Guadalquivir
BALEARIC IS.
Miles
100 200

1212
Compostella
LEON
NAVARRE
ARAGON
Saragossa
CATALONIA
CASTILE
PORTUGAL
Toledo
Valencia
Lisbon
Cordova
Las Navas de Tolosa
Seville
Granada
Mediterranean Sea

1300
GALICIA
NAVARRE
LEON AND CASTILE
ARAGON
Barcelona
PORTUGAL
CASTILE
Toledo
Valencia
Cordova
Seville
GRANADA
TO CASTILLE 1492

vanced from Toledo with a powerful pan-Iberian army, winning a decisive victory over the Moors at the battle of Las Navas de Tolosa. Thereafter Moorish power was permanently crippled. Cordova fell to Castile in 1236, and by the later thirteenth century the Moors were confined to the small southern kingdom of Granada where they remained until 1492. Castile now dominated central Spain, and the work of re-Christianization proceeded apace as Christian peasants were imported en masse into the reconquered lands. Aragon, in the meantime, was conquering the islands of the western Mediterranean from the Moslems and establishing a powerful maritime empire.

Thus the High Middle Ages witnessed the Christianization of nearly all the Iberian Peninsula and its organization into two powerful Christian kingdoms and several weaker ones. The long crusade against the Moslems was the chief factor in the molding of Spanish life in the Middle Ages, and its ultimate result was to produce the intense blend of piety and patriotism which inspired

147

the saints, soldiers, and *conquistadores* of Spain's sixteenth-century Golden Age.

SOUTHERN ITALY AND SICILY

Probably the most vigorous and militant force in Europe's eleventh-century awakening was the warrior-aristocracy of Normandy—largely Viking in ancestry but now thoroughly adapted to French culture. These Norman knights, French in tongue, Christian in faith, feudal in social organization, plied their arms across the length and breadth of Europe: in the reconquest of Spain, on the Crusades to the Holy Land, on the battlefields of England and France, and in southern Italy and Sicily. Normandy itself was growing in prosperity and political centralization, and an ever-increasing population pressure drove the greedy and adventurous Norman warriors far and wide on distant enterprises. The impression that they made on contemporaries is suggested by a passage from an Italian chronicler:

> The Normans are a cunning and revengeful people; eloquence and deceit seem to be their hereditary qualities. They can stoop to flatter, but unless curbed by the restraint of law they indulge in the licentiousness of nature and passion and, in their eager search for wealth and power, despise whatever they possess and seek whatever they desire. They delight in arms and horses, the luxury of dress, and the exercise of hawking and hunting, but on pressing occasions they can endure with incredible patience the inclemency of every climate and the toil and privation of a military life.

Early in the eleventh century the Normans began to try their luck in the chaotic politics of southern Italy. Here, Byzantine coastal cities—a legacy of Justinian's conquests—struggled with old Lombard principalities and rising seaport republics such as Naples and Amalfi. The great offshore island of Sicily was controlled by the Moslems—or rather it was divided among several mutually hostile Moslem princes who had been compounding the confusion of southern Italy by mounting raids against it. The whole area was a bewildering mixture of at least four peoples: Greek, Lombard, Latin-Italian, and Arab—and three major religions: Roman Catholic,

Eastern Orthodox, and Islamic—in addition to which there existed an important and vigorous Jewish minority. It was, in short, a chaotic melting pot, politically unstable and, from the standpoint of the Normans, enormously promising.

First hiring themselves out as mercenaries to one side or another, the Norman adventurers quickly began to found states of their own. During the 1030s and 1040s a group of eight brothers, sons of a relatively insignificant Norman lord named Tancred d'Hauteville, began wandering into southern Italy and gradually assumed leadership in the movement of conquest. These eight d'Hauteville brothers illustrate vividly the dynamism engendered in Europe by the adventurous enterprises of landless younger sons of the Northern European nobility. For although they were nobodies in Normandy, the d'Hautevilles rose to supreme power in southern Italy. In the early 1040s the district of Apulia was thrown into chaos by a Lombard insurrection against Byzantine control; when the dust had cleared, it was found that most of Apulia was dominated by neither Byzantines nor Lombards but by three of Tancred d'Hauteville's sons, bearing the formidable names: William Iron-Hand, Humphrey, and Drogo.

The papacy, fearing the ominous rise of Norman power to the south of the Papal States and spurred on by stories of Norman atrocities, mounted an army against the Normans and engaged them in battle at Civitate in 1053. The Normans defeated the army, captured the pope himself, and, after paying him due reverence, obliged him to confirm their conquests and become their lord—in short, to legitimize them. No longer free-booters, the Normans now enjoyed the status of respectable landholders and vassals of St. Peter.

In the meantime the greatest of the d'Hauteville brothers, Robert Guiscard (the Cunning), had arrived in the area and had carved out a patrimony for himself in the southern province known as Calabria. Robert was proud, ambitious, ruthless, calculating, and dishonest—possessed, in other words, of all the qualities of the successful statesman and empire builder. As master of Calabria he lived like a brigand, inviting distinguished guests to dinner only to have them robbed. In 1054 he won control of Apulia and thereby rose to a position of dominance in Norman Italy. A treaty which he executed with the papacy in 1059 gave him the title, "By the grace of God and St. Peter, duke of Apulia, Calabria, and hereafter Sicily."

The Capella Palatina in Palermo (1132–1140); note the mosaics on
the inside of the arches and on the floor.

This last phrase was in effect a papal suggestion that Robert and
his fellow Normans might well direct their energies to the conquest
of the Sicilian Moslems.

Robert Guiscard's newly conquered duchy was wealthy and
powerful by the standards of the age. It included an important
center of medical studies at Salerno and several thriving commercial

Mosaic of Christ from the Cathedral in Monreale.

cities such as Amalfi which carried on an extensive trade with Africa, Arabia, and Constantinople. But the Normans, who "despise whatever they possess and seek whatever they desire," were not satisfied with dominion over Apulia and Calabria. In 1060 Guiscard, taking up the papal challenge, landed with a Norman army in Sicily. Shortly afterward he turned the enterprise over to his brother Roger, the youngest of the d'Hautevilles. In later years Guiscard, although hard-pressed to suppress the incessant revolts of his Apulian nobles, found time to launch a major attack against Byzantine lands and to come to the papacy's rescue by driving a hostile Holy Roman emperor from Rome. His death in 1085 terminated a career that reflected in full measure the limitless confidence, enterprise, and ambition of his age.

While Robert Guiscard was occupied in his farflung projects, his brother Roger was proceeding with the subjugation of Sicily. The Norman conquest of the island was difficult and prolonged, but in 1072 the rich Sicilian city of Palermo, with one of the finest harbors in the Mediterranean, fell to the Normans. By 1091 the conquest was completed and Roger d'Hauteville stood as undisputed master of Sicily.

By now the entire area of Sicily and southern Italy was in Norman hands, yet it remained for a time politically divided. Robert Guiscard's heterogeneous, rebellious state passed first to his son, then to his grandson who died without direct heirs in 1127. Under these two successors, southern Italy became ever more turbulent. Sicily, on the contrary, was much less prone to rebellion. Roger d'Hauteville wisely instituted a policy of toleration which placated the Sicilian Moslems and won their support for the new Norman dynasty. When Roger died in 1101 he passed on to his heirs a well-organized state and a sophisticated administration which combined Moslem, Byzantine, and feudal elements and was backed by an obedient Saracen army.

In 1105 Sicily passed to Roger d'Hauteville's son, Roger II or Roger the Great (d. 1154), a brilliant administrator and empire builder of a rather different type than Guiscard. Roger the Great was able, ambitious, tolerant, and cruel—less the adventurous feudal warrior than his predecessors had been, and far more sophisticated than they. In 1127 Roger undertook a campaign for the mastery of southern Italy, and by 1129 he assumed control of all the Norman domains, Apulia and Calabria as well as Sicily. In the following year he was elevated to royal status by papal coronation and the lands won by the Normans were thereby fused into a kingdom.

Although Roger the Great's new realm embraced both Sicily and southern Italy, it was called simply the Kingdom of Sicily; it would later be called the Kingdom of the Two Sicilies. Roger ruled strongly but tolerantly over the assorted peoples of his realm with their variety of faiths, customs, and languages. The Sicilian capital of Palermo, with its superb harbor and magnificent palace, its impressive public buildings and luxurious villas, was at once a great commercial center and a crucial point of cultural exchange. Known as the city of the threefold tongue, Palermo drew its administrators and scholars from the Latin, Byzantine, and Arabic cultural traditions.

The legal structure of the kingdom included elements from Justinian's *Corpus Juris* and subsequent Byzantine law, from Lombard law, and from Norman feudalism. The royal court or *curia* was the core of an efficient, centralized bureaucracy with special departments of justice and finance. The administration profited from the inclusion of an important non-noble professional class, devoted to the king and to the efficient execution of its duties. Drawing on the long experience of Byzantium and Islam, Roger's government was far in advance of the other states of Latin Christendom.

The kingdom's splendid and varied architecture was similarly multi-cultural in inspiration. The Capella Palatina (Palace Church) at Palermo, built on a marble foundation and opulently decorated with mosaics, was a source of wonder and admiration. Not far from the capital, the magnificent cathedral at Monreale, begun several decades after Roger's death, synthesizes Italian, Norman-French, Moslem, and Byzantine artistic traditions with wonderful artistry. The nave of the cathedral is built on the pattern of the Italian basilica, but the building is enlivened with rich Islamic and Byzantine decorations. It contains a remarkable set of brass doors executed in the Byzantine style, and its interior sparkles with some 70,000 square feet of Byzantine mosaics. This remarkable structure, the cathedral church of the archbishop of Sicily, remains today in an excellent state of preservation. It epitomizes in stone the multiform civilization of twelfth-century Norman Sicily.

Under Roger and his successors the kingdom enjoyed a vital and diverse intellectual life. Its history was well chronicled by talented contemporary historians—in particular, Hugo Falcandus who produced an illuminating biography of Roger the Great. The Moslem scholar Idrisi, the greatest geographer of his age, produced a comprehensive geographical work which drew from classical and Islamic sources. Characteristically, Idrisi dedicated his masterpiece to Roger the Great, and the work bears the title, "The Book of Roger." Sicily, like Spain, became a significant source of translations from Arabic and Greek into Latin. The Sicilian translators provided Western European scholars with a steady stream of texts drawn from both classical Greek and Islamic sources, and these texts, together with those passing into Europe from Spain, served as the essential foundations for the impressive intellectual achievements of thirteenth-century Christendom.

In many ways Norman Sicily was Western Europe's most interesting and fruitful frontier state. Having been carved out partially at Moslem expense, it was representative of twelfth-century Europe's advancing territorial frontier, and as a vibrant center of cultural interplay it demonstrated that the frontier was not only advancing

but also open. Europe besieged had given way to a new Europe—
buoyant, expanding, and exposed to the invigorating influences of
surrounding civilizations. And nowhere was this stimulating cultural contact more intense than in Norman Sicily. East and West
met in Roger the Great's glittering, sun-drenched realm, and worked
creatively side by side to make his kingdom the most sophisticated
European state of its day.

THE CRUSADES

The Crusades to the Holy Land were the most spectacular and
self-conscious acts of Western Christian expansionism in the High
Middle Ages, although by no means the most lasting. They arose
in response to a major political crisis in the Near East. During the
eleventh century a new warlike tribe from Central Asia, the Seljuk
Turks, swept into Persia, took up the Islamic faith, and turned the
Abbasid caliphs of Baghdad into their pawns. In 1071 the Seljuk
Turks inflicted a nearly fatal blow upon the Byzantine Empire,
smashing a Byzantine army at the battle of Manzikert and seizing
Asia Minor, the essential reservoir of Byzantine manpower. Stories
began filtering into the West of Turkish atrocities against Christian
pilgrims to Jerusalem, and when the desperate Byzantine emperor,
Alexius Comnenus, swallowed his pride and appealed to the West
for help, Europe, under the leadership of a reinvigorated papacy, was
only too glad to respond.

The Crusades represented a fusion of three characteristic impulses
of medieval man: sanctity, pugnacity, and greed. All three were
essential. Without Christian idealism the Crusades would be incon-
ceivable, yet the pious dream of liberating Jerusalem and the Holy
Land from the infidel was reinforced mightily by the lure of new
lands and unimaginable wealth. The Crusades provided a superb
opportunity for the Christian warrior-aristocracy to perform their
knightly skills in the service of the Lord—and to make their fortunes
in the bargain.

It was to Pope Urban II that Emperor Alexius Comnenus sent
his envoys asking for military aid against the Turks, and Urban II,
a masterful reform pope, was quick to grasp the opportunity. The
Crusade presented many advantages to the Church. It enabled the
papacy to put itself at the forefront of an immense popular movement

and to grasp thereby the moral leadership of Europe. Moreover, the Church may well have seen in the Crusade a partial solution to the problem of endemic private warfare in Europe—a means of drawing off many of the more warlike and restive members of the European nobility and turning their ferocity outward against the Moslems rather than inward against each other. And as a rescue mission to Byzantium, the Crusade opened the possibility of reuniting the Eastern and Western Churches which had been in schism for more than a generation. Finally, Urban shared with many other Europeans of his day the beguiling dream of winning Jerusalem for Christendom.

Therefore in 1095 Pope Urban II summoned the European nobility to take up the Cross and reconquer the Holy Land. He delivered a powerful, epoch-making address to the Frankish aristocracy at Clermont-Ferrand, calling upon them to emulate the brave deeds of their ancestors, to avenge the Turkish atrocities (which he described in gory detail), to win the Biblical "land of milk and honey" for Christendom, and drive the infidel from the holy city of Jerusalem. Finally, he promised those who undertook the enterprise the highest of spiritual rewards: "Undertake this journey for the remission of your sins, with the assurance of the imperishable glory of the kingdom of Heaven."

The response was overwhelming. With shouts of "God wills it!" Frankish warriors poured into the crusading army. By 1096 the First Crusade was under way. A great international military force— with a large nucleus of feudal knights from central and southern France, Normandy, and Sicily—made their way across the Balkans and assembled at Constantinople. Altogether the warriors of the First Crusade numbered around 25,000 or 50,000, a relatively modest figure by modern standards but immense in the eyes of contemporaries. Emperor Alexius was gravely disturbed by the magnitude of the Western European response. Having asked for a certain amount of military support, he had, as he put it, a new barbarian invasion on his hands. Cautious and apprehensive, he demanded and obtained from the Crusaders a promise of homage for all the lands they might conquer.

From the beginning there was friction between the Crusaders and the Byzantines. They differed in temperament and also in aim, for the Byzantines wished only to recapture the lost provinces of

Asia Minor, whereas the Crusaders were determined on nothing less than the conquest of the Holy Land. Alexius promised military aid, but it was never forthcoming, and not long after the Crusaders left Constantinople they broke with the Byzantines altogether. Hurling themselves southeastward across Asia Minor into Syria, they encountered and defeated Moslem forces, captured ancient Antioch after a long and complex siege, and in the summer of 1099 took Jerusalem itself. Urban II, who had remained behind, died just before the news of Jerusalem's fall reached Rome.

The Crusaders celebrated their capture of Jerusalem by plundering the city and pitilessly slaughtering its inhabitants. As a contemporary eyewitness describes it,

> If you had been there you would have seen our feet colored to our ankles with the blood of the slain. But what more shall I relate? None of them were left alive; neither women nor children were spared . . . . Afterward, all, clergy and laymen, went to the Sepulcher of the Lord and His glorious temple, singing the ninth chant. With fitting humility they repeated prayers and made their offering at the holy places that they had long desired to visit.

With the capture of Jerusalem, after only three years of vigorous campaigning, the goal of the First Crusade had been achieved. No future crusade was to enjoy such notable success, and during the two centuries that followed, the original conquests were gradually lost. For the moment, however, Europe rejoiced at the triumph of its Crusaders. Some of them returned to their homes and received heroes' welcomes. Others remained in Latin Syria to enjoy the fruits of their conquests. A long strip of territory along the eastern Mediterranean shore had been wrested from Islam and was now divided, according to feudal principles, among the Crusader knights. These warriors consolidated their conquests by erecting large and elaborate castles whose ruins still excite the admiration of travelers.

The conquered lands were organized into four Crusader States: the County of Edessa, the Principality of Antioch, the County of Tripolis, and the Kingdom of Jerusalem. This last was the most important of the four states, and the king of Jerusalem was theoretically the feudal overlord of all the Crusader territories. In fact, however, he had difficulty enforcing his authority outside his own kingdom. Indeed, the feudal knights who settled in the Holy Land were far too proud and warlike for their own good, and the Crusader States were characterized from the beginning by dangerous rivalries and dissensions.

Gradually, over the years, the Moslems began to reconquer their lost lands. Jerusalem fell to them in 1187, less than a century after its capture by the Christians. Europe sent new Crusading armies eastward, but to no avail. In later years some of Europe's most illustrious monarchs took up the Cross—Richard the Lion-Hearted of England, Emperor Frederick Barbarossa of Germany, St. Louis of France—but always in vain. In 1291 the last Christian bridgehead on the Syrian coast fell to the Moslems, and the Crusader States came to an end.

Yet the Crusades were more than simply a splendid failure. For the greater part of the High Middle Ages, Christian Crusaders ruled portions of the Holy Land. Their activities caught the imagination of Europe and held it for two centuries. During the Crusading age European merchants established permanent bases in Syria and vastly enlarged their role in international commerce. As a surprising side effect of the Crusading movement, a considerable portion of the Byzantine empire passed for a time into Western Christian hands. This came about as a consequence of the Fourth Crusade (1201–1204), which, by a curious series of circumstances, was diverted from the Holy Land to Constantinople. The Crusaders took the city by siege in 1204, succeeding where so many armies before them had failed, and actually established a dynasty of Western emperors in Constantinople which ruled the city for half a century until a Greek dynasty displaced them. In the Latin Empire of Constantinople as well as in the Holy Land, Christian knights broadened their horizons by contacts with other civilizations. The effect of such contacts in dissolving the provincial narrow-mindedness of the Western European nobility is incalculable.

Finally, the Crusades gave rise to several semi-monastic orders of Christian warriors—for example, the Knights Templars, the Knights Hospitallers, and the Teutonic Knights—which represented the ultimate synthesis of the military and the Christian life. In the thirteenth century the Teutonic Knights transferred their activities from the Holy Land to northern Germany and devoted themselves to the eastward thrust of German-Christian civilization against the heathen Slavs.

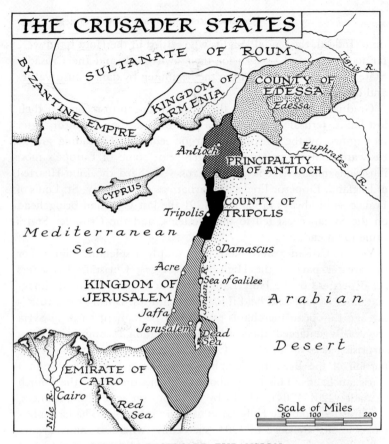

THE CRUSADER STATES

THE CRUSADER STATES

SULTANATE OF ROUM

BYZANTINE EMPIRE

KINGDOM OF ARMENIA

COUNTY OF EDESSA

Edessa

Tigris R.

Euphrates R.

Antioch

PRINCIPALITY OF ANTIOCH

CYPRUS

Tripolis

COUNTY OF TRIPOLIS

M e d i t e r r a n e a n
S e a

○*Damascus*

Acre

Sea of Galilee

KINGDOM OF JERUSALEM

Jordan R.

A r a b i a n

Jaffa

Jerusalem

Dead Sea

D e s e r t

EMIRATE OF CAIRO

Nile R. ○*Cairo*

Red Sea

Scale of Miles
0   50   100   200

THE GERMAN EASTWARD EXPANSION

Eastern Germany was still another of Europe's expanding frontiers. The German expansion eastward was not a product of active royal policy but rather a movement led by enterprising local aristocrats. They succeeded, over a long period running from *c.* 1125 to *c.* 1350, in moving the eastern boundary of Germany from the Elbe River past the Oder to the Vistula at Slavic expense. They consolidated their gains by building innumerable agrarian villages and encouraging a massive eastward migration of German peasants. Consequently, the new areas were not only conquered; they were in large part Christianized and permanently Germanized.

The later phases of the German push were spearheaded by the Teutonic Knights who penetrated temporarily far northward into

THE GERMAN EASTWARD PENETRATION

■	German before 800
▨	800–1400
▥	Large minorities 1400
▧	Small minorities 1400

FINNS

SWEDES

DANES

Baltic Sea

ESTONIANS

LETTS

Dvina R.

RUSSIANS

Lübeck

Königsberg

Elbe R.

Niemen R.

Berlin

Vistula R.

G E R M A N S

Magdeburg

Weser R.

Oder R.

POLES

Leipzig

Breslau

Dresden

Rhine R.

Prague

Cracow

BOHEMIANS

Dniester

MORAVIANS

Danube R.

Vienna

ITALIANS

Buda

Venice

Thoiss R.

Po R.

Drave R.

H U N G A R I A N S

CROATS

Adriatic Sea

Danube R.

Scale of Miles

0   100   200   300   400

Lithuania, Latvia, and Estonia and even made an unsuccessful bid to conquer Byzantine Russia. During the fourteenth and fifteenth centuries the Teutonic Knights were forced to forfeit many of their conquests, but much of the great German expansion proved to be permanent. The epoch between 1125 and 1350 witnessed the conquest and Germanization of what ultimately became the eastern two-fifths of modern Germany.*

In the later thirteenth and early fourteenth centuries the great European expansion was clearly coming to an end. The internal frontiers of forest and swamp had by then been won, and the external frontiers were everywhere hardening, sometimes even receding as in the Holy Land. The closing of the frontiers was accompanied by diminishing prosperity and a drying up of high medieval culture. The brilliant cultural achievements of the High Middle Ages were products of a buoyant, expanding, frontier society, fired by a powerful faith, driven by immense ambitions, and beguiled by a world in which, so it seemed, anything was possible.

* Before World War II.

CHRONOLOGY OF THE EUROPEAN FRONTIER MOVEMENT

Spain	*Sicily*	*Holy Land*
1002: Breakup of Caliphate of Cordova	1016: Norman infiltration begins	
	1060–1091 Sicily conquered	
1085: Capture of Toledo	1085: Death of Robert Guiscard	1095: Calling of First Crusade
1140: Aragon unites with Catalonia	1130: Coronation of Roger the Great	1099: Crusaders take Jerusalem
	1154: Death of Roger the Great	
		1187: Crusaders lose Jerusalem
1212: Great Christian victory at Las Navas de Tolosa		1204: Crusaders take Constantinople
1236: Castile takes Cordova		1291: Crusaders driven from Holy Land

10

New Dimensions in Medieval Christianity

THE CHURCH IN THE HIGH MIDDLE AGES

The expansion of civilization during the High Middle Ages has been viewed thus far as a series of advancing economic and territorial frontiers. However, frontiers of all sorts were being explored and extended in this dynamic epoch. Scholars were pioneering in new intellectual frontiers, artists and writers were adding ever-new dimensions to Western culture, administrators were pushing forward the art of government. And underlying all these phenomena was an intense deepening of the religious impulse which manifested itself in many different ways: in the rise of a vigorous papacy dedicated to reform and the creation of a Christian world order, * in the development of new and different monastic orders, in the rapid expansion of ecclesiastical administration and Church activities, in the intensification of lay piety, and in the growth of religious heterodoxy.

Medieval religion followed many different paths. It could be devoutly orthodox, it could be anticlerical, and it could be openly heretical. Yet its basic institutional expression was the Catholic Church, and the most obvious thing that the preponderant majority

* See Chapter 11.

162

of Western Christians had in common was the fact of their being Catholics. Nationalism was scarcely yet alive, and the allegiance of Europeans tended to be either local or international. In the twelfth and thirteenth centuries the majority of Europeans were still intensely local in their outlook, only vaguely aware of what was going on beyond their immediate surroundings. But alongside their localism was an element of cosmopolitanism—a consciousness of belonging to the great international commonwealth of Western Christendom, fragmented politically, but united culturally and spiritually by the Church.

The Church in the High Middle Ages was a powerful unifying influence. It had made notable progress since the half-heathen pre-Carolingian era. A flourishing parish system was by now spreading across the European countryside to bring the sacraments and a modicum of Christian instruction to the peasantry. New bishoprics and archbishoprics were formed, and old ones were becoming steadily more active. The papacy never completely succeeded in breaking the control of kings and secular lords over their local bishops, but by the twelfth century it was coming to exercise a very real control over the European episcopacy, and the growing efficiency of the papal bureaucracy evoked the envy and imitation of the rising royal governments.

THE SACRAMENTS

The buoyancy of high medieval Europe is nowhere more evident than in the accelerating impact of Christian piety on European society. The sacraments of the Church introduced a significant religious dimension into the life of the typical European layman: his birth was sanctified by the sacrament of *baptism* in which he was cleansed of the taint of original sin and initiated into the Christian fellowship. At puberty, he received the sacrament of *confirmation* which reasserted his membership in the Church and gave him the additional grace to cope with the problems of adulthood. His wedding was dignified by the sacrament of *marriage*. If he chose the calling of the ministry, he was spiritually transformed into a priest by the sacrament of *holy orders*. At his death, he received the sacrament of *extreme unction* which prepared his soul for its journey into the next world. And throughout his life he could receive forgiveness from the damning consequences of mortal sin by repenting his past transgressions and humbly receiving the comforting sacrament of *penance.* Finally, he might partake regularly of the central sacrament of the Church—the *eucharist*—receiving the body of Christ into his own body by consuming the eucharistic bread. Thus the Church, through its seven sacraments, brought God's grace to all Christians, great and humble, at every critical juncture of their lives. The sacramental system, which only assumed final form in the High Middle Ages, was a source of immense comfort and reassurance: it brought hope of salvation not simply to the saintly elite but to the sinful majority; it made communion with God not merely the elusive goal of a few mystics but the periodic experience of all believers. And, of course, it established the Church as the essential intermediary between God and man.

THE EVOLUTION OF PIETY

The ever-increasing scope of the Church, together with the rising vigor of the new age, resulted in a deepening of popular piety throughout Europe. The High Middle Ages witnessed a profound shift in religious attitude from the awe and mystery characteristic of earlier Christianity to a new emotionalism and dynamism. This shift is evident in ecclesiastical architecture, as the stolid, earthbound Romanesque style gave way in the later twelfth century to the tense, upward-reaching Gothic.* A parallel change is evident in devotional practices as the divine Christ sitting in judgment gave way to the tragic figure of the human Christ suffering on the Cross for man's sins. And it was in the High Middle Ages that the Virgin Mary came into her own as the compassionate intercessor for hopelessly lost souls. No matter how sinful a person might be, he could be redeemed if only he won the sympathy of Mary, for what son could refuse the petition of his mother? Indeed, a legend of the age told of the devil complaining to God that the tender-hearted Queen of Heaven was cheating Hell of its most promising candidates. In this atmosphere of religious romanticism, Christianity became, as never before, a doctrine of love, hope, and compassion. The God of Justice became the merciful, suffering God who died in agony to atone for the sins of men and to bring them everlasting life.

* See pp. 248-259.

Like all other human institutions, the medieval Church fell far short of its ideals. Corrupt churchmen were in evidence throughout the age, and certain historians have delighted in cataloguing instances of larcenous bishops, gluttonous priests, and licentious nuns. But cases such as these were clearly exceptional. The great shortcoming of the medieval Church was not gross corruption but rather a creeping complacency which resulted sometimes in a shallow, even mechanical attitude toward the Christian religious life. The medieval Church had more than its share of saints, but among much of the clergy the profundity of the Faith was often lost in the day-to-day affairs of the pastoral office and the management of far-flung estates.

THE CRISIS IN BENEDICTINISM

The drift toward complacency has been a recurring problem in Christian monasticism. Again and again, the lofty idealism of a monastic reform movement has been eroded and transformed by time and success until, at length, new reform movements arose in protest against the growing worldliness of the old ones. This cycle has been repeated countless times. Indeed, the sixth-century Benedictine movement was itself a protest against the excesses and inadequacies of earlier monasticism. Saint Benedict had regarded his new order as a means of withdrawing from the world and devoting full time to communion with God. But Benedictinism, despite Benedict's ideal, quickly became involved in teaching, evangelism, and ecclesiastical reform, and by the tenth and eleventh centuries the whole Benedictine movement had become deeply immersed in worldly affairs. Benedictine monasteries controlled vast estates, supplied significant contingents of knights to the feudal armies of the period, and worked closely with secular princes in affairs of state. Early in the tenth century the Cluniac movement, which was itself Benedictine in spirit and rule, arose as a protest against the worldliness and complacency of contemporary Benedictine monasticism, but by the later eleventh century the Congregation of Cluny had definitely come to terms with the secular establishment and was beginning to display traces of the very complacency against which it had originally rebelled. Prosperous, respected, and secure, Cluny was too content with its majestic abbeys and priories, its elaborate liturgical program, and its bounteous fields to support the radical transformation of

Christian society for which many Christian reformers were now struggling.

Saint Benedict had sought to create monastic sanctuaries in which Christians might retire from the world, but the High Middle Ages witnessed an endeavor to sanctify society itself. The new goal, pioneered by the reform papacy of the eleventh century, was not *withdrawal* but *conversion*. Rather than making Christians safe from the world, the world would be made safe for Christianity. During the eleventh and twelfth centuries, these two contrary tendencies— withdrawal and conversion—both had a profound impact upon monastic reform.

In the opening decades of the High Middle Ages the Benedictine movement was showing signs of exhaustion. During the long, troubled centuries of the Early Middle Ages, Benedictine teachers and missionaries, scribes and political advisors, had provided indispensable services to society. Benedictine monasteries had served as the spiritual and cultural foci of Christendom. But in the eleventh and twelfth centuries, the Benedictines saw their pedagogical monopoly broken by the rising cathedral schools and universities of the new towns. These urban schools produced increasing numbers of well-trained scholars who gradually superseded the Benedictine monks as scribes and advisers to princes. In other words, the great urbanizing impulse of the High Middle Ages drastically diminished the traditional Benedictine contribution to the functioning of society.

Still, the Benedictines retained their great landed wealth. The Benedictine monastery was scarcely the sanctuary from worldly concerns that St. Benedict had planned. Nor was it any longer the vital force it once had been in Christianizing the world. Twelfth-century Benedictinism followed neither the path of withdrawal nor the path of conversion, and even in the arena of secular affairs it was losing its grip. The Benedictine life was beginning to appear tarnished and unappealing to sensitive religious spirits caught up in the soaring piety of the new age.

CARTHUSIANS AND CISTERCIANS

The monastic revolt against Benedictinism followed the two divergent roads of uncompromising withdrawal from society and ardent participation in the Christianization of society. The impulse toward withdrawal pervaded the Carthusian order which arose in eastern France in the later eleventh century and spread across Christendom in the twelfth. Isolated from the outside world, the Carthusians lived in small groups, worshiping together in communal chapels but otherwise living as hermits in individual cells. This austere order exists to this day and, unlike most monastic movements, its severe spirituality has seldom waned. Yet even in the spiritually charged atmosphere of the twelfth century it was a small movement, offering a way of life for only a minority of heroically holy men. Too ascetic for the average Christian, the Carthusian order was much admired but seldom joined.

The greatest monastic order of the twelfth century, the Cistercian, managed for a time to be both austere and popular. The mother house of the order, Cîteaux, was established in 1098 on a wild, remote site in eastern France. The Cistercian order grew very slowly at first, then gradually acquired momentum. In 1115 it had four daughter houses; by the end of the century it had 500.

The spectacular success of the Cistercians demonstrates the immense appeal of the idea of withdrawal to the Christians of the twelfth century. Like Cîteaux, the daughter houses were deliberately built in remote wilderness areas. The abbeys themselves were stark and primitive in dramatic contrast to the elaborate Cluniac architecture. Cistercian life was stark and primitive too—less severe than that of the Carthusians but far more so than that of the Cluniacs. The Cistercians sought to resurrect the strict, simple life of primitive Benedictinism, but in fact they were more austere than Benedict himself. The numerous Cistercian houses were bound together tightly, not by the authority of a central abbot as at Cluny, but by an annual council of all Cistercian abbots meeting at Cîteaux. Without such centralized control it is unlikely that the individual houses could have clung for long to the harsh, ascetic ideals on which the order was founded.

The key figure in twelfth-century Cistercianism was St. Bernard, who joined the community of Cîteaux in 1112 and three years later became the founder and abbot of Clairvaux, one of Cîteaux's earliest daughter houses. Saint Bernard of Clairvaux was the leading Christian of his age—a profound mystic, a brilliant religious orator, and a crucial figure in the meteoric rise of the Cistercian order. His moral influence was so immense that he became Europe's leading

arbiter of political and ecclesiastical disputes. He persuaded the king
of France and the Holy Roman Emperor to participate in the Second Crusade. He persuaded Christendom to accept his candidate in
a hotly disputed papal election in 1130. On one occasion he even
succeeded in reconciling the two great warring families of Germany:
the Welfs and Hohenstaufens. He rebuked the Pope himself: "Re-
member, first of all, that the Holy Roman Church, over which you
hold sway, is the mother of churches, not their sovereign mistress—
that you yourself are not the lord of bishops but one among them...."
And he took an uncompromising stand against one of the rising
movements of his day: the attempt to reconcile the Catholic faith
with human reason, which was led by the brilliant twelfth-century
philosopher, Peter Abelard. In the long run Bernard failed to halt
the reconciliation of faith with reason, but he succeeded in making
life miserable for the unfortunate Abelard and in securing the
official condemnation of certain of Abelard's teachings.*

Above and beyond all his obvious talents as a leader and persuader
of men, St. Bernard won the devotion and admiration of twelfth-
century Europe through his reputation for sanctity. He was widely
regarded as a saint in his own lifetime, and stories circulated far and
wide of miracles that he performed. Pilgrims flocked to Clairvaux
to be healed by his touch. This aspect of St. Bernard's reputation
made his admittedly skillful preaching and diplomacy even more
effective than it would otherwise have been. For here was a holy
man, a miracle worker, who engaged in severe fasts, overworked
himself to an extraordinary degree, wore coarse and humble clothing, and quite obviously devoted himself totally to the service of God.

Humble and prayerful though he was, he could also overawe men
with his energy and iron will. On one occasion, for example, he
commanded Duke William of Aquitaine to reinstate certain bishops
whom the duke had driven from their sees. When, after much
persuasion, the duke proved obdurate, St. Bernard celebrated a high
mass for him. Holding the consecrated host in his hands, Bernard
advanced from the altar toward the duke and said, "We have be-
sought you, and you have spurned us. The united multitude of the
servants of God, meeting you elsewhere, has entreated you and you
have scorned them. Behold! Here comes to you the Virgin's Son,

* See pp. 274-276.

the Head and Lord of the Church which you persecute! Your Judge is here, at whose name every knee shall bow . . . . Your Judge is here, into whose hands your soul is to pass! Will you spurn him also? Will you scorn him as you have scorned his servants?" The duke threw himself on the ground and submitted to St. Bernard's demands.

Bernard's career demonstrates vividly the essential paradox of Cistercianism. For although the Cistercians strove to dissociate themselves from the world, Bernard was drawn inexorably into the vortex of secular affairs. Indeed, as the twelfth century progressed, the entire Cistercian movement became increasingly worldly. Like the later Puritans, the Cistercians discovered that their twin virtues of austere living and hard work resulted in an embarrassing accumulation of wealth and a concomitant corrosion of their spiritual simplicity. Their efforts to clear fields around their remote abbeys placed them in the vanguard of the internal frontier movement. They became pioneers in scientific farming and introduced notable improvements in the breeding of horses, cattle, and sheep. The English Cistercians became the great wool producers of the realm. Altogether the Cistercians exerted a powerful, progressive influence on European husbandry and came to play a prominent role in the European economy. Economic success brought ever-increasing wealth to the Order. Cistercian abbey churches became steadily more elaborate and opulent, and the primitive austerity of Cistercian life was progressively relaxed. In later years there appeared new offshoots, such as the Trappists, which returned to the strict observance of original Cistercianism.

MONASTICISM IN THE WORLD

The Cistercians had endeavored to withdraw from the world, but despite their goal they became a powerful force in twelfth-century Europe. At roughly the same time, other orders were being established with the deliberate aim of participating actively in society and working toward its regeneration. The Augustinian Canons, for example, submitted to the rigor of a rule, yet carried on normal ecclesiastical duties in the world, serving in parish churches and cathedrals. The fusion of monastic discipline and worldly activity culminated in the twelfth-century Crusading orders—the Knights Templars, the Knights Hospitallers, the Teutonic Knights, and similar groups—whose ideal was a synthesis of the monastic and the military life for the purpose of expanding the political frontiers of Western Christendom. These and other efforts to direct the spiritual vigor of monastic life toward the Christianization of society typify the bold visions and lofty hopes of the new, emotionally charged religiosity that animated twelfth-century Europe.

HERESIES AND THE INQUISITION

The surge of popular piety also raised serious problems for the Church and society, for it resulted in a flood of criticism against churchmen. It was not that churchmen had grown worse, but rather that laymen had begun to judge them by harsher standards. Popular dissatisfaction toward the workaday Church manifested itself in part in the rush toward the austere twelfth-century monastic orders. Yet the majority of Christians could not become monks, and for them, certain new heretical doctrines began to exert a powerful appeal.

The heresies of the High Middle Ages flourished particularly in the rising towns of Southern Europe. The eleventh-century urban revolution had caught the Church unprepared; whereas the new towns were the real centers of the burgeoning lay piety, the Church, with its roots in the older agrarian feudal order, seemed unable to minister effectively to the vigorous and widely literate new burgher class. Too often the urban bishops appeared as political oppressors and foes of *burghal* independence rather than as inspiring spiritual directors. Too often the Church failed to understand the townsmen's problems and aspirations or to anticipate their growing suspicion of ecclesiastical wealth and power. Although the vast majority of medieval townsmen remained loyal to the Church, a troublesome minority, particularly in the south, turned to new, anticlerical sects. In their denunciation of ecclesiastical wealth, these sects were doing nothing more than St. Bernard and the Cistercians had done. But many of the anticlerical sects crossed the boundary between orthodox reformism and heresy by preaching without episcopal or papal approval; far more important, they denied the exclusive right of the priesthood to perform sacraments.

One such sect, the Waldensians, was founded by a merchant of Lyons named Peter Waldo who, about 1173, gave all his possessions to the poor and took up a life of apostolic poverty. He and his followers worked at first within the bounds of orthodoxy, but gradually their anticlericalism and their denial of special priestly powers earned them the condemnation of the Church. Similar groups, some orthodox, some heretical, arose in the communes of Lombardy and were known as the *Humiliati*. Naturally these groups proved exceedingly troublesome and embarrassing to the local ecclesiastical hierarchies, but generally they escaped downright condemnation unless they themselves took the step of denying the authority of the Church. Many of them did take that step, however, and by the thirteenth century heretical, anticlerical sects were spreading across northern Italy and southern France, and even into Spain and Germany.

The most popular and dangerous heresy in southern France was sponsored by a group known as the *Cathari* (the pure) or *Albigensians* —after the town of Albi where they were particularly strong. The Albigensians represented a fusion of two traditions: (1) the anticlerical protest against ecclesiastical wealth and power, and (2) an exotic theology derived originally from Persian dualism. The Albigensians recognized two gods: the god of good who reigned over the universe of the spirit, and the god of evil who ruled the world of matter. The Old Testament God, as creator of the material universe, was their god of evil; Christ, who was believed to have been a purely spiritual being with a phantom body, was the god of good. Albigensian morality stressed a rigorous rejection of all material things—of physical appetites, wealth, worldly vanities, and sexual intercourse— in the hope of one day escaping from the prison of the body and ascending to the realm of pure spirit. In reality this severe ethic was practiced only by a small élite known as the *perfecti*; the rank and file, who were called *credentes* (believers), normally begat children, amassed worldly goods, and participated only vicariously in the rejection of the material world— by criticizing the affluence of the Church. Indeed, their opponents accused them of gross licentiousness, and it does seem to be true that certain Provençal noblemen were attracted to the new teaching by the opportunity of appropriating Church property in good conscience.

However, Albigensianism was spreading rapidly as the thirteenth century dawned and was becoming an ominous threat to the unity of Christendom and the authority of the Church. Pope Innocent III, recognizing the extreme gravity of the situation, tried with every means in his power to eradicate Albigensianism. At length, in 1208, he responded to the murder of a papal legate in southern France by summoning a crusade against the Albigensians—the first crusade ever to be called against European Christians. The Albigensian Crusade was a ruthless, savage affair which succeeded in its purpose but only at the cost of ravaging the vibrant civilization of southern France. The French monarchy intervened in the Crusade's final stages, brought it to a bloody conclusion, and thereby extended the sway of the Capetian kings to the Mediterranean. The Albigensian Crusade was an important event in the development of French royal power, and it succeeded in reversing the trend toward heresy in Southern Europe. It also disclosed the brutality of which the Church was capable when sufficiently threatened.

In the years immediately following the Albigensian Crusade, there emerged an institution that will always stand as a grim symbol of the medieval Church at its worst: the Inquisition. The Christian persecution of heretics dates from the later fourth century, but it was not until the High Middle Ages that heterodox views presented a serious problem to European society. Traditionally, the problem of converting or punishing heretics was handled at the local level, but in 1233 the papacy established a permanent central tribunal for the purpose of standardizing procedures and increasing efficiency in the suppression of heresies. The methods of the Inquisition included the use of torture, secret testimony, conviction on the testimony of only two witnesses, the denial of legal counsel to the accused, and other procedures offensive to the Anglo-American legal tradition but not especially remarkable by standards of the times. Indeed, many of these procedures—including torture—were drawn from the customs of Roman Law. In defense of the Inquisition it might be said that convicted heretics might escape death by renouncing their "errors," and that far from establishing a reign of terror, the Inquisition seems to have enjoyed popular support.

Some historians have adduced other arguments in an attempt to defend an indefensible institution. Let us say here merely that the Christian faith was far more important to the people of medieval Europe than national allegiance—that the medieval Church, with its elaborate charitable activities, its hospitals and universities, and its other social services, performed many of the functions of the modern state, and that therefore medieval heresy was analogous to modern treason. To the medieval Christian, heresy was a hateful, repugnant thing, an insult to Christ, and a source of contamination to others. Today, when political and economic doctrines are more important to most people than religious creeds, the closest parallel to medieval Waldensianism or Albigensianism is to be found in the Communist and Nazi parties in modern America. In examining popular opposition toward extremist groups such as these, perhaps we can gain an inkling of the state of mind that produced the medieval Inquisition.

MENDICANTISM

The thirteenth-century Church found an answer to the heretical drift in urban piety which was far more compassionate and effective than the Inquisition. In the opening decades of the century two radically new orders emerged—the Dominican and the Franciscan —which were devoted to a life of poverty, preaching, and charitable deeds. Rejecting the life of the cloister, they dedicated themselves to religious work in the world—particularly in the towns. Benedictines and Cistercians had traditionally taken vows of personal poverty, but the monastic orders themselves could and did acquire great corporate wealth. The Dominicans and Franciscans, on the contrary, were pledged to both personal and corporate poverty, and were therefore known as mendicants (beggars). Capturing the imagination of thirteenth-century Christendom, they drained urban heterodoxy of much of its former support by demonstrating to the townsmen of Europe that Christian orthodoxy could be both relevant and compelling.

THE DOMINICANS

Saint Dominic (1170–1221), a well-educated Spaniard, spent his early manhood as an Augustinian canon at a cathedral in Castile. In his mid-thirties he traveled to Rome, met Pope Innocent III, and followed the Pope's bidding to preach in southern France against the Albigenisans. For the next decade, between 1205 and 1215, he worked among the heretics, leading an austere, humble life, and winning considerable renown for his eloquence and simplicity. For the most part the Albigensians seem to have been unaffected by Dominic's preaching; they respected him but did not follow him.

   The Dominican Order evolved out of a small group of volunteers who joined Dominic in his work among the Albigensians. Gradually, Dominic came to see the possibility of a far greater mission for his followers: to preach and win converts to the faith throughout the world. In 1215, Dominic's friend, the bishop of Toulouse, gave the group a church and a house in the city, and shortly thereafter the papacy recognized the Dominicans as a separate religious order and approved the Dominican Rule. The congregation founded by Dominic was to be known as the Order of Friars Preachers. It assumed its permanent shape during the years between its formal establishment in 1216 and Dominic's death in 1221 by which time it had grown to include some 500 friars and 60 priories organized into eight provinces embracing the whole of Western Europe. The Dominicans stood in the vanguard of the thirteenth-century upsurge of piety. Their order attracted men of imagination and unusual religious dedication, men who could not be satisfied with the enclosed and tradition-bound life of earlier monasticism but who were challenged by the austerity of the Dominican Rule, the disciplined vitality of the order, and the stimulating goal of working toward the moral regeneration of society rather than withdrawing from the world.

   The Dominican Rule drew freely from the earlier rule of the Augustinian Canons which Dominic had known in his youth, but added new elements and provided a novel direction for the religious life. The order was to be headed by a minister-general, elected for life, and a legislative body that met annually and consisted sometimes of delegates from the Dominican provinces, sometimes of priors from all the Dominican houses. The friars themselves belonged not to a particular house or province but to the order, and their place of residence and activity was determined by the minister-general. Their life, strictly regulated and austere, included such rigors as regular midnight services, total abstinence from meat, frequent fasts, and prolonged periods of mandatory silence. And the entire order was strictly bound by the rule of poverty which Dominic had learned from his contemporary, St. Francis. Not only should poverty be the condition of individual Dominicans as it was of individual Benedictines; it was to be the condition of the order itself. The

Dominican order was to have no possessions except churches and priories. It was to have no fixed incomes, no manors, but was to subsist through charitable gifts. It was, in short, a mendicant order.

The Dominican order expanded at a phenomenal rate during the course of the thirteenth century. Dominican friars carried their evangelical activities across the length and breadth of Europe and beyond, into the Holy Land, Central Asia, Tartary, Tibet, and China. Joining the faculties of the rising universities they became the leading proponents of Aristotelian philosophy and included in their numbers such notable scholars as St. Albertus Magnus and St. Thomas Aquinas. Dominic himself had insisted that his followers acquire broad educations before undertaking their mission of preaching and that each Dominican priory include a school of theology. Within a few decades after his death his order included some of the most brilliant intellects of the age.

The Dominicans were, above all, preachers, and their particular mission was to preach among heretics and non-Christians. Their contact with heretics brought them into close involvement with the Inquisition, and in later years their reputation was darkened by the fact that they themselves became the leading inquisitors. The grand inquisitor of Spain, for example, was customarily a Dominican. They acquired the ominous nickname, *"Domini canes"*—hounds of God— by their willingness to supplement St. Dominic's policy of persuasion with the easier and crueler policy of force.

The Dominican order still flourishes. The rule of corporate poverty was softened increasingly and finally, in the fifteenth century, dropped altogether, for it was recognized that full-time scholars and teachers could not beg or do odd jobs or be in doubt as to the source of their next meal. But long after their original mendicant ideals were modified, the Dominicans remained faithful to their essential mission of championing Catholic orthodoxy by word and pen.

SAINT FRANCIS

Dominic's remarkable achievement was overshadowed by that of his contemporary, St. Francis (*c.* 1182–1226)—a warm and appealing man who is widely regarded as Christianity's ideal saint. Francis was a true product of the medieval urban revolution. He was the son of a wealthy cloth merchant of Assisi, a northern Italian town

with an influential Albigensian minority. As a youth he was generous, high-spirited, and popular, and in time he became the leader
of a boisterous but essentially harmless "teen-age gang." He was by
no means a rake or a dissolute young man but rather, as one writer
has aptly expressed it, he "seems altogether to have been rather a
festive figure."

In his early twenties, St. Francis underwent a profound religious
conversion which occurred in several steps. It began on the occasion
of a banquet which he was giving for some of his friends. After the
banquet Francis and his companions went out into the town with
torches, singing in the streets. Francis was crowned with garlands as
king of the revellers, but after a time he disappeared and was found
in a religious trance. Thereafter he devoted himself to solitude,
prayer, and service to the poor. He went as a pilgrim to Rome where
he is reported to have exchanged clothes with a beggar and spent the
day begging with other beggars. Returning to Assisi, he encountered
an impoverished leper and, notwithstanding his fear of leprosy, he
gave the poor man all the money he was carrying and kissed his hand.
Thenceforth he devoted himself to the service of lepers and hospitals.

To the confusion and consternation of his bourgeois father,
Francis now went about Assisi dressed in rags, giving to the poor.
His former companions pelted him with mud, and his father, fearing that Francis' incessant almsgiving would consume the family
fortune, disinherited him. Undaunted, Francis left the family house
gaily singing a French song. He spent the next three years of his life
in the environs of Assisi, living in abject poverty, ministering to
lepers and social outcasts, and continuing to embarrass his family by
his unconventional behavior. It was at this time that he began to
frequent a crumbling little chapel known as the Portiuncula. One
day, in the year 1209, while attending mass there, he was struck by
the words of the Gospel which the priest was reading: "Everywhere
on your road preach and say, 'The kingdom of God is at hand.'
Cure the sick, raise the dead, cleanse the lepers, drive out devils.
Freely have you received; freely give. Carry neither gold nor silver
nor money in your girdles, nor bag, nor two coats, nor sandals, nor
staff, for the workman is worthy of his hire." (Matt. X, vii-x).
Francis at once accepted this injunction as the basis of his vocation
and immediately thereafter—even though a layman—began to
preach to the poor.

This painting of St. Francis, ascribed to the half-legendary thirteenth-century Italian painter Cimabue (*c.* 1240–1302), is taken from a series of frescoes in the Upper Church of St. Francis in Assisi.

Disciples now joined him, and when he had about a dozen followers he is said to have remarked, "Let us go to our Mother, the Holy
Roman Church, and tell the pope what the Lord has begun to do
through us and carry it out with his sanction." This may have been
a naive approach to the masterful, aristocratic Pope Innocent III,
yet when Francis came to Rome in 1210, Innocent sanctioned his
work. Doubtless the Pope saw in the Franciscan mission a possible
orthodox counterpoise to the Waldensians, Albigensians, and other
heretical groups who had been winning masses of converts from the
Church by the example of their poverty and simplicity. For here
was a man whose loyalty to Catholicism was beyond question and
whose own artless simplicity of life might bring erring souls back into
the Church. Already Innocent III had given his blessing to movements similar to that of Francis. An orthodox group of *Humiliati* had
received his sanction in 1201, and in 1208 he permitted a converted
Waldensian to found an order known as the "Poor Catholics," which
was dedicated to lay preaching. In Francis' movement the pope
must have seen still another opportunity to encourage a much-
needed wave of radical reform within the orthodox framework. And
it may well be that Francis' glowing spirituality appealed to the
sanctity of Innocent himself, for the pope, even though a great man
of affairs, was a genuinely pious person. However, thirteenth-century
Europe deserves some credit for embracing a movement which in
many other ages would have been persecuted or ridiculed. Rome
crucified Christ, but high medieval Europe took Francis to its heart
and made him a saint.

Immediately after the papal interview Francis and his followers
returned to the neighborhood of Assisi. They were given the Portiuncula as their own chapel, and over the years it continued to serve
as the headquarters of the Franciscan movement. Around it the friars
built huts of branches and twigs. The Portiuncula was a headquarters
but not a home, for the friars were always on the move, wandering in
pairs over the country, dressed in peasants' clothing, preaching, serving, and living in conscious imitation of the life of Christ. During
the next decade the order expanded at a spectacular rate. Franciscans
were soon to be found throughout northern Italy; by 1220 Franciscan missions were active in Germany, France, Spain, Hungary,
and the Holy Land, and the friars numbered in the thousands. The
immensely attractive personality of Francis himself was doubtless

a crucial factor in his order's popularity, but it also owed much to the fact that its ideals appealed with singular effectiveness to the highest religious aspirations of the age. Urban heresy lost some of its allure as the cheerful, devoted Franciscans began to pour into Europe's cities, preaching in the crowded streets and setting a living example of Christian sanctity.

The Franciscan ideal was based above all on the imitation of Christ. Fundamental to this ideal was the notion of poverty, both individual and corporate. The Franciscans subsisted by working and serving in return for their sustenance. Humility was also a part of the ideal; Francis named his followers the "Friars Minor" (little brothers). Preaching was an important part of their mission, and it answered an urgent need in the rising cities where the Church had hitherto responded inadequately to the deepening religious hunger of townsmen. Perhaps most attractive of all was the quality of joyousness, akin to the joyousness that Francis had shown before his conversion, but directed now toward spiritual ends. Contemporaries referred to Francis affectionately as "God's own troubadour."

Pious men of other times have fled the world; the Albigensians renounced it as the epitome of evil. But Francis embraced it joyfully as the handiwork of God. In his "Song of Brother Sun," he expressed poetically his holy commitment to the physical universe:

> Praise be to Thee, my Lord, for all thy creatures,
> Above all Brother Sun
> Who brings us the day, and lends us his light;
> Beautiful is he, radiant with great splendor,
> And speaks to us of Thee, O most high.
> Praise to Thee, my Lord, for Sister Moon and for the stars;
> In heaven Thou hast set them, clear and precious and fair.
> Praise to Thee, my Lord, for Brother Wind.
> For air and clouds, for calm and all weather
> By which Thou supportest life in all Thy creatures.
> Praise to Thee, my Lord, for Sister Water
> Which is so helpful and humble, precious and pure.
> Praise to Thee, my Lord, for Brother Fire,
> By whom Thou lightest up the night.
> And fair is he, and gay and mighty and strong.
> Praise to Thee, my Lord, for our sister, Mother Earth,

Who sustains and directs us,
And brings forth varied fruits, and plants and flowers bright . . .
Praise and bless my Lord, and give Him thanks,
And serve Him with great humility.

Early Franciscanism was too good to last. The order was becoming
too large to retain its original disorganized simplicity. Francis was
a holy man rather than an organization man, and well before his
death the movement was passing beyond his control. In 1219–1220
he traveled to Egypt in an effort to convert its Moslem inhabitants—
a hopeless task, but Francis was never dismayed by the impossible—
and while he was away it became apparent that his order required a
more coherent organization than he had seen fit to provide it. Many
perplexing questions now arose: With thousands of friars invading
the begging market, what would become of the poor common tramp?
Would Europe's generosity be overstrained? Above all, how could
these multitudes of friars be expected to cleave to the ideal without
an explicit rule and without Francis' personal presence to inspire and
guide them? In short, could the Franciscan ideal be practical on a
large scale? For the movement was proliferating at a remarkable
rate. Besides the Friars Minor themselves, a Second Order was
established—a female order directed by Francis' friend, St. Clare—
known as the Poor Clares. And there was a peripheral group of
part-time Franciscans, known as Tertiaries, who dedicated themselves to the Franciscan way while continuing their former careers
in the world. The little band of Franciscan brothers had evolved into
a vast and complex body.

On his return from the Near East, Francis prevailed upon a powerful friend, Cardinal Hugolino—later Pope Gregory IX—to become
the order's protector. On Hugolino's initiative a formal rule was
drawn up in 1220 which provided a certain degree of administrative structure to the order. A novitiate was established, lifetime
vows were required, and the rule of absolute poverty was mitigated.
In 1223 a shorter and somewhat laxer rule was instituted, and over
the years and decades that followed, the movement continued to
evolve from the ideal to the practical.

St. Francis himself withdrew more and more from involvement in
the order's administration. At the meeting of the general chapter in
1220 he resigned his formal leadership of the movement with the

words, "Lord, I give thee back this family that Thou didst entrust to me. Thou knowest, most sweet Jesus, that I have no more the power and the qualities to continue to take care of it." In 1224, St. Francis underwent a mystical experience atop Mt. Alverno in the Apennines, and legend has it that he received the stigmata* on that occasion. It is not entirely clear how St. Francis reacted to the evolution of his order, but in his closing years his mysticism deepened, his health declined, and he kept much to himself. At his death in 1226 he was universally mourned, and the order which he had founded remained the most powerful and attractive religious movement of its age.

As Franciscanism became increasingly modified by the demands of practicality it also became increasingly rent with dissension. Some friars, wishing to draw on Francis' prestige without being burdened with his spiritual dedication, advocated an exceedingly lax interpretation of the Franciscan way. Others insisted on the strict imitation of Francis' life and struggled against its modification. These last, known in later years as "Spiritual Franciscans," sought to preserve the apostolic poverty and artless idealism of Francis himself, and by the fourteenth century they had become vigorously antipapal and anticlerical.

The majority of Franciscans, however, were willing to meet reality halfway. Although Francis had disparaged formal learning as irrelevant to salvation, Franciscan friars began devoting themselves to scholarship and took their places alongside the Dominicans in the thirteenth- and fourteenth-century universities. Indeed, Franciscan scholars such as Roger Bacon in thirteenth-century England played a crucial role in the revival of scientific investigation, and the minister-general of the Franciscan order in the later thirteenth century, St. Bonaventure, was one of the most illustrious theologians of the age. The very weight and complexity of the Franciscan organization forced it to compromise its original ideal of corporate poverty. Although it neither acquired nor sought the immense landed wealth of the Benedictines or Cistercians, it soon possessed sufficient means to sustain its members. It is interesting to

---

* The stigmata, which has been attributed to several saints, consists of a person receiving, by divine grace, wounds on his hands, feet, and side corresponding to the wounds of Christ.

see how the minister-general Bonaventura, a holy man and also a brilliant philosopher, instituted and justified some of the changes that the order underwent in the thirteenth century. Although an intense admirer of St. Francis, Bonaventure was not himself a beggar by nature, nor a wandering minstrel, nor a day laborer, but a scholar-administrator burdened with the task of adapting a way of life designed for a dozen friars living in huts of twigs to an international order of many thousands. Contrary to Francis, Bonaventure encouraged scholarship as an aid to preaching and evangelism. St. Francis had urged his followers that "manual labor should be done with faith and devotion." Bonaventure, after demonstrating the superiority of contemplation over manual labor, concluded that Franciscans were under no compulsion to engage in physical work, though if any wished to do so he should by all means do it, "with faith and devotion."

Necessary though they were, these compromises robbed the Franciscan movement of a good measure of the radical idealism that Francis had instilled in it. In the progress from huts of twigs to halls of ivy something very precious was left behind. The Franciscans continued to serve society, but by the end of the thirteenth century they had ceased to inspire it.

THE PASSING OF THE HIGH MIDDLE AGES

The pattern of religious reform in the High Middle Ages is one of rhythmic ebb and flow. A reform movement is launched with high enthusiasm and lofty purpose, it galvanizes society for a time, then succumbs gradually to complacency and gives way to a new and different wave of reform. But with the passing of the High Middle Ages one can detect a gradual waning of spiritual vigor. The frontiers were closing as the fourteenth century dawned. Western political power was at an end in Constantinople and the Holy Land, and the Spanish reconquest had ground to a halt. The economic boom was giving way to an epoch of depression, declining population, peasants' rebellions, and debilitating wars. And until the time of the Protestant Reformation, no new religious order was to attain the immense social impact of the thirteenth-century Franciscans and Dominicans. Popular piety remained strong, particularly in Northern Europe where succeeding centuries witnessed a

significant surge of mysticism. But in the south a more secular attitude was beginning to emerge. Young men no longer flocked into
monastic orders; soldiers no longer rushed to crusades; papal excommunications no longer wrought their former terror. The electrifying
appeal of a St. Bernard, a St. Dominic, and a St. Francis was a
phenomenon peculiar to their age. By the fourteenth century, their
age was passing.

CHRONOLOGY OF HIGH MEDIEVAL
MONASTICISM AND HETERODOXY

     910: Founding of Cluny
   1084: Establishment of Carthusian Order
   1098: Establishment of Cîteaux
1112–1153: Career of St. Bernard of Clairvaux as a Cistercian.
   1128: Original rule of Knights Templars.
  c.1173: Beginning of Waldensian sect.
   1208: Innocent III calls Albigensian Crusade.
   1210: Innocent III authorizes Franciscan Order.
   1216: Dominican Rule sanctioned by papacy.
   1226: Death of St. Francis.
   1233: Inquisition established.

11

Empire and Papacy

PAPACY AND CHURCH IN THE
MID-ELEVENTH CENTURY

The role of the papacy in the changing religious configurations of
the High Middle Ages was scarcely touched upon in the previous
chapter, for although it was fundamental to the spiritual development of the period, it was also closely associated with the politics
of empire and kingdom which is the central topic of this chapter.
We must therefore go back to the mid-eleventh century, the age
when Cluny still stood in the vanguard of European monasticism,
when Cîteaux was yet an untouched wilderness and the mendicant
movement lay in the distant future. With the dawning of the High
Middle Ages there emerged a newly invigorated papacy, dedicated
to ecclesiastical reform and the spiritual regeneration of Christian
society. Almost at once the reform papacy became involved in an
epic struggle with the Holy Roman Empire—a tragic conflict which
dominated European politics for more than two centuries. On the
eve of the conflict Germany was the mightiest monarchy in Western
Christendom and the German king or Holy Roman emperor was
appointing popes. By 1300 the Holy Roman Empire was reduced
to a specter of its former greatness and the papacy, after 250 years
of political prominence, was exhausted, battle-scarred, and on the
brink of a prolonged decline.

Before the beginnings of papal reform in the mid-eleventh century, a chasm existed between the papal theory of Christian society and the realities of the contemporary Church. The papal theory, with a venerable tradition running all the way back to the fifth-century pope, Leo the Great,* envisaged a sanctified Christian commonwealth in which lords and kings accepted the spiritual direction of priests and bishops who, in turn, submitted to the leadership of the papacy. The popes claimed to be the successors—the vicars—of St. Peter. Just as St. Peter was the chief of Christ's apostles, they argued, the pope was the monarch of the apostolic Church. And as eternal salvation was more important than earthly prosperity—as the soul was more important than the body—so the priestly power was greater than the power of secular lords, kings, and emperors. The properly ordered society, the truly Christian society, was one dominated by the Church which, in turn, was dominated by the pope. In the intellectual climate of the High Middle Ages this view had great pertinence and caught the imagination of many thinking men. It provided the papacy with a dynamic, convincing, almost irresistible intellectual position.

The reality of mid-eleventh-century society was far different. Almost everywhere the Church was under the control of aristocratic lay proprietors. Petty lords appointed their priests; dukes and kings selected their bishops and abbots. As we have seen, the Holy Roman emperors used churchmen extensively in the administration of Germany. In France, the Church provided warriors from its estates for the feudal armies, clerks for the feudal chanceries, and shrewd political advisers for the feudal princes. The Church played a vital role in the operation of tenth- and early-eleventh-century society, but it was always subordinate to the lay ruling class. Its spiritual and sacramental role was compromised by its secular administrative responsibilities. As was bound to happen under such conditions, the Church tended to neglect its sacred mission. From the lay standpoint it was an effective administrative tool, but from the spiritual standpoint it was inadequate and often corrupt. Monasteries all too frequently ignored the strict Benedictine Rule. Some priests had concubines, and a great many had wives, despite the canonical requirement of priestly celibacy. Married priests often bequeathed

* See p. 26.

their churches and church lands to their own offspring, and reformers began to fear the danger of an hereditary priesthood. Moreover, lay lords often sold important ecclesiastical offices to the highest bidder, and the new prelate customarily recouped the expense of buying his office by ruthlessly exploiting his tenants and subordinates. This flourishing commerce in ecclesiastical appointments was known as *simony*. It was regarded by some contemporary reformers as the arch sin of the age.

Ecclesiastical corruption was nowhere more evident than in Rome itself. The papacy of the earlier eleventh century had fallen into the soiled hands of the Roman nobility and had become a prize disputed among the several leading aristocratic families of the city. In 1032 the prize fell to a callow, sensuous young man, Pope Benedict IX, whose outrageous pontificate was scandalous even by contemporary Roman standards. Pope Benedict sold the papacy, then changed his mind and reclaimed it. By 1046 his claim to the papal throne was challenged by two other claimants; the papacy had degenerated into a three-way schism.

ECCLESIASTICAL REFORM

Such were the conditions of the European Church as the mid-eleventh century approached. A Church dominated by lay proprietors had long existed in Europe and had long been accepted. But with the powerful upsurge of lay piety that accompanied the opening of the High Middle Ages, the comfortable Church-state relationship of the previous epoch seemed profoundly wrong to many sensitive spirits. This was the epoch in which Christians were beginning to join hermit groups such as the Carthusians; they would soon be flocking into the new, austere Cistercian order. Such men as these were responding to the spiritual awakening of their age by following the path of withdrawal from worldly society. Others chose the more novel and adventurous approach of *conversion* and took up the onerous task of reforming the Church and the world. The dream of sanctifying society, which was later to find such vivid expression in the career of St. Francis, was shared by many Christians of the High Middle Ages. During the second half of the eleventh century it manifested itself in a powerful movement of ecclesiastical reform which was beginning to make itself felt across the length and breadth of Western Christendom. At the heart of this movement was the reform papacy.

In general, the reformers fell into two groups: (1) a conservative group which sought to eliminate simony, enforce clerical celibacy, and improve the moral calibre of churchmen but without challenging the Church's traditional subordination to the lay aristocracy— a subordination that had been sweetened by countless generous gifts of lands and powers to submissive prelates, and (2) a radical group which sought to demolish the tradition of lay control and to rebuild society on the pattern of the papal monarchy theory. The radical reformers struggled to establish an ideal Christian commonwealth in which laymen no longer appointed churchmen—in which kings deferred to bishops and a reformed papacy ruled the Church. The conservative reformers endeavored to heal society; the radicals wished to overturn it.

The Congregation of Cluny, firm in its spiritual rectitude yet at peace with the existing social order, was one of the chief centers of conservative reform in the eleventh century. Its ideals were shared by several of the more enlightened rulers of the age, among them Emperor Henry III, the powerful Salian monarch of Germany. Shocked by the disgraceful antics of Pope Benedict IX and the three-way tug-of-war for the papal throne, Henry III intervened in Italy in 1046, arranged the deposition of Benedict and his two rivals, and drastically improved the quality of papal leadership by appointing the first of a series of reform popes. The ablest of these imperial appointees, Pope Leo IX (1049–54), carried on a vigorous campaign against simony and clerical marriage, holding yearly synods at Rome, sending legates far and wide to enforce reform, and traveling constantly himself to preside over local councils and depose guilty churchmen. Leo IX's reform pontificate opened dramatically when, at the Roman Synod of 1049, the bishop of Sutri was condemned for simony and promptly fell dead in the presence of the whole assembly—a victim, it was assumed, of the divine wrath.

Leo IX labored mightily for reform, and his pontificate constitutes the opening phase in the evolution of the dynamic high-medieval papacy. His concern for a secure territorial position in central Italy prompted him to lead an army against the enterprising Norman adventurer to the south, Robert Guiscard, but being defeated and captured at Civitate he was forced to recognize the Normans and give them the status of papal vassals.* His insistence on a vigorous assertion of papal authority led him into a conflict with the Eastern Orthodox Church, and in 1054 the conflict culminated in a permanent schism between the two communions. More than anything else, Leo struggled to enforce canon law and to purge the Church of simony and incontinence. In all his enterprises, he could count on the general support of Emperor Henry III. In these early years empire and papacy worked together to raise the moral level of the European Church.

But however successful this reform movement might have been, there were those who felt that it was not going far enough. The real evil, in the view of the radical reformers, was lay supremacy over the Church, and Henry III's domination of papal appointments, however well-intentioned, was the supreme example of a profound social sin. A number of ardent reformers were to be found among the cardinals whom Pope Leo IX appointed and gathered around him. These new men, who dominated the reform papacy for the next several decades, came for the most part from monastic backgrounds. Many of them were deeply influenced by the strong piety surging throughout the towns of eleventh-century northern Italy: a piety that was stimulating a widespread revival of eremitic monasticism.

These radical reformers had their opportunity when Henry III died prematurely in 1056, leaving behind him an infant son and a weak queen-regent. By then many of them had become captivated by the radical reform ideology and, above all, by the notion of a papacy free of both imperial and Roman aristocratic control. At the death of Henry III's last papal appointee in 1057, the cardinals began electing reform popes on their own. In 1059 they issued a daring and momentous declaration of independence known as the *Papal Election Decree*, which stated that thenceforth emperors and Roman laymen would merely give formal approval to the candidate whom the cardinal bishops elected. In the years that followed, this revolutionary proclamation was challenged by both the Empire and the Roman aristocracy, but in the end the cardinals won out.

* See p. 149.

The papacy had been wrested free of lay control. The first step toward papal monarchy had been taken.

THE INVESTITURE CONTROVERSY

The next step was infinitely more difficult. It involved nothing less than the annihilation of lay control over the entire Church. At a time when the Church possessed untold wealth, including perhaps a third of the land in Europe, the total realization of such a goal would cripple secular power and revolutionize European society. Yet only by its realization, so the radical reformers believed, could a true Christian commonwealth be achieved.

The immense struggle over lay appointments broke out in earnest in 1075 when Gregory VII (1073–1085), the greatest of the reform popes, issued a proclamation banning lay investiture. Traditionally, a newly chosen bishop or abbot was invested by a lay lord with a ring and a pastoral staff, symbolic of his marriage to the Church and his duty toward his Christian flock. Pope Gregory VII attacked this custom of lay investiture as the crucial symbol of lay authority over churchmen. Its prohibition was a grave threat to every ruler in Christendom but especially to the Holy Roman Emperor, whose administrative system depended on his control of the German Church. By Gregory VII's time, Henry III's infant son, Henry IV, had grown to vigorous manhood and was showing promise of being as strong a ruler as his father. Refusing to accept the decree against lay investiture, Henry IV sent a flaming letter of defiance to Gregory VII. The pope responded with a startling and unprecedented exercise of spiritual authority: he excommunicated and deposed Henry IV. In so doing, he was repudiating the traditional concept of sacred, divinely commissioned kingship. The king, in Gregory's view, was in no sense God's earthly vicar; he was a purely secular figure, charged with keeping order in the Christian society. It was for the pope, the supreme spiritual monarch of Christendom, to judge whether or not the king was fit to rule. Gregory's actions were nothing less than revolutionary, for in banning lay investiture and deposing the king of Germany he was putting into practice the papal theory in its most radical form and striking at the very bedrock of the established order.

Gregory's deposition of Henry IV shook Germany to its foundations and unleashed a powerful aristocratic reaction that had long been building up against the centralizing policies of the Salian dynasty. Many Germans, churchmen and laymen alike, refused to serve an excommunicated sovereign. The great aristocrats took the revolutionary step of threatening to elect a new king in Henry's place, thereby challenging the ingrained German tradition of hereditary kingship with the fateful counter-doctrine of elective monarchy.

Desperate to keep his throne, Henry IV crossed into Italy to seek the pope's forgiveness. In January, 1077, at the castle of Canossa in Tuscany, the two men met in what was perhaps medieval history's most dramatic encounter—Henry IV barefoot and humble, clothed in rough, penitential garments, Gregory VII torn between his conviction that Henry's change of heart was insincere and opportunistic, and his priestly duty to forgive a repentant sinner. Finally, Pope Gregory lifted Henry's excommunication, and the monarch, promising to amend his ways, returned to Germany to rebuild his authority.

Down through the centuries Canossa has symbolized the ultimate royal degradation before the power of the Church. Perhaps it was. But in the immediate political context it was a victory—and a much-needed one—for Henry IV. It did not prevent a group of German nobles from electing a rival king; it did not restore the powerful centralized monarchy of Henry III; but it did save Henry IV's throne. Restored to communion, he was able to rally support, to check for a time the forces of princely particularism, and to defeat the rival king. As his power waxed, however, he ignored his promises at Canossa and continued to support lay investiture. In 1080 Gregory VII excommunicated the defiant king a second time, only to find that this potent spiritual weapon was losing its strength through overuse. In the early 1080s Henry IV returned to Italy, this time with an army at his back. In the confusion that followed, Gregory VII was forced to flee Rome and seek refuge among the Normans in southern Italy. In 1085 Gregory died, consumed by bitterness and a conviction of failure. His last words were these: "I have loved justice and hated iniquity; therefore I die in exile."

Although Gregory VII failed to transform Europe into what he conceived to be a proper Christian society, his theory of papal monarchy retained its potency. The reform papacy soon fell into the able hands of Urban II (1088–99), a former prior of Cluny, who seized the moral leadership of Europe by calling the First Crusade. Urban II and his successors made life miserable for the unlucky Henry IV, stirring up rebellions in Germany and eroding the power of the imperial government. In 1106 Henry IV died as unhappily as had Gregory VII. In the end, Henry's own son and heir, Henry V, led an army of hostile aristocrats against his father. As Henry IV died, the German Empire seemed to be collapsing in ruins around him.

Henry V (1106–1125) enjoyed a happier reign than his father's, but only because he forsook his father's struggle to recover the fullness of imperial power as it had existed in the mid-eleventh century. The independence-minded aristocracy consolidated the gains it had made during the preceding era of chaos, and Henry V could do nothing about it.

Toward the end of his reign, Henry V worked out a compromise settlement with the Church which brought the Investiture Controversy to an end at last. Already the Controversy had been settled by compromise in England and France, where the Church-state struggle had been considerably less bitter than in Germany. As time progressed both papacy and Empire tended to withdraw somewhat from the extreme positions they had taken during Gregory VII's pontificate. At length they reconciled their differences in the Concordat of Worms of 1122. Henry V agreed that the investiture ceremony would no longer be performed by laymen, but the pope conceded to the emperor the important privilege of bestowing on the new prelate the symbols of his *territorial* and *administrative* jurisdiction. Bishops and abbots were thenceforth to be elected according to the principles of canon law, by the monks of a monastery or the canons of a cathedral, but the emperor had the right to be present at such elections and to make the final decision in the event of a dispute. These reservations enabled the emperor to retain a considerable degree of *de facto* control over the appointment of important German churchmen. The reconciliation of royal control and canonical election is illustrated in a delightful twelfth-century charter of King Henry II of England to the monks at Winchester: "I order you to hold a free election, but nevertheless I forbid you to elect anyone except Richard, my clerk, the archdeacon of Poitiers."

There was no real victor in the Investiture Controversy. The Church had won its point—lay investiture was banned—but monarchs still exercised very real control over their churches. The theory of papal monarchy over a reconstituted Christian society remained unrealized.

Still, the papal-imperial balance of power had changed radically since the mid-eleventh century. The papacy was now a mighty force in Europe, and the power of the emperor had declined sharply. During the chaotic half-century between the onset of the Investiture Controversy in 1075 and Henry V's death in 1125, feudalism came to Germany. In these decades of civil strife a powerful new aristocracy emerged. Ambitious landowners rose to great power, built castles, extended their estates, and usurped royal rights. They forced minor neighboring noblemen to become their vassals and, in some instances, forced free peasants to become their serfs. The monarchy was helpless to curb this ominous process of fragmentation.

In northern Italy the emperors had traditionally exercised their power through the pro-imperial Lombard bishops who possessed wide jurisdictional rights over their cities and the surrounding countryside. In the anarchy wrought by the papal-imperial struggle, the pious and fiercely independent inhabitants of the rising commercial cities on the Lombard Plain took up the cause of papal reform, rebelled against episcopal and imperial control, and established quasi-independent communes or city states. By 1125 they had broken the power of the Lombard bishops and had reduced imperial control to little more than a formality. Lombardy had become a region of free urban communes.

In Germany and Italy alike, imperial power was receding before the whirlwind of local particularism, invigorated by the soaring popular piety of the age. Long before the Concordat of Worms, the downfall of the medieval empire had begun.

THE AGE OF FREDERICK BARBAROSSA (1152–1190)

The Salian dynasty died out with the passing of Henry V in 1125. During the next quarter-century Germany reaped the bitter harvest of princely particularism. The great nobles ignored the principle of hereditary royal succession and reverted to the elective principle which they had asserted at the time of Canossa. Their choice always fell to a man of royal blood but never to the most direct heir. In the turbulent decades between 1125 and 1152 a great rivalry developed between two powerful families who had risen to power in the anarchic era of the Investiture Controversy: the Welfs of Saxony and the Hohenstaufens of Swabia. In 1152 the princes elected as king a powerful and talented Hohenstaufen, Frederick Barbarossa (the Red-Bearded), duke of Swabia, who took as his mission the revival and reconstruction of the German monarchy.

Emperor Frederick Barbarossa recognized fully that the mighty imperial structure of Henry III was beyond recovery. His goal was to harness the new feudal forces of his age to the royal advantage. He actually encouraged the great princes of the realm to expand their power and privileges at the expnse of the lesser lords, but at the same time he forced them to recognize his own feudal lordship over all the kingdom. In other words, he succeeded in establishing the leading feudal magnates as his vassals—his tenants-in-chief. He was the supreme overlord at the apex of the feudal pyramid.

But as the sorry state of the early French monarchy well illustrates, feudal overlordship was an ephemeral thing if the royal overlord lacked the power and resources to support his position. Therefore Frederick Barbarossa set about to increase his revenues and extend the territories under his direct authority. A strong feudal monarchy required a substantial territorial core under exclusive royal control—an extensive royal demesne to act as a counterweight to the great fiefs of the chief vassals of the realm. Frederick enlarged his demcsne territories, most of which were concentrated in Swabia, by bringing many of the new monasteries and rising towns under imperial jurisdiction. The crux of his imaginative policy was the reassertion of imperial authority over the wealthy cities of Lombardy. With Lombardy under his control and its revenues pouring into the imperial treasury, no German lord could challenge him.

Barbarossa's Lombard policy earned him the hostility of the papacy which had always feared the consolidation of imperial power in Italy, and of the intensely independent Lombard cities which were determined to give up as little of their wealth and autonomy as they possibly could. And should he become too deeply involved in Italy, Barbarossa exposed himself to rebellion on the part of the German aristocrats and high nobility—in particular, the Welf family which was vigorously represented at the time by Duke Henry the Lion of Saxony.

The papacy of the mid-twelfth century was having problems of its own. Pope Hadrian IV (1154–59), who was to become one of Frederick Barbarossa's most ardent foes, was faced at the beginning of his pontificate with the problem of maintaining the papacy's hold on Rome itself. A gifted man of humble origins, Hadrian IV was the one Englishman ever to occupy the papal throne. Rome was turbulent during his years, for the revolutionary social forces that had earlier allied with the papacy in breaking the power of the pro-imperial Lombard bishops were now challenging the Pope's authority over Rome. In the 1140s the city was torn by a lower-class rebellion whose leaders struggled to drive out the Pope and dreamed of reestablishing the ancient Roman Republic. Very quickly this antipapal communal movement spread to other cities in the Papal States, and for a time the papacy itself was forced into exile. Before long, the Roman rebellion fell under the leadership of Arnold of Brescia, a gifted scholar and spiritual revolutionary, whose goal it was to strip the Church of its wealth and secular authority. Suppressed by the Norman troops of Roger the Great in the 1140s, Arnold of Brescia's revolution reasserted itself under Hadrian IV, and the Pope was driven to the desperate expedient of placing Rome under interdict, ordering the suspension of church services throughout the city. The interdict proved an effective weapon; among other things, it severely curtailed the influx of pilgrims and thereby had an adverse effect on Rome's economy. The revolution collapsed and Arnold of Brescia was driven from the city. Hadrian and Barbarossa joined forces to hunt him down, and no sooner had he fallen into their hands than he was hanged, burned, and thrown into the Tiber (1155). Thus Arnold was emphatically eliminated and his relics were put out of the reach of any future admirers. But his movement persisted as an anticlerical heresy—an early example of the opposition to ecclesiastical wealth and power that was soon to find expression among the Waldensians and Albigensians and, by implication, among the Franciscans.

The growing split between the papacy and the Roman townsmen was an ominous indication that papal leadership over urban reform movements was at an end. The papacy was no longer able to make common cause with the explosive forces of popular piety as it had done in the age of Gregory VII but was now beginning to suppress them. Pope Hadrian IV actually had little choice but to defend himself in whatever way possible against Arnold of Brescia, yet, in

THE HOLY ROMAN EMPIRE IN 1190

North Sea

Baltic Sea

KINGDOM OF DENMARK

LITHUANIA

PRUSSIANS

Elbe

Lübeck

POMERANIA

RUSSIA

SAXONY

BRANDENBURG

KINGDOM

OF

POLAND

Rhine

Cologne

NASSAU

BOHEMIA

KINGDOM OF FRANCE

LORRAINE

Worms

FRANCONIA

MORAVIA

Danube

ALSACE

SWABIA

Augsburg

Constance

BAVARIA

KINGDOM OF BURGUNDY

Milan

LOMBARDY

Venice

KINGDOM OF HUNGARY

TUSCANY

Pisa

Adriatic Sea

Danube

BULGARIANS

Sutri

Rome

Anagni

SERBIA

CORSICA

BYZANTINE EMPIRE

SARDINIA

KINGDOM OF SICILY

Palermo

Mediterranean Sea

MILES
0 100 200 300 400

laying Rome under interdict, he was following a path that would lead within a century to the Albigensian Crusade and the Inquisition. This tragic schism between papal leadership and popular piety was a factor of no small importance in the ultimate downfall of the later medieval papacy.

Hadrian IV and Frederick Barbarossa first met on the occasion of the imperial coronation in Rome in 1155. The two men had collaborated against Arnold of Brescia, but thereafter they became enemies. At their initial encounter, Hadrian insisted that Frederick follow ancient tradition and lead the papal mule.* At first Frederick haughtily refused to humble himself in such a manner, but when it appeared that there would be no coronation at all he grudgingly submitted. This small conflict was symbolic of far greater ones, for Hadrian IV and his successors proved to be implacable opponents of Frederick's drive to win control of the Lombard cities.

The Lombard struggle reached its climax under the pontificate of Alexander III (1159–1181), Hadrian's successor. Wise, shrewd, and learned, Alexander III was the greatest pope of the twelfth century and Frederick Barbarossa's most formidable opponent. Whereas most of the early reform popes had been monks, Alexander III and many of his successors were canon lawyers. Gregory VII himself had urged the study of canon law and the formulation of canonical collections in order to provide intellectual ammunition to support papal claims to authority. During the later eleventh and twelfth centuries the study of canon law was pursued vigorously in northern Italian schools, particularly the great law school at Bologna, and a good number of twelfth- and thirteenth-century popes were products of these schools. Alexander III was one of the ablest of them.

Determined to prevent Frederick Barbarossa from establishing himself strongly in northern Italy, Alexander III rallied the Lombard towns which had long been engaged in intercity warfare but now combined forces against the Empire. They formed an association called the Lombard League and organized a powerful interurban army to oppose Frederick. The emperor had meanwhile thrown his support behind a rival claimant to the papal throne,

---

* The tradition of the ceremonial mule-leading seems to have originated in the eighth-century forgery, the "Donation of Constantine."

and Alexander III responded by excommunicating and deposing Frederick. There followed a bitter, prolonged struggle involving Alexander III, Frederick Barbarossa, and the Lombard League, which ended in the total victory of the Lombard army at the battle of Legnano in 1176. Barbarossa submitted as graciously as he could, granting *de facto* independence to the Lombard cities in return for their admission of a vague imperial overlordship. Pope and emperor tearfully embraced; Barbarossa led Alexander's mule and promised thereafter to be a dutiful son of the Roman See.

Barbarossa had lost a battle, but he had by no means lost the war. Leaving Lombardy severely alone, he shifted his operations southward to Tuscany, establishing administrative control over this rich province immediately to the north of the Papal States. At the same time he arranged a fateful marriage between his son and the future heiress of the Norman Kingdom of southern Italy and Sicily —a marriage which ultimately brought that opulent kingdom within the imperial fold. The papacy had been outwitted and was in grave danger of being encircled and stifled by the Empire. In 1180 Barbarossa consolidated his power in Germany by crushing the greatest and most hostile of his vassals, Henry the Lion, the Welf duke of Saxony. After Alexander III's death in 1181, the papacy ceased for a time to be a serious threat, and the far-sighted Emperor was at the height of his power in 1190 when he died while leading his army toward the Holy Land to participate in the Third Crusade.

Barbarossa had taken pains to circumvent the princely policy of elective monarchy by forcing the princes, prior to his death, to elect his son, Henry VI. In 1190 Henry VI succeeded to the German throne without difficulty, and in 1194 he made good his claim to the Kingdom of Sicily. The Papal States were now an island completely surrounded by Holy Roman Empire, and the papacy was powerless to alter the situation. The bounteous revenues of southern Italy and Sicily fattened the imperial purse. The territories under imperial rule had never been so extensive.

But, for an age in which the emperor had to remain ever vigilant against the centrifugal forces of local particularism and, above all, against the ambitions of the great German vassals, the imperial frontiers had become dangerously overextended. It remained ominously uncertain whether a single man could rule Italy and Germany concurrently. Whether Henry VI could have accomplished this task we shall never know, for he died prematurely in 1197 leaving as his heir his infant son, Frederick II. The problems the Empire faced in 1197 would have taxed the ablest of leaders, yet at this crucial moment imperial leadership failed. The papacy had its opportunity at last.

THE HIGH NOON OF THE MEDIEVAL PAPACY

During the twelfth century, the papacy lost much of its former zealous reform spirit as it evolved into a huge, complex administrative institution. Revenues flowed into its treasury from all the states of Western Christendom; bishops traveled vast distances to make their spiritual submission to the Roman pontiff; the papal curia served as a court of last appeal for an immense network of ecclesiastical courts. Papal authority over the European Church had increased immeasurably since the mid-eleventh century. As the dream of a papal monarchy came ever nearer to realization, the traditional theory of papal supremacy over Christian society was increasingly magnified and elaborated by the canon lawyers. These subtle ecclesiastical scholars were beginning to dominate the papal curia, and, like Alexander III, to occupy the papal throne itself.

Innocent III (1198–1216), the greatest of all the lawyer popes, came to power in the year following Emperor Henry VI's death. It was he who seized the opportunity offered by the succession of an infant to the throne of the overextended Empire. Innocent III was history's most powerful pope—a brilliant, astute diplomat, an imperious, self-confident aristocrat who, although genuinely pious, was distinctly aloof from the surging religious emotionalism of the humbler folk of his age. He had the wisdom and sensitivity to support the Franciscans, and the ruthlessness to mount the Albigensian Crusade. *

Animated by the theory of papal monarchy in its most uncompromising form, Innocent III forced his will on the leading monarchs of Europe, playing off one king against another with consummate skill. In the course of a long struggle with King John of England over the appointment of an archbishop of Canterbury, Innocent laid John's entire kingdom under interdict, threatened to depose

* See pp. 171-172.

John himself, and endeavored to persuade King Philip Augustus of France to send an army against him. The struggle ended with John's complete submission, the installation of Innocent's man in the archbishopric of Canterbury, and the establishment of papal lordship over England. Innocent had earlier clashed with Philip Augustus over the king's refusal to repudiate an uncanonical second marriage and return to his first wife. After laying France under interdict and excommunicating Philip, Innocent obtained his submission.† Innocent instigated the Fourth Crusade, which was aimed at Jerusalem but ended in Constantinople, and mounted crusades against the Albigensians and the Spanish Moors. These diverse activities illustrate clearly the unprecedented political and moral sway which he exercised over Christendom.

A mighty force in the secular politics of his age, Innocent III also dominated the Church more completely than any of his predecessors had done. In 1215 he summoned a general Church council in Rome —the Fourth Lateran Council—which produced a remarkable quantity of significant ecclesiastical legislation: clerical habit was strictly regulated, a moratorium was declared on new religious orders, the ancient Germanic legal procedure of the ordeal was condemned, fees for the administration of sacraments were forbidden, cathedral churches were ordered to maintain schools and to provide sermons at their chief services, and all Catholics were bound to receive the sacraments of penance and the eucharist at least once a year. The efficient organization of the Fourth Lateran Council, and the degree to which Pope Innocent dominated and directed it are clearly illustrated by the fact that the churchmen in attendance—more than 1200 bishops, abbots, and priests—produced their important new legislation in meetings that lasted a total of only three weeks. By contrast, the fifteenth century Council of Basel met off and on for 18 years and the Council of Trent for 19 years.

The range of Innocent III's activities was seemingly boundless, but throughout his pontificate one political issue took precedence over all others: the problem of the German imperial succession. It

---

† Philip Augustus' submission was less complete, however, than might have been wished. His controversial second wife had died—conveniently but naturally —and his reconciliation with his first wife was a mere formality.

was a marvellously complex problem which taxed even Pope Innocent's diplomatic skill. Involved in it were the questions of whether or not the kingdom of Sicily would remain in imperial hands, whether the imperial throne would pass to the Welfs or the Hohenstaufens, and whether an accommodation could be achieved between the traditionally hostile forces of papacy and Empire. The German succession problem also touched the interests of the French and English monarchies: the Welf claimant, Otto of Brunswick, was a nephew of King John of England and could usually count on his support, whereas the Hohenstaufens enjoyed the friendship of the French king, Philip Augustus.

The direct Hohenstaufen heir was the infant Frederick, son of the late Henry VI. But since a child could hardly be expected to wage a successful fight for the throne in these turbulent years, the Hohenstaufen claim was taken up by Frederick's uncle, Philip of Swabia, brother of the former emperor. The young Frederick remained in Sicily while Philip of Swabia and the Welf, Otto of Brunswick, contended for the imperial throne. Innocent recognized the principle that the German princes had the right to elect their own monarch, but, as it happened, Philip and Otto had both been elected, each by a different group of German nobles. In the case of a disputed election such as this, Innocent claimed the right to intervene by virtue of the traditional papal privilege of crowning the emperor. He delayed his decision considerably, and in the meantime, civil war raged in Germany. At length he settled on Otto of Brunswick. Otto had promised to support the papal interests in Germany and to abandon almost entirely the policy of imperial control of the German Church which had been spelled out in the Concordat of Worms of 1122. Further, a Welf emperor would have no claim on the Hohenstaufen Kingdom of Sicily, and Otto's coronation would therefore realize the papal goal of separating the two realms.

Despite Innocent's decision, the civil war continued in Germany until, in 1208, Philip of Swabia died. Otto was crowned emperor in 1209, but now, having no rival to oppose him, he repudiated his promises to Innocent III, asserted his mastery over the German Church, and even launched an invasion of southern Italy. Innocent responded to this breach of faith by deposing and anathematizing Otto and throwing his support behind the young Frederick. From the beginning, the kingdom of Sicily had been, at least nominally, a papal vassal state, and Innocent III, as overlord, claimed the feudal privilege of guardianship over its minor king. Frederick, in other words, was Innocent's ward. Before undertaking to back Frederick, Innocent wrung a number of promises from him, making him swear to abdicate as king of Sicily and sever the Sicilian kingdom from the Empire, to go on a crusade, to follow the spiritual direction of the papacy, and in general to confirm the promises that Otto of Brunswick had made and later repudiated.

Innocent's decision in favor of Frederick resulted in a revival of the Hohenstaufen cause in Germany and a renewal of the civil war. Innocent employed all his diplomatic skill and leverage to win over German nobles to Frederick's cause. He was supported in these maneuverings by King Philip Augustus of France, now on friendly terms with the papacy, traditionally sympathetic to the Hohenstaufens, and hostile to the English and their Welf allies.

The complex currents of international politics in Innocent's pontificate reached their climax and their resolution in 1214; King John invaded France from the west while Otto of Brunswick led a powerful army against Philip Augustus from the east—an army heavily subsidized by England and consisting of the combined forces of pro-Welf princes from Germany and the Low Countries. John's invasion bogged down and accomplished nothing; Otto's army met the forces of Philip Augustus in pitched battle at Bouvines and was decisively defeated. The battle of Bouvines of 1214 was an epoch-making engagement. Philip Augustus of France emerged as Europe's mightiest monarch, Otto's imperial dreams were demolished, and Frederick became emperor in fact as well as in theory. Bouvines was a triumph not only for Philip Augustus and Frederick but also for Innocent III. His ward was now emperor-elect and was pledged to sever the kingdom of Sicily from Germany and free the German Church of imperial control.

Germany itself was in a state of chaos. The solid achievements of Frederick Barbarossa, which might have served as the foundation for a powerful revival of imperial power, were compromised by the subsequent imperial involvement in the affairs of the Sicilian kingdom and were demolished by 19 years of civil strife during which the German princes usurped royal privileges and royal lands on a vast scale. By the time of Innocent III's death, the imperial authority that Barbarossa had achieved was all but unrecoverable.

The policies of Innocent III were everywhere triumphant. Yet

Innocent, by the very range and breadth of his political activities, had involved the papacy in secular affairs to such a degree that its spiritual authority was becoming tarnished. Innocent had won his battles, but he had chosen a dangerous battlefield. His successors, lacking both his skill and his luck, could do little to arrest the gradual decline of papal political authority during the middle and later decades of the thirteenth century and over the centuries that followed. For papal power was based ultilmately on spiritual prestige, and the thirteenth-century popes, despite their piety, despite their continuing concern for ecclesiastical reform, were lawyers, administrators, and diplomats rather than charismatic spiritual leaders. The papacy was a mighty force in the world of the thirteenth century, but it was failing more and more to satisfy the spiritual hunger of devoted Christians. Piety remained strong, but many of the pious were coming to doubt that the papal government, with its vast wealth and bureaucratic efficiency, was indeed the true spiritual center of the apostolic Church and the citadel of Christ's kingdom on earth. The popes were doing what they had to do, and in playing the game of international politics they continued to dream of a regenerated Christian society led and inspired by the Church. But as time went on they dreamed less and, perhaps understandably, permitted their political means to overshadow their spiritual ends.

The impressive diplomatic success of Innocent III's pontificate ended abruptly with his death in 1216. Once Innocent was gone, his former ward and candidate, Frederick II, now a grown man, made it clear that he would ignore his promises as completely as Otto of Brunswick had earlier done. Frederick ruled exactly as he pleased, and as his reign progressed he became the medieval papacy's most ferocious adversary. In choosing Frederick and supporting his candidacy to the imperial throne, Innocent III had made a fearful miscalculation.

FREDERICK II (1211–1250)

Frederick II, whose Sicilian childhood exposed him to several faiths, grew up to be a brilliant, anticlerical skeptic, more concerned with his harem and his exotic menagerie than with his soul. He dazzled his contemporaries and earned the name *Stupor Mundi*, the

"Wonder of the World." His dream of unifying all Italy and making it the nucleus of the Empire won him the undying hatred of the papacy. Indeed, some churchmen regarded Frederick quite literally as the incarnate Anti-Christ.

Frederick II was a talented, many-sided man—perhaps the most flamboyant product of an intensely creative age. He was a writer of considerable skill and an amateur scientist, curious about the world around him, but in some matters deeply superstitious. After much delay he kept his promise to lead a crusade (1228), but instead of fighting the Moslems he negotiated with them, and did so with such success that Jerusalem itself came into his hands for a time. The amicable spirit of Frederick's crusade against the infidel struck many churchmen as unholy, and its success infuriated them. That this irreverent skeptic should win the crown of Jerusalem was almost more than they could stand.

Frederick II ruled his kingdom of Sicily in the autocratic but enlightened manner of a Renaissance despot, establishing a uniform legal code, tightening and broadening the centralized administrative system of his Norman-Sicilian predecessors, encouraging agriculture, industry, and commerce, abolishing interior tariffs and tolls, and founding a great university at Naples. He had promised Innocent III that he would cut Sicily off from the Empire, but he made no effort to keep his promise. He had always preferred his urbane, sunny Sicilian homeland to the cold forests and gloomy castles of Germany. Although he tried to follow Frederick Barbarossa's policy of strengthening the royal demesne and enforcing the feudal obligations of his great German vassals, he did so half-heartedly. To him, Germany was important chiefly as a source of money and military strength with which to carry out his policy of bringing all Italy under his rule.

As it happened, this policy proved disastrous to the Holy Roman Empire. Frederick's aggressions in Italy evoked the opposition of a revived Lombard League and the implacable hostility of the papacy. He gave up lands and royal rights in Germany with an almost careless abandon in order to keep the peace with the German princes and win their support for his persistent but inconclusive Italian campaigns. In the end, he was even obliged to tax his beloved Sicily to the point of impoverishment in order to support his endless wars. Brilliant lawyer-popes such as Gregory IX and

Innocent IV devoted all their diplomatic talents and spiritual sanctions to blocking Frederick's enterprises, building alliances to oppose him and hurling anathemas against him. In 1245 Pope Innocent IV presided over a universal council of the Church at Lyons which condemned and excommunicated the emperor. Frederick II was deposed, a rival emperor was elected in his place, and a crusade was called to rid the Empire of its ungodly tyrant. Revolts now broke out against Frederick throughout his Empire. The royal estates in Germany slipped more and more from his grasp, and his Italian holdings were ridden with rebellion. Against this unhappy background Frederick II died in 1250.

THE DECLINE OF THE MEDIEVAL EMPIRE

In a very real sense, the hopes of the medieval Empire died with him. His son succeeded him in Germany but died in 1254 after a brief and unsuccessful reign. For the next 19 years, Germany endured a crippling Interregnum (1254–1273) during which no recognized emperor held the throne. In 1273 a vastly weakened Holy Roman Empire reemerged with papal blessing under Rudolph of Hapsburg, the first emperor of a family that was destined to play a crucial role in modern European history. Rudolph attempted to rebuild the shattered royal demesne and shore up the foundations of imperial rule, but it was much too late. The monarch's one hope had been to strengthen and extend the crown lands, gradually transforming them into the nucleus of a modern state. This was the policy on which the medieval French monarchy had risen to a position of dominance in France; it was the policy that Frederick Barbarossa had pursued so promisingly in Germany. But it was a policy that aroused the unremitting opposition of the great princes who had no desire to see their own rights and territories eaten away by royal expansion. On the contrary, they longed to extend their own principalities at the expense of the crown.

The civil strife during Innocent's pontificate, the Italian involvements of Frederick II, and the Interregnum of 1254–1273 gave the princes their opportunity, and by 1273 the crown lands were hopelessly shrunken and disorganized. Germany was now drifting irreversibly toward the loose confederation of principalities and the anemic elective monarchy that characterized its constitutional structure from the fourteenth to the later nineteenth century. The tragic failure of the medieval Empire doomed Germany to 600 years of agonizing disunity—a bitter heritage that may well have contributed to her catastrophic career in the twentieth century.

Italy, too, emerged from the struggles of the High Middle Ages hopelessly fragmented. The Papal States continued to divide the peninsula, but they were torn with unrest and disaffection, and the papacy had trouble enough maintaining its authority over the turbulent inhabitants of Rome itself. North of the Papal States, Tuscany and Lombardy had become a chaos of totally independent warring city-states—Florence, Siena, Venice, Milan, and many others—whose rivalries would form the political backdrop for the Italian Renaissance.

The Kingdom of Sicily, established by the Normans and cherished by the Hohenstaufens, passed shortly after Frederick II's death to his illegitimate son, Manfred. The papacy, determined to rid Italy of Hohenstaufen rule, bent all its energies toward securing Manfred's downfall. At length it offered the Sicilian crown to Charles of Anjou, a cadet member of the French royal house, with the intention that Charles should drive Manfred out of the Sicilian kingdom. Charles of Anjou, a dour, cruel man of enormous ambition, defeated and killed Manfred in 1266 and established a new, French dynasty on the throne of the kingdom.

The inhabitants of the realm, particularly those on the island of Sicily, had become accustomed to Hohenstaufen rule and deeply resented Charles of Anjou. They looked upon his French soldiers as an army of occupation. When, on Easter Monday, 1282, a French soldier mishandled a young married woman on her way to evening services in Palermo, he was struck down, and on all sides was raised the cry, "Death to the French." The incident resulted in a spontaneous uprising and a general massacre of the French which quickly spread throughout the island. When the French retaliated, the Sicilians offered the crown to Peter III of Aragon, Manfred's son-in-law, who claimed the Hohenstaufen inheritance and led an army to Sicily.

There resulted a long, bloody, indecisive struggle known by the romantic title, "The War of the Sicilian Vespers." For twenty years, Charles of Anjou and his successors, backed by the French monarchy and the papacy, fought against the Sicilians and Aragonese.

In the end, southern Italy remained Angevin and its kings ruled from Naples, while Sicily passed under the control of the kings of Aragon. The dispute between France and Aragon over southern Italy and Sicily persisted for generations and was an important factor in the politics of the Italian Renaissance. The chaotic and destructive strife of the thirteenth century destroyed the prosperity of the region. Once the wealthiest and most enlightened state in Italy, the kingdom of Sicily became backward, pauperized, and divided—a victim of international politics and of the ruthless struggle between Church and state.

THE PAPACY AFTER INNOCENT III

To judge by the disintegration of the Holy Roman Empire in the thirteenth century, one would conclude that the papacy had won an overwhelming victory. But the victory was an empty one. For as popes like Innocent III, Gregory IX, and Innocent IV became increasingly involved in power politics, their spiritual role was more and more obscured. In the thirteenth century the papacy's international religious mission was being steadily subordinated to its local political interests. Slowly, almost imperceptibly, it was losing its hold on the heart of Europe. Papal excommunication, after several centuries of overuse—often for political purposes—was no longer the terrifying weapon it once had been. To call a crusade against Frederick II was doubtless an effective means of harassing that troublesome emperor, but the crusading ideal was debased in the process. The time would come when a pope would call a crusade and nobody would answer.

As the papacy became a great political power and a big business, it found itself in need of ever-increasing revenues. By the end of the thirteenth century the papal tax system was admirably efficient, with the result that the papacy acquired an unsavory reputation for boundless greed. As one contemporary observer complained, the supreme pastor of Christendom was supposed to lead Christ's flock but not to fleece it. Ironically, the fiscal and political cast of the later medieval papacy came as a direct consequence of its earlier dream of becoming the spiritual dynamo of a reformed Christendom. Rising to prominence in the eleventh century upon the flood-tide of the new popular piety, the papacy became in the twelfth and thirteenth centuries increasingly insensitive to the deep spiritual aspirations of European Christians as it became more and more absorbed in the external problems of political power.

The papacy humbled the Empire only to be humbled itself by the rising power of the new centralized monarchies of Northern Europe. By the end of the thirteenth century a new concept of royal sovereignty was in the air. The kings of England and France were finding it increasingly difficult to tolerate the existence of a semi-independent, highly privileged, internationally controlled Church within their realms. By endeavoring to bring these ecclesiastical "states within states" under royal control, the two monarchies encountered vigorous papal opposition. The issue of papal versus royal control of the Church was an old one, but the ancient controversy now took on a new form. The growing monarchies of the late thirteenth century found themselves increasingly in need of money. This was particularly true after 1294 when England and France became locked in a series of costly wars. Both monarchies adopted the novel policy of systematically taxing the clergy of their realms. Pope Boniface VIII (1294–1303) retaliated in 1296 with the papal bull *Clericis Laicos* that forbade royal taxation of the clergy without express papal permission. Once again, Church and state were at an impasse.

Boniface VIII was another lawyer-pope—a man of ability but not of genius—proud and intransigent, with a vision of absolute papal power that transcended even the notions of Innocent III, but with a fatal blindness to the momentous implications of the new centralized monarchies of late thirteenth-century Europe. His great weakness was his inability to bend his stupendous concepts of papal authority to the hard realities of contemporary European politics.

In King Philip the Fair* of France (1285–1314), Boniface had a powerful and ruthless antagonist. Philip ignored the papal bull prohibiting clerical taxation; he set his agents to work spreading scandalous rumors about the Pope's morals, and exerted serious financial pressure on Rome by cutting off all papal taxes from his

---

* Fair in the sense of "handsome."

French realm. Boniface VIII was obliged to submit for the moment, and Philip taxed his clergy unopposed. But a vast influx of pilgrims into Rome in the Jubilee year of 1300 restored the Pope's confidence. He withdrew his concession to Philip the Fair on clerical taxation and in 1302 issued the famous bull *Unam Sanctam* which asserted the doctrine of papal monarchy in uncompromising terms: ". . . we declare, announce, affirm, and define that for every human creature, to be subject to the Roman pontiff is absolutely necessary for salvation."

Philip the Fair now summoned an assembly of the realm and accused Pope Boniface of every imaginable crime from murder to black magic. A small French military expedition crossed into Italy in 1303 and took Pope Boniface prisoner at his palace at Anagni with the intention of bringing him to France for trial. Anagni, the antithesis of Canossa, symbolized the humiliation of the medieval papacy. The French plan failed—Boniface was freed by local townsmen a few days after his capture—but the proud old Pope died shortly thereafter, outraged and chagrined that armed Frenchmen should have dared to lay hands on his person.

The great age of the medieval papacy was now at an end. In 1305 the cardinals elected the Frenchman Clement V (1305–1314) who pursued a policy of timid subservience to the French throne. Clement V submitted on the question of clerical taxation, repudiated *Unam Sanctam*, and abandoned faction-ridden Rome for a new papal capital at Avignon on the Rhone. Here the popes remained for the next several generations, their independence often limited by the power of the French monarchy and their spiritual prestige continuing to decline.

It is easy to criticize the inflexibility of a Boniface VIII or the limpness of a Clement V, but the waning of papal authority in the later Middle Ages did not result primarily from personal shortcomings. Rather it stemmed from an ever-widening gulf between papal government and the spiritual hunger of ordinary Christians, combined with the hostility to Catholic internationalism on the part of increasingly powerful centralized states such as England and France. It would be grossly unfair to describe the high medieval papacy as "corrupt." Between 1050 and 1300 men of good intentions and high purposes sat on the papal throne. Not satisfied merely to chide the society of their day by innocuous moralizing from the sidelines, they plunged boldly into the world and struggled vigorously to transform and sanctify it. Tragically, perhaps inevitably, they soiled their hands.

CHRONOLOGY OF THE PAPAL-IMPERIAL CONFLICT

1039–1056: Reign of Henry III
    1046: Henry III deposes 3 rival popes, inaugurates papal reform movement
1049–1054: Pontificate of Leo IX
1056–1106: Reign of Henry IV
    1059: Papal Election Decree
1073–1085: Pontificate of Gregory VII
    1075: Gregory VII bans lay investiture.
    1076: Gregory VII excommunicates and deposes Henry IV.
    1077: Henry IV humbles himself at Canossa.
    1080: Second excommunication and deposition of Henry IV.
1088–1099: Pontificate of Urban II
1106–1125: Reign of Henry V
    1122: Concordat of Worms
1152–1190: Reign of Frederick I, "Barbarossa"
1154–1159: Pontificate of Hadrian IV
    1155: Execution of Arnold of Brescia
1159–1181: Pontificate of Alexander III
    1176: Lombards defeat Barbarossa at Legnano.
    1180: Barbarossa defeats Duke Henry the Lion of Saxony.
1190–1197: Reign of Henry VI
    1194: Henry VI becomes king of Sicily.
1198–1216: Pontificate of Innocent III
1211–1250: Reign of Frederick II
    1214: Philip Augustus defeats Otto of Brunswick at Bouvines.
    1215: Fourth Lateran Council
1227–1241: Pontificate of Gregory IX
1243–1254: Pontificate of Innocent IV
    1245: Council of Lyons
1254–1273: Interregnum
1273–1291: Reign of Rudolph of Hapsburg
1282–1302: War of the Sicilian Vespers
1294–1303: Pontificate of Boniface VIII
    1302: Boniface VIII issues *Unam Sanctam.*
    1303: Boniface VIII humiliated at Anagni.
1305–1314: Pontificate of Clement V. Papacy moves to Avignon.

12

England and France

THE ANGLO-NORMAN MONARCHY

While Empire and papacy were engaged in their struggle, France and England were evolving into centralized states. Strong monarchy came earlier to England than to France; yet it was the English who were most successful in imposing constitutional limitations on the crown. French royal absolutism and English parliamentary monarchy are both rooted in the High Middle Ages.

The Anglo-Saxon period of English history came to an end when Duke William of Normandy won the English crown with his victory at Hastings in 1066. In the centuries that followed, England was more closely tied to the Continent than before; her rulers were at once kings of England and great feudal vassals of the kings of France. England's involvement in France continued from 1066 until the mid-sixteenth century. It was a source of cultural enrichment to the English, but it also led to centuries of hostilities between the two monarchies.

William the Conqueror brought a number of fundamental changes to his new kingdom. He divided much of the conquered land among the leading warriors of his victorious army, thereby introducing into England a new, knightly, French-speaking aristocracy. He established a feudal regime in England more or less on the Norman pattern by transforming most English estates, both lay and ecclesiastical, into fiefs, held by crown vassals in return for a specified number of mounted knights and various other feudal services. The crown vassals or tenants-in-chief, in order to raise the numerous knights required by the monarchy, subdivided portions of their fiefs into smaller fiefs and granted them to knightly subvassals. In other words, the process of subinfeudation proceeded in much the way that it had centuries earlier on the Continent. As a natural by-product of the establishment of feudalism in England, scores of castles were hastily erected across the land.

But feudalism in England was not accompanied by political disintegration as it had been in Carolingian Frankland. The Norman kings of England were careful to reserve vast stretches of land for their own demesne and to keep their vassals under tight rein. Indeed, under William the Conqueror and his energetic successors, royal centralization—which had progressed far under the Anglo-Saxon kings—was significantly accelerated. William had come to England not as a mere aggressor but as a legitimate claimant to the throne, related (distantly) to the Anglo-Saxon royal family and designated—so he claimed—by King Edward the Confessor, who had died childless early in 1066.

Taking up the role of Edward the Confessor's rightful successor, William promised to preserve the laws and customs of Edward's day. Indeed, it was only natural that he should do so, for many of these customs were highly beneficial to the monarchy. The dane-geld, for example, had evolved into a unique and highly lucrative royal land tax. King William faithfully preserved it, although he did not hesitate to augment it with various new feudal dues imposed on his tenants-in-chief. The Anglo-Saxon custom of general allegiance to the crown was even more valuable to the Norman kings than the danegeld. It enabled them to demand oaths of loyalty from every vassal and subvassal in the English feudal hierarchy. A knight's allegiance to his lord was now secondary to his direct allegiance to the crown. Private war between vassals was prohibited, and private castles could be built only by royal license. In brief, the new institution of feudalism was molded by the powerful Anglo-Saxon tradition of royal supremacy into something far more centralized—far less centrifugal—than the feudalism of the Continent.

On the Conqueror's death, his kingdom passed in turn to his two sons, William II (1087–1100) and Henry I (1100–1135). Both were strong, ruthless men, but Henry I was the abler of the two. A skillful general and brilliant legal and administrative innovator, Henry I rid England of rebellion and exploited the growing prosperity of his day by a policy of severe taxation. He was not a kindly man, but his was an age in which firmness and military skill were the chief requisites to successful rule and excessive geniality was a grave weakness. His great service to his English subjects was his pitiless enforcement of the peace.

The reigns of William the Conqueror and his sons witnessed a significant growth in royal administrative institutions. The unique survey of land holdings known as Domesday Book—the product of a comprehensive census of the realm undertaken by royal order in 1086—testifies eloquently to the administrative vigor of William the Conqueror. Between 1066 and 1135 royal administration became steadily more elaborate and efficient. By Henry I's reign, royal justices were traveling around England, hearing cases in the various counties, and thereby extending the king's jurisdiction far and wide across the land. The baronial courts and the ancient folk courts of the counties and local districts continued to function. But the extension of royal jurisdiction under Henry I was the initial step in a long and profoundly significant process whereby folk justice and baronial justice were overshadowed and finally superseded by the king's justice.

Administrative efficiency and royal centralization were the keynotes of Henry I's reign. Royal dues were collected systematically by local noblemen in the king's service—the sheriffs—who passed the money on to a remarkably effective accounting agency known as the Exchequer. A powerful royal bureaucracy was gradually coming into being. The growing efficiency of the Exchequer and the expansion of royal justice were both motivated chiefly by the king's desire for larger revenues. For the more cases the royal justices handled, the more fines went into the royal coffers; the more closely the sheriffs were supervised, the less likely it was that royal taxes would stick to their fingers. The Norman kings discovered that strong government was good business.

HENRY II (1154–1189)

Henry I's death in 1135 was followed by a period of unrest and a disputed royal succession. He was survived by a daughter, Matilda, who was wed to Geoffrey Plantagenet, count of Anjou. Henry I had

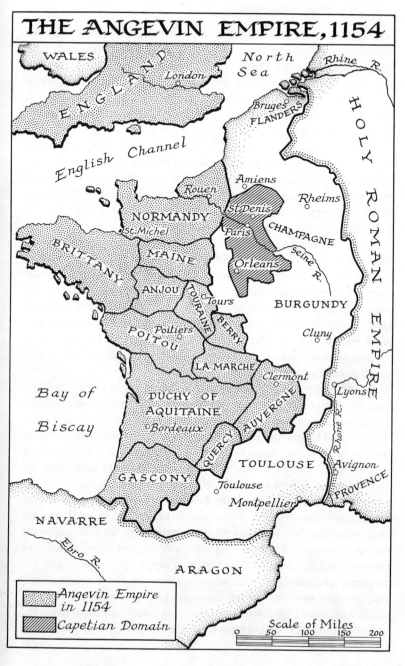

THE ANGEVIN EMPIRE, 1154

WALES

North Sea

Rhine R.

ENGLAND

London

Bruges

FLANDERS

HOLY ROMAN EMPIRE

English Channel

Rouen

Amiens

St.Denis

Rheims

NORMANDY

St.Michel

Paris

CHAMPAGNE

BRITTANY

MAINE

Orleans

Seine R.

ANJOU

TOURAINE

Tours

BURGUNDY

POITOU

Poitiers

BERRY

Cluny

LA MARCHE

Clermont

Bay of

DUCHY OF

AUVERGNE

Lyons

Biscay

AQUITAINE

Bordeaux

QUERCY

Rhone R.

Avignon

TOULOUSE

PROVENCE

GASCONY

Toulouse

Montpellier

NAVARRE

Ebro R.

ARAGON

Angevin Empire
in 1154

Capetian Domain

Scale of Miles

0   50   100   150   200

213

arranged the marriage with the hope of healing the bitter rivalry between the two great powers of northern France: Normandy and Anjou. Shortly before Henry I's death, his daughter Matilda bore him a grandson, Henry Plantagenet, who was destined ultimately to inherit a vast territory including Anjou, Normandy, and England. But when the old king died, his grandson was still an infant, and the English crown was seized by Henry I's nephew, Stephen of Blois (king of England 1135–1154). For two turbulent decades Stephen and Matilda struggled for control of England while the English barons, often playing one side against the other, threw up unlicensed castles and usurped royal rights. English churchmen and commoners, tormented by the endemic warfare of the period, looked back longingly toward the peaceful days of Henry I.

During Stephen's troubled reign Henry Plantagenet grew to vigorous manhood and established control over Anjou and Normandy. A marriage with Eleanor of Aquitaine, the heiress of that large, heterogeneous southern duchy, extended still further the territories under his jurisdiction. And at King Stephen's death in 1154 Henry peacefully acquired the English throne and became King Henry II of England. He now held sway over an immense constellation of territories north and south of the English Channel which has been called the Angevin Empire. It was not an integrated realm but rather a medley of individual states held together only by their subordination to a single man. On the map, the Angevin Empire dwarfs the modest territory controlled by the King of France. But Henry II, and his sons who succeeded him, had difficulty in keeping order throughout their vast, diverse territories. The Angevin Empire was doubtless a source of power and prestige to the English monarchy, but it was also a grave burden.

Henry II was an energetic, brilliant man—short, burly, and red-headed. Named after his grandfather, he ruled in Henry I's imperious tradition and consciously imitated him. In many respects he was a creature of his age—a product of the great intellectual and cultural outburst of twelfth-century Europe. He was a literate monarch who consorted with scholars, promoted the growing towns, and presided over an age of economic boom. A chaos of feverish activity pervaded his court, which was constantly on the move and, in the opinion of one contemporary observer, "a perfect portrait of Hell."

Henry II's goals were the preservation of the Angevin Empire, the strengthening of royal power, and the increasing of his revenues. During his thirty-five year reign the royal administration grew steadily in complexity and effectiveness. The illegal baronial castles of Stephen's reign were destroyed, and traditional royal privileges were recovered and expanded. More and more, the older feudal relationship of service in return for land gave way, under the pressure of royal ambition and a growing money economy, to wage service. The Exchequer grew, the sheriffs were kept under strict royal control, separate administrative departments evolved, and public records became fuller and more extensive. Many Englishmen were delighted at the return of peace and order; others were uneasy over the steady rise of "Big Government."

Henry II has been called the father of English common law. Like his predecessors, he favored the extension of royal jurisdiction chiefly for its financial rewards to the crown, and in his quest for ever-greater judicial revenues he was able to push the powers of the royal courts far beyond their former limits. His Assize of Clarendon of 1166 provided that local inquest juries should meet periodically under royal auspices to identify and denounce notorious neighborhood criminals. The inquest jury had been used before but never in such a systematic fashion. He also extended royal jurisdiction over the vast and turbulent field of land disputes, employing local juries to determine the rightful possessors of disputed estates. Previous kings had intervened in territorial quarrels but never in a consistent, systematic way. Now, itinerant royal justices made periodic circuits of the countryside, bringing the king's law to vast numbers of Englishmen who had previously been untouched by it. Henry II's subjects learned to turn to his courts for quick, modern, rational justice. Feudal law, with its archaic and time-consuming procedures, had little chance in the competition. Gradually the patchwork of local laws and customs which had so long divided England gave way to a uniform royal law—a *common* law by which all Englishmen were governed. The political unification of the tenth century was consummated by the legal unification under the Angevin kings.

Predictably, Henry II also sought to expand royal justice at the expense of the ecclesiastical courts. In this matter he was opposed by his implacable archbishop of Canterbury, Thomas Becket. King and archbishop became locked in a furious quarrel which centered on the issue of whether churchmen accused of crimes should be subject to royal jurisdiction or tried by Church courts alone. The issue was brought to a violent climax in 1170 when four overenthusiastic knightly supporters of Henry II, acting without royal order, murdered Becket in Canterbury Cathedral. This dramatic crime made a profound impact on the age. Becket became a martyr; miracles were alleged to have occurred at his tomb, and he was quickly canonized. Acutely embarrassed by the episode, Henry II was obliged to do penance by walking barefoot through the streets of Canterbury and submitting to a flogging by the Canterbury monks. But his campaign against the ecclesiastical courts was delayed only momentarily. By the end of his reign, royal justice had made significant inroads on the authority of the Church courts, and the crown had succeeded in bringing the English Church under tight rein. Here, as elsewhere, Henry II was remarkably successful in steering England toward administrative and legal centralization.

RICHARD AND JOHN

Henry II was succeeded by his eldest surviving son, Richard the Lion-Hearted (1189–1199), a cruel, skillful warrior who devoted himself chiefly to two great projects: defending the Angevin Empire against the French crown and crusading against the Moslems. He was a superb general but a second-rate administrator who spent less than six months of his ten-year reign in England. During his protracted absences, the administrative system of Henry II proved its worth; it governed England more or less satisfactorily for ten years without a king. Meanwhile Richard was engaging in romantic but fruitless adventures in the Holy Land and was successfully defending the Angevin Empire against the remorseless pressure of King Philip Augustus of France.

The fortunes of the Angevin Empire veered sharply with the accession of King John (1199–1216), Richard the Lion-Hearted's younger brother. John is an enigmatic figure—brilliant in certain respects, a master of administrative detail, but a suspicious and unscrupulous leader. He trusted nobody, and nobody trusted him. Consequently, his subjects never supported him more than half-heartedly in moments of crisis.

In Philip Augustus of France (1180–1223) John had a shrewd and unremitting antagonist. Philip took full advantage of his position as feudal overlord over John's continental possessions. In 1202 John was summoned to the French royal court to answer charges brought against him by one of his own Aquitainian vassals. When John refused to come, Philip Augustus declared his French lands forfeited and proceeded to invade Normandy. The duchy quickly fell into Philip's hands (1203–4) as John's demoralized vassals defected, one after another, and John himself fled ignominiously to England. In the chaos that followed Philip Augustus was able to wrest Anjou and most of the remaining continental possessions of the Angevin Empire from John's control. Only portions of distant Aquitaine retained their connection with the English monarchy. King John had sustained a monstrous political and military disaster.

For the next ten years John nursed his wounds and wove a dextrous web of alliances against King Philip in hopes of regaining his lost possessions, but his careful plans were shattered by Philip's decisive victory over John's Flemish and German allies at the battle of Bouvines in 1214. With Bouvines went John's last hope of reviving the Angevin Empire.

These catastrophies destroyed what remained of John's royal prestige and paved the way for the epoch-making English baronial uprising that culminated in the signing of Magna Carta in 1215. John's barons had good reason to oppose him. He had pushed the centralizing tendencies of his Norman and Angevin predecessors to new limits and was taxing his subjects as they had never been taxed before. The baronial reaction of 1215 may be regarded both as a protest against John and as an effort to reverse the trend toward royal authoritarianism of the past 150 years. Magna Carta has been interpreted in contradictory ways: as the fountainhead of English constitutional monarchy, and as a reactionary, backward-looking document designed to favor the particularistic feudal aristocracy at the expense of the enlightened Angevin monarchy.

In reality, Magna Carta was both feudal and constitutional—both backward-looking and forward-looking. Its more important clauses were designed to keep the king within the bounds of popular tradition and feudal custom. Extraordinary taxes, for example, were to be levied only by the common council of the kingdom. But implicit in the traditional feudal doctrine that the lord had to respect the rights of his vassals—and in the age-old Germanic notion that the monarch had to adhere to the customs of his people—was the profound constitutional principle of government under the law. In striving to make King John a good feudal lord, the barons in 1215 were moving uncertainly, perhaps unconsciously, toward constitutional monarchy. For this was the crucial moment when the English nobles were just beginning to represent a national point of view. In the past, baronial opposition to royal autocracy had taken the form of a selfish insistence on local aristocratic autonomy. But one finds in Magna Carta the notion that the king is bound by traditional legal limitations in his relations with all classes of free Englishmen. It would be misleading to lay too much stress on the underlying principles of this intensely practical document, which was concerned primarily with correcting specific abuses of royal power, but it would be equally misleading to ignore the momentous implication in Magna Carta of an overarching body of law which limited and circumscribed royal authority.

The chief constitutional problem in the years following Magna Carta was the question of how an unwilling king might be forced to stay within the bounds of law. A series of royal promises was obviously insufficient to control an ambitious monarch who held all the machinery of the central government in his grasp. Magna Carta itself relied on a committee of 25 barons who were empowered, should the king violate the Charter, to call upon the English people "to distrain and distress him in every possible way." Thus the monarch was to be restrained by the crude sanction of baronial and popular rebellion—a desperate and unwieldy weapon against an unscrupulous king.

John himself seems to have had no intention of carrying out his promises. He repudiated Magna Carta at the first opportunity, with the full backing of his papal overlord, Innocent III. At his death in 1216 England was in the midst of a full-scale revolt. John's death ended the revolt, and the crown passed to his nine-year-old son, Henry III (1216–1272) who was supervised during his minority by a baronial council. In the decades that followed, Magna Carta was reissued many times, but the great task of the new age was to create political institutions capable of limiting royal autocracy by some means short of rebellion. The ultimate solution to this problem was found in Parliament.

HENRY III

Henry III was a petulant, erratic monarch: pious without being holy, bookish without being wise. Surrounding himself with foreign favorites and intoxicated by grandiose, impractical foreign projects, he ignored the advice of his barons and gradually lost their confidence.

Ever since its beginning, the English monarchy had customarily arrived at important decisions of policy with the advice of a royal council of nobles and officials. In Anglo-Saxon times, this council was called the *witenagemot*; after 1066 it was known as the *curia regis*. Its composition had always been vague, and it had never possessed anything resembling a veto power over royal decisions, but many Englishmen, particularly noblemen, put much importance in the fact that royal policies were framed in consultation with the barons.

Traditionally, English royal councils were of two types. Ordinary royal business was conducted in a small council consisting of the king's household officials and whatever barons happened to be at court at the time. But in moments of crisis, or when some important decision was pending, the kings supplemented their normal coterie of advisers by summoning the important noblemen of the realm to meet as a great council. It was this great baronial council that eventually evolved into Parliament.

A key factor in the evolution from great council to Parliament was the trend in the thirteenth century toward including representatives of the county gentry and the townsmen alongside the great barons. This notable development resulted from the royal policy, particularly evident after Magna Carta, of summoning the great council for the purpose of obtaining approval for some uncustomary tax. As wealth gradually seeped downward into the sub-baronial classes, the king found it expedient to obtain the consent of these lesser orders to new royal taxes by summoning their representatives to the great council.

The vigorous baronial opposition to Henry III arose from the fact that he summoned the great council not for the purpose of consulting his magnates on policy matters but chiefly for the purpose of obtaining their consent to new taxes. The barons resented being asked to finance chimerical foreign schemes in which they had not been consulted and of which they disapproved. They might well have chosen as their motto, "No taxation without consultation." They responded to Henry III's fiscal demands with increasing reluctance, until at last, in 1258, the monarch's soaring debts brought on a financial crisis of major proportions. In order to obtain desperately needed financial support from his barons, King Henry submitted to a set of baronial limitations on royal power known as the Provisions of Oxford.

These Provisions went far beyond Magna Carta in providing machinery to force the king to govern according to good custom and in consultation with his magnates. The great council was to be summoned at least three times a year and was to include, along with its usual membership, 12 men "elected" by the "community"—in other words, chosen by the barons. These 12 were empowered to speak for the magnates in the great council, so that even if heavily outnumbered their authority would be great. The Provisions of Oxford also established a Committee of Fifteen, chiefly baronial in composition, which shared with the king control over the royal administration. Specifically, the Council of Fifteen was given authority over the exchequer and was empowered to appoint the chancellor and other high officers of state.

The Provisions of Oxford proved premature, and the governmental system which they established turned out to be unworkable because of baronial factionalism. Their importance lies in the fact that they disclose clearly the attitude of many mid-thirteenth-century barons toward the royal administration. These magnates had no thought of abolishing the enlightened administrative and legal achievements of the past two centuries or of weakening the central government. Their interests were national rather than parochial, and they merely sought to exert a degree of control over the royal administration. Most of them acted as they did, not on the basis of theoretical abstractions, but because they thought it necessary to curb an incompetent, arbitrary, spendthrift king.

With the failure of the Provisions, Henry III resumed exclusive control over his government and returned to the arbitrary policies that his barons found so distasteful. At length, baronial discontent exploded into open rebellion. The barons, led by Simon de Montfort, defeated the royal army at Lewes in 1264 and captured Henry himself. For the next 15 months Simon ruled England in the king's name, sharing authority with two baronial colleagues and a committee of magnates similar to that of the Provisions of Oxford. The rule of Simon de Montfort and his committee was augmented periodically by meetings of the great council—now commonly called "parliaments." Simon's government was a product of the same philosophy that underlay the Provisions of Oxford, and like the government of the Provisions, it was weakened and ultimately brought to ruin by baronial factionalism.

In 1265 the monarchy rallied under the leadership of Henry III's talented son, Edward, defeated a baronial army at Evesham, and crushed Simon de Montfort's faltering rebellion.

THE EVOLUTION OF PARLIAMENT

But the effect of the uprising proved to be lasting. England had undergone an interesting experience in baronial government and, far more important, a significant step had been taken in the development of Parliament. For earlier in 1265, Simon de Montfort had summoned a great council—a parliament—which included for the first time all three of the classes that were to characterize the parliaments of the later Middle Ages. Simon de Montfort's parliament included, in addition to the barons, two knights from every shire and two burghers from every town. Simon's chief motive in summoning this parliament was probably to broaden the base of his rebellion, but in later years parliaments were summoned for many purposes: to sit as a high court of law, to advise the king on important matters of policy, to declare their support in moments of crisis, and to give their consent to the ever-increasing royal taxes.

The English Parliament was built upon a sturdy foundation of local government, and all three of the major parliamentary orders—barons, burghers, and shire knights—brought with them a wealth of local political experience. The burghers in Parliament were usually veterans of town government. The shire knights had long been involved in the administration of the counties and the county courts. Intermediate between the baronial nobility and the peasantry, these men constituted a separate class—a country gentry—rooted to their shires and their ancestral estates, experienced in local government, and well suited to represent their counties in Parliament.

In 1272 Henry III was succeeded by his son, Edward I (1272–1307), a far wiser man than his father. Edward I was a monarch of strong will and independence, but he had the sagacity to take the barons into his confidence and he was successful by and large in winning their support. Although he, like his father, regarded parliaments chiefly as means of winning approval for new taxes, he used them for many other purposes as well. He summoned parliaments frequently and experimented endlessly in their composition. In the later years of his reign the inclusion of shire knights and townsmen became customary. It was not until the fourteenth century, however, that the knights and burghers began meeting separately from the barons, thereby giving birth to the great parliamentary division into Lords and Commons.

As the thirteenth century closed, the actual powers of parliaments remained exceedingly vague and their composition was still fluid. At best, they might bargain discreetly with the king for concessions in return for financial aid. Still, a beginning had been made. The deep-rooted medieval concept of limited monarchy had given rise to an institution that would develop over the centuries into a keystone of representative government. There was obviously nothing remotely democratic about the parliaments that Edward I summoned. He regarded them as instruments of royal policy, and used them to aid and strengthen the monarchy rather than limit it. Yet ultimately, Parliament was to be the crucial institutional bridge between medieval feudalism and modern democracy.

EDWARD I

The reign of Edward I witnessed the culmination of many trends that had been developing throughout the High Middle Ages. Through his creative legislation Edward completed the great work of his predecessors in creating an effective and complex royal administrative system and building an enlightened, comprehensive body of common law. He was a skillful general who added Wales to the English realm, came close to conquering Scotland and fought vigorously but inconclusively with King Philip the Fair over the remaining English territories in southern France. But his most significant contribution, in the long run, was his policy of developing Parliament into an integral organ of government. It is ironic, therefore, that King Edward regarded Parliament primarily as a useful instrument for raising the necessary revenues to support his far-flung projects. He would have been appalled to learn that his royal descendants would one day be figurehead kings and that Parliament was destined to rule England.

THE EARLY CAPETIANS

When William of Normandy conquered England in 1066, the French monarchy exerted a feeble control over a small territory around Paris and Orleans known as the Ile de France and was virtually powerless in the lands beyond. To be sure, the French kings had as their vassals great feudal magnates such as the dukes of Normandy and Aquitaine and the counts of Anjou, Flanders, and Champagne, but vassalage was a slender bond indeed when the king lacked the power to enforce his lordship. In theory the anointed king of the French, with his priestly charisma, with the sovereign power traditionally associated with royalty, and with the supreme feudal overlordship, was a mighty figure indeed. But in grim reality he was impotent to control his great vassals and unable to keep order even in the Ile de France itself.

Since 987 the French crown had been held by the Capetian dynasty. The achievement of the Capetians in the first century or so of their rule was modest enough. Their one triumph was their success in keeping the crown within their own family. The Capetians had gained the throne originally by virtue of being elected by the magnates of the realm, but from the first they sought to purge the monarchy of its elective character and to make it hereditary. This they accomplished by managing to produce male heirs at the right moment and by arranging for the new heir to be crowned before the old king died. They may have been aided by the fact that the crown was not a sufficiently alluring prize to attract powerful usurpers.

In the early twelfth century the Capetians remained weaker than several of their own vassals. While vassal states such as Normandy and Anjou were becoming increasingly centralized, the Capetian Ile de France was still ridden with fiercely insubordinate robber barons. If the Capetians were to realize the immense potential of their royal title, they had three great tasks before them: (1) to master and pacify the Ile de France, (2) to expand their political and economic base by bringing additional territories under direct royal authority, and (3) to make their lordship over the great vassals real rather than merely theoretical.

During the twelfth and thirteenth centuries a series of remarkable Capetian kings pursued and achieved these goals. Their success was so complete that by the opening of the fourteenth century the Capetians controlled all France, either directly or indirectly, and had developed an efficient and sophisticated royal bureaucracy. They followed no hard and fast formula. Rather their success depended on a combination of luck and ingenuity—on their clever exploitation of the powers which, potentially, they had always possessed as kings and feudal overlords. They were surprisingly successful in avoiding the family squabbles that had at times paralyzed Germany and England. Unlike the German monarchs, they maintained comparatively good relations with the papacy. They had the enormous good fortune of an unbroken sequence of direct male heirs from 987 to 1328. Above all, they seldom overreached themselves: they avoided grandiose schemes and spectacular strokes of policy, preferring instead to pursue modest, realistic goals. They extended their power gradually and cautiously by favorable marriages, by confiscating the fiefs of vassals who died without heirs, and by dispossessing vassals who violated their feudal obligations toward the monarchy. Yet the majority of the Capetians had no desire to absorb all the territories of their vassals. Rather, they sought to build a kingdom with a substantial core of royal domain lands surrounded by the fiefs of loyal, obedient magnates.

LOUIS VI AND LOUIS VII

The first Capetian to work seriously toward the consolidation of royal control in the Ile de France was King Philip I (1060–1108), a bloated, repugnant man who grasped the essential fact that the Capetian monarchy had to make its home base secure before turning to loftier goals. Philip's realistic policy was pursued far more vigorously by his son, Louis VI, "the Fat" (1108–1137). Year after year Louis the Fat battled the petty brigand-lords of the Ile de France, besieged their castles one after another, and at last reduced them to obedience. At his death in 1137 the Ile de France was relatively orderly and prosperous, and the French monarchy was beginning to pull abreast of its greater vassals.

Louis the Fat received invaluable assistance in the later part of his reign from Abbot Suger of the great royal abbey of Saint-Denis. As chief royal adviser from 1130 to 1151, this talented statesman labored hard and effectively to extend the king's sway, to systematize the royal administration, and, incidentally, to augment the wealth and prestige of Saint-Denis. Suger provided an invaluable element of continuity between the reigns of Louis the Fat and his son, Louis VII (1137–1180), who pursued his father's goals with less than his father's skill. Pious and gentle, Louis VII was, in the words of a contemporary observer, "a very Christian king, if somewhat simpleminded."

When Abbot Suger died in 1151, Louis VII was left to face unaided a new and formidable threat to the French monarchy. The Angevin Empire was just then in the process of formation, and in 1154 the ominous configuration was completed when Henry Plantagenet, Count of Anjou and Duke of Normandy and Aquitaine, acceded to the English throne as King Henry II. Louis VII sought to embarrass his mighty vassal by encouraging Henry's sons to rebel, but his efforts were too half-hearted to be successful. Still, Louis VII's reign witnessed a significant extension of royal power. Indeed, as one historian has aptly said, it was under Louis VII that "the prestige of the French monarchy was decisively established."* The great vassals of the crown, fearful of their powerful Angevin colleague and respectful of Louis VII's piety and impartiality, began for the first time to bring cases to the court of their royal overlord and to submit their disputes to his judgment. Churchmen and townsmen alike sought his support in struggles with the nobility. These developments resulted not so much from royal initiative as from the fundamental trends of the age toward peace, order, and increased commercial activity. Frenchmen in increasing numbers were turning to their genial, unassuming monarch for succor and justice, and, little by little, Louis VII began to assume his rightful place as feudal suzerain and supreme sovereign of the realm.

PHILIP AUGUSTUS (1180–1223)

The French monarchy came of age under Louis VII's talented son, Philip II "Augustus" (1180–1223). By remorseless insistence on his feudal rights, and by a policy of dextrous and ruthless opportunism, Philip Augustus enlarged the royal territories enormously and, beyond the districts of direct royal jurisdiction, transformed

* R. Fawtier, *The Capetian Kings of France* (London, 1962), p. 23.

the chaotic anarchy of the vassal states into an orderly feudal hierarchy subordinate to the king.

Philip Augustus' great achievement was his destruction of the Angevin Empire and his establishment of royal jurisdiction over Normandy, Anjou, and their dependencies. For two decades he plotted with dissatisfied members of the Angevin family against King Henry II and King Richard the Lion-Hearted, but it was not until the reign of King John (1199–1216) that his efforts bore fruit. Against John's notorious faithlessness and greed, Philip was able to play the role of the just lord rightfully punishing a disobedient vassal. And when Philip Augustus moved against Normandy in 1203–4, John's remarkable unpopularity played into his hands. The prize which Philip had sought so long fell with surprising ease, and once Normandy was his, John's remaining fiefs in northern France fell like dominoes. Ten years later, in 1214, Philip extinguished John's last hope of recovering the lost territories by winning a decisive victory over John's German allies at Bouvines. Settling the fate of Normandy and Anjou, Bouvines was also a turning point in the power balance between France and Germany in the High Middle Ages. For thereafter, the waxing Capetian monarchy of France replaced the faltering kingdom of Germany as the great continental power in Western Europe.

Under Philip Augustus and his predecessors significant developments were occurring in the royal administrative system. The *curia regis* had assumed its place as the high feudal court of France and was proving an effective instrument for the assertion of royal rights over the dukes and counts. Hereditary noblemen, who had traditionally served as local administrators in the royal territories, were gradually replaced by salaried middle-class officials known as *baillis*. These new officials, whose functions were at once financial, judicial, military, and administrative, owed their positions to the royal favor and were therefore fervently devoted to the interests of the crown. Throughout the thirteenth century the *baillis* worked tirelessly and often unscrupulously to erode the privileges of the feudal aristocracy and extend the royal sway. This intensely loyal and highly mobile bureaucracy, without local roots and without respect for feudal and local traditions, became in time a powerful instrument of royal absolutism. The *baillis* stood in sharp contrast to the local officials

of England—the sheriffs and the shire knights—who were customarily drawn from the local gentry and whose loyalties were divided
between the monarch whom they served and the region and class
from which they sprang.

LOUIS VIII (1223–1226)

The closing years of Philip Augustus' reign were concurrent with
the savage Albigensian Crusade in southern France, called by
Philip's great contemporary, Pope Innocent III, against the supporters of the Albigensian heresy which was spreading rapidly through
Languedoc and northern Italy (see pp. 171). Philip Augustus
declined to participate personally in the Crusade, but his son,
Prince Louis, took an active part in it, and when the prince succeeded
to his father's throne in 1223 as Louis VIII (1223–1226), he threw
all the resources of the monarchy behind the southern campaign.
The Crusade succeeded in eliminating the Albigensian threat to
Western Christendom but only by devastating large portions of
southern France and exterminating the brilliant culture which
previously had flourished there. Thenceforth southern France
tended to be dominated by northern France, and the authority of
the French monarchy was extended to the Mediterranean.

It may perhaps be surprising to discover that Louis VIII, who
inherited a vastly expanded royal jurisdiction from his father and
extended it still further himself, granted about a third of the hard-
won royal territories as fiefs to junior members of the Capetian
family. These family fiefs, created out of the royal domain, are
known as *appanages*. Their emergence should serve as a warning that
the growth of the Capetian monarchy cannot be understood simply
as a linear process of expanding the royal territories. The Capetians
had no objection to vassals as long as they were obedient and subject
to royal control. Indeed, given the limited transportation and
communication facilities of twelfth- and thirteenth-century France,
the kingdom was far too large to be controlled directly by the
monarchy. The new vassals, bound to the crown by strong family
ties, played an essential role in the governance of the realm and
strengthened rather than weakened the effectiveness of Capetian
rule.

SAINT LOUIS (1226–1270)

Louis VIII died prematurely in 1226, leaving the land in the capable hands of his stern and pious Spanish widow, Blanche of Castile, who acted as regent for the boy-king Louis IX (1226–1270) —the later St. Louis. Even after St. Louis came of age in 1234 he remained devoted to his mother, and Queen Blanche continued for years to be a dominant influence in the royal government.

St. Louis possessed both his mother's sanctity and his mother's firmness. Unlike many saint-kings, he was a strong monarch, obsessed with the obligation to rule justly and firmly and to promote moral rectitude throughout the kingdom of France. His sanctity, although thoroughly genuine, was perhaps too orthodox—too conventional. He persecuted heretics and crusaded against the Moslems. He once remarked that the only possible response for a Christian toward Jews who blasphemed was "to plunge his sword into their bellies as far as it would go." Still, in asserting these attitudes he was merely mirroring his age. His reign was far different from that of Philip Augustus, for he oriented his life not toward political ends but toward what he conceived to be religious ends. He believed in war against the infidel, but he believed just as fervently in peace among Christian rulers. Accordingly, he arranged treaties with Henry III of England and with the king of Aragon which settled peacefully all outstanding disputes. He played the role of peacemaker among Christian princes and was even called on to arbitrate between King Henry III and his barons.

St. Louis was content, in general, to maintain the royal rights established by his predecessors. His *baillis* and other officials were actually far more aggressive than he in extending the royal power; as one modern historian puts it, "In this reign monarchial progress was the complex result of the sanctity of a revered ruler, and the patient and obstinately aggressive policy of the king's servants." Indeed, St. Louis went to the length of establishing a system of itinerant royal inspectors—*enquêteurs*—who reported local grievances and helped keep the ambitious local officials in check.

In France under Louis IX medieval culture reached its climax. Town life flourished under St. Louis' rule, and in the towns magnificent Gothic cathedrals were being erected. This was the great age of the medieval universities, and at the most distinguished

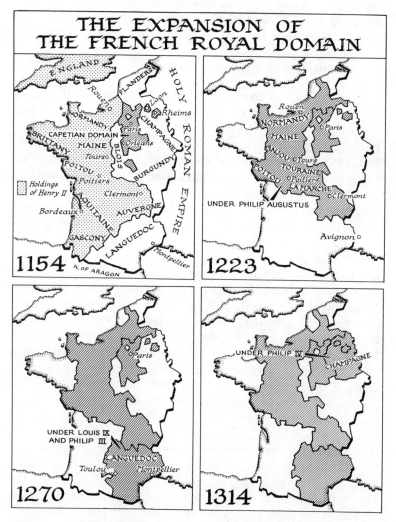

THE EXPANSION OF
THE FRENCH ROYAL DOMAIN

1154

ENGLAND

Rouen
FLANDERS
Laon
HOLY
NORMANDY
Rheims
CAPETIAN DOMAIN
Paris
CHAMPAGNE
BRITTANY
MAINE
BLOIS
Orleans
ROMAN
Tours
Holdings
of Henry II
POITOU
Poitiers
BURGUNDY
EMPIRE
Clermont
Bordeaux
AQUITAINE
AUVERGNE
GASCONY
LANGUEDOC
Montpellier
K. OF ARAGON

1223

Rouen
NORMANDY
MAINE
Paris
ANJOU
Tours
TOURAINE
POITOU
Poitiers
LA MARCHE
UNDER PHILIP AUGUSTUS
Clermont
Avignon

1270

Paris
UNDER LOUIS IX
AND PHILIP III
LANGUEDOC
Toulou
Montpellier

1314

UNDER PHILIP IV
CHAMPAGNE

university of the age, the University of Paris, some of the keenest
intellects of medieval Europe—St. Bonaventure, Albertus Magnus,
Thomas Aquinas—were assembled concurrently. The universities
produced brilliant and subtle theologians, but they also produced
learned and ambitious lawyers—men of a more secular cast, who
devoted their talents to the king and swelled the ranks of the royal

bureaucracy. The Capetian government became steadily more complex, more efficient and, from the standpoint of the feudal nobility, more oppressive.

PHILIP THE FAIR (1285–1314)

St. Louis died in the midst of his second Crusade. Under his successors the bureaucracy pursued its ruthless centralizing policies without restraint. The saint-king was succeeded by his inept son, Philip III (1270–1285), and his frigid, unscrupulous grandson, Philip IV, "the Fair" or "the Handsome" (1285–1314). Philip the Fair was a mysterious, silent figure, conventionally pious but with a real flair for choosing able, aggressive, and thoroughly unprincipled ministers—chiefly middle-class lawyers from southern France —who devoted themselves with remarkable singlemindedness to the exaltation of the French monarchy.

The reign of Philip the Fair was an age of unceasing royal aggression—against the territories of neighboring states, against the papacy, and against the traditional privileges of the French nobility. Philip waged an indecisive war against King Edward I of England over Edward's remaining fiefs in southern France. He made a serious effort to absorb Flanders, imprisoning the Flemish count and ruling the district directly through a royal agent, but he was foiled by a bloody Flemish revolt in 1302. He pursued a successful policy of nibbling aggression to the east against the Holy Roman Empire. He suppressed unscrupulously the rich Crusading order of Knights Templars, ruined their reputation by an astonishingly modern campaign of vituperative propaganda, and confiscated their wealth. We have seen in Chapter II how he struggled with Pope Boniface VIII, how his agents held Boniface captive for a brief time, and how he finally engineered the election of the pliable French Pope Clement V who took up residence at Avignon. Against his nobles he pursued a rigorously anti-feudal policy. He short-circuited the feudal hierarchy and demanded direct allegiance and obedience from all Frenchmen. All these activities were manifestations of the prevailing political philosophy of his reign: that the French king was by rights the secular and spiritual master of France and the dominating figure in Western Europe. We encounter this same philosophy in ambitious French statesmen of succeeding centuries—in Cardinal Richelieu, in Louis XIV, and, stripped of its monarchial trappings, in Napoleon and de Gaulle.

Throughout the thirteenth century the French royal bureaucracy had been developing steadily. The royal revenues came to be handled by a special accounting bureau, roughly parallel to the English Exchequer, called the *Chambre des Comtes*. The king's judicial business became the responsibility of a high court known as the *Parlement of Paris*, which was to play a highly significant political role in later centuries. Under Philip the Fair the bureaucracy became an exceedingly refined and supple tool of the royal interest, and its middle-class background and fanatical royalism gave the king a degree of independence from the nobility that was quite unknown in contemporary England.

Still, the king could not rule without a degree of support from his subjects. Philip's victory over the papacy on the issue of royal taxation of the clergy and his rape of the Knights Templars brought additional money into his treasury, but the soaring expenses of government and warfare forced him to seek ever-new sources of revenue and, as in England to secure his subjects' approval for extraordinary taxation. But instead of summoning a great assembly —a parliament—for this purpose, he usually negotiated individually with various tax-paying groups in local assemblies.

Nevertheless, it was under Philip the Fair that France's first great representative assemblies were summoned. Beginning in 1302, the Estates General was assembled from time to time, primarily for the purpose of giving formal support to the monarchy in moments of crisis—during the height of the struggle with Pope Boniface VIII, for example, or in the midst of the Knights Templars controversy. The assembly included members of the three great social classes or "estates"—the clergy, the nobility, and the townsmen. It continued to meet occasionally during the succeeding centuries, but it never became a real organ of government as did the English Parliament. Its failure resulted in part from a premature and unsuccessful bid for power during the fourteenth century in the midst of the Hundred Years' War. But even under Philip the Fair, the Estates General lacked the potential of the contemporary parliaments of England. It had no real voice in royal taxation and was therefore not in a position to bargain with the king through increasing control of the purse strings. It was not, as in England, an evolutionary outgrowth of the royal council but rather an entirely separate and therefore somewhat exotic body. There was no real opportunity for the bourgeoisie and the gentry to join ranks as in the English House of Commons; lacking the important responsibilities in local government which fell on the English shire knights, the knights in France remained an inarticulate and subordinate part of the aristocratic class. Above all, the French nobility and bourgeoisie lagged far behind the English in developing a national consciousness or a feeling of cohesion. Late-thirteenth-century France was too large, too heterogeneous, and too recently consolidated under royal authority, for its inhabitants to have acquired a meaningful sense of identification as a people; their outlook remained provincial and parochial.

Yet despite the significant differences between the English Parliament and the French Estates General, the two institutions had much in common. Both were products of a European-wide evolution out of feudal monarchy and out of the vague but pervading medieval notion of government by the consent of the realm. Similar representative institutions were emerging concurrently all over Western Christendom: in the Christian kingdoms of Spain, in Italy under Frederick II, in the rising principalities of Germany, and in innumerable counties, duchies, and communes across the length and breadth of Europe. Of these many experiments, only the English Parliament survives today. But Parliament was not merely the outgrowth of an isolated English experience; it was one particular manifestation of a broad and fundamental trend in European civilization during the High Middle Ages.

CHRONOLOGY OF THE ENGLISH AND FRENCH MONARCHIES
IN THE HIGH MIDDLE AGES

England	*France*
1066: Norman Conquest of England	987–1328: Rule of the Capetian Dynasty
1066–1087: Reign of William the Conqueror	1060–1108: Reign of Philip I
1087–1100: Reign of William II	
1100–1135: Reign of Henry I	1108–1137: Reign of Louis VI, "the Fat"
1135–1154: Disputed succession; King Stephen	
1154–1189: Reign of Henry II	1137–1180: Reign of Louis VII
1189–1199: Reign of Richard the Lion-Hearted	1180–1223: Reign of Philip II, "Augustus"
1199–1216: Reign of John	
1203–1204: Loss of Normandy	1214: Battle of Bouvines
1215: Magna Carta	1223–1226: Reign of Louis VIII
1216–1272: Reign of Henry III	1226–1270: Reign of St. Louis IX
1264–1265: Simon de Montfort's rebellion	1270–1285: Reign of Philip III
1272–1307: Reign of Edward I	1285–1314: Reign of Philip IV, "the Fair"

13

Literature and Art

THE DYNAMICS OF HIGH MEDIEVAL CULTURE

Thirteenth-century Paris has been described as the Athens of medieval Europe. It is true, of course, that a vast cultural gulf separates the golden age of Periclean Athens from the golden age of thirteenth-century France, but it is also true that these two golden ages had something in common. Both developed within the framework of traditional beliefs and customs which had long existed but were being challenged and transformed by powerful new forces. The socio-religious world of the Early Middle Ages, like the socioreligious world of the early Greek polis, was parochial and tradition-bound. As the two cultures passed into their golden ages, the values of the past were being challenged by new intellectual currents, and the old economic patterns were breaking down before a sharp intensification of commercial activity. Yet, for a time, these dynamic new forces resulted in a heightened cultural expression of the old values. The Parthenon, dedicated to the venerable civic goddess Athena, and the awesome Gothic cathedral of Notre Dame (Our Lady) are both products of a boundless new creativity harnessed to the service of an older ideology. In the long run, the new creative impulses would prove subversive to the old ideologies, but for a time both ancient Greece and medieval Europe achieved an elusive equilibrium between old and new. The results, in both cases, were spectacular.

Thus twelfth- and thirteenth-century Europe succeeded, by and large, in keeping its vibrant and audacious culture within the bounds of traditional Catholic Christianity. And the Christian world view gave form and orientation to the new creativity. Despite the intense dynamism of the period, it can still be called, with some semblance of accuracy, an Age of Faith.

Europe in the High Middle Ages underwent a profound artistic and intellectual awakening which affected almost every imaginable form of expression. Significant creative work was done in literature, architecture, sculpture, law, philosophy, music, drama, and even in science. By the close of the period, the foundations of the Western cultural tradition were firmly established. The pages that follow will provide only a glimpse at a few of the remarkable achievements of this fertile era.

LATIN LITERATURE

The literature of the High Middle Ages was abundant and richly varied. Poetry was written both in the traditional Latin—the universal scholarly language of medieval Europe—and in the vernacular languages of ordinary speech that had long been evolving in the various districts of Christendom. Traditional Christian piety found expression in a series of somber and majestic Latin hymns, whose mood is illustrated—through the clouded glass of translation —by these excerpts from "Jerusalem the Golden" (twelfth century):

> The world is very evil, the times are waxing
>   late,
> Be sober and keep vigil; the judge is at the
>   gate . . . .
> Brief life is here our portion; brief sorrow,
>   short-lived care.
> The life that knows no ending, the tearless
>   life, is there . . . .
> Jerusalem the Golden, with milk and honey
>   blessed,
> Beneath thy contemplation sink heart and
>   voice oppressed.
> I know not, O I know not, what social joys
>   are there,
> What radiancy of glory, what light beyond
>   compare.

At the opposite end of the spectrum of medieval Latin literature we encounter poetry of quite a different sort, composed by young, wandering scholars and aging perpetual-undergraduate types. The deliberate sensuality and blasphemy of their poems is an expression of student rebelliousness against the ascetic ideals of their elders:

> For on this my heart is set, when the hour
>   is neigh me,
> Let me in the tavern die, with a tankard
>   by me,
> While the angels, looking down,
>   joyously sing o'er me . . . etc.

One of these wandering-scholar poems is an elaborate and impudent expansion of the Apostles' Creed. The phrase from the Creed, "I believe in the Holy Ghost, the Holy (Catholic) Church . . ." is embroidered as follows:

> *I believe* in wine that's fair to see,
> And in the tavern of my host
> More than *in the Holy Ghost*
> The tavern will my sweetheart be,
> And *the Holy Church* is not for me.*

These sentiments should not be regarded as indicative of a sweeping trend toward agnosticism. Rather, they are distinctively medieval expressions of the irreverent student radicalism that all ages know.

VERNACULAR LITERATURE: THE EPIC

For all its originality, the Latin poetry of the High Middle Ages was overshadowed both in quantity and in variety of expression by vernacular poetry. The drift toward emotionalism, which we have already noted in medieval piety, was closely paralleled by the evolution of vernacular literature from the martial epics of the eleventh century to the delicate and sensitive romances of the thirteenth. Influenced by the sophisticated and somewhat feminine romanticism of the Southern troubadour tradition, the bellicose spirit of Northern France gradually softened.

* My italics.

In the eleventh and early twelfth centuries, heroic epics known as *chansons de geste* (songs of great deeds) were enormously popular among the feudal nobility of Northern France. These *chansons* arose out of the earlier heroic tradition of the Teutonic North that had produced such moody and violent masterpieces as *Beowulf*. The hero Beowulf is a lonely figure who fights monsters, slays dragons, and pits his strength and courage against a wild, wind-swept wilderness. The *chansons de geste* reflect the somewhat more civilized and Christianized age of feudalism. Still warlike and heroic in mood, they often consisted of exaggerated accounts of events surrounding the reign of Charlemagne. The most famous of all the *chansons de geste*, the *Song of Roland*, tells of a heroic and bloody battle between a hoard of Moslems and the detached rearguard of Charlemagne's army as it was withdrawing from Spain. Like old-fashioned Westerns, the *chansons de geste* were packed with action, and their heroes tended to steer clear of sentimental entanglements with ladies. Warlike prowess, courage, and loyalty to one's lord and fellows-in-arms were the virtues stressed in these heroic epics. The battle descriptions, often characterized by gory realism, tell of Christian knights fighting with almost superhuman strength against fantastic odds. The heroes of the *chansons* are not only proud, loyal and skilled at arms, but also capable of experiencing deep emotions—weeping at the death of their comrades and appealing to God to receive the souls of the fallen. In general, the *chansons de geste*, and the *Song of Roland* in particular, mirror the bellicose, masculine spirit and sense of military brotherhood that characterized the feudal knighthood of eleventh-century Europe:

> Turpin of Reims, his horse beneath him slain,
> And with four lance wounds he himself in pain,
> Hastens to rise, brave lord, and stand erect.
> He looks on Roland, runs to him, and says
> Only one thing: "I am not beaten yet!
> True man fails not, while life in him is left."
> He draws Almace, his keen-edged steel-bright brand

And strikes a thousand strokes amid the
press . . . .

Count Roland never loved a recreant,
Nor a false heart, nor yet a braggart
jack,
Nor knight that was not faithful to his
lord.
He cried to Turpin—churchman militant—
"Sir, you're on foot, I'm on my horse's
back.
For love of you, here will I make my
stand,
And side by side we'll take both good and
bad.
I'll not leave you for any mortal man. . . ."

Now Roland feels that he is nearing death;
Out of his ears the brain is running forth.
So for his peers he prays God call them
all,
And for himself St. Gabriel's aid implores.

Roland's rearguard is slain to a man, but the Lord Charlemagne
returns to avenge him, and a furious battle ensues:

Both French and Moors are fighting with a
will.
How many spears are shattered! lances
split!
Whoever saw those shields smashed all to
bits,
Heard the bright hauberks grind, the mail
rings rip,
Heard the harsh spear upon the helmet
ring,
Seen countless knights out of the
saddle spilled,
And all the earth with death and death-
cries filled,
Would long recall the face of suffering!

The French are victorious, Charlemagne himself defeats the Moorish emir in single combat, and Roland is avenged:

> The Moslems fly, God will not have them
>   stay.
> All's done, all's won, the French have
>   gained the day.

THE LYRIC

During the middle and later twelfth century the martial spirit of Northern French literature was gradually transformed by the influx of the romantic troubadour tradition of Southern France. In Provence, Toulouse, and Aquitaine, a rich and colorful culture had been developing in the eleventh and twelfth centuries, and out of this vivacious society came a lyric poetry of remarkable sensitivity and enduring value. The lyric poets of the South were known as *troubadours*. Many of them were courts minstrels, but some, including Duke William IX of Aquitaine himself, were members of the upper nobility. Their poems were far more intimate and personal than the *chansons de geste*, and placed much greater emphasis upon romantic love. The wit, delicacy, and romanticism of the troubadour lyrics betoken a more genteel and sophisticated nobility than that of the feudal North—a nobility that preferred songs of love to songs of war. Indeed, medieval Southern France, under the influence of Islamic courtly poetry and ideas, was the source of the romantic-love tradition of Western civilization. It was from Southern France that Europe derived such concepts as the idealization of women, the importance of male gallantry and courtesy, and the impulse to embroider relations between man and woman with potent emotional overtones of eternal oneness, undying devotion, agony, and ecstasy. One of the favorite themes of the lyric poets was the hopeless love—the unrequited love from afar:

> I die of wounds from blissful blows,
> And love's cruel stings dry out my
>   flesh,
> My health is lost, my vigor goes,
> And nothing can my soul refresh.
> I never knew so sad a plight,
> It should not be, it is not right . . . .

> I'll never hold her near to me
> My ardent joy she'll ever spurn,
> In her good grace I cannot be
> Nor even hope, but only yearn.
> She tells me nothing, false or
>   true,
> And neither will she ever do.

The author of these lines, Jaufré Rudel (flourished 1148), unhappily and hopelessly in love, finds consolation in his talents as a poet, of which he has an exceedingly high opinion. The poem from which the lines above are taken concludes on a much more optimistic note:

> Make no mistake, my song is fair,
> With fitting words and apt design.
> My messenger would never dare
> To cut it short or change a line . . . .
>
> My song is fair, my song is good,
> 'Twill bring delight, as well it
>   should.

Many such poems were written in Southern France during the twelfth century. The recurring theme is the poet's passionate love for a lady. Occasionally, however, the pattern is reversed, as in the following lyric poem by the poetess Beatritz de Dia (flourished 1160):

> I live in grave anxiety
> For one fair knight who loved me so.
> It would have made him glad to know
> I loved him too—but silently.
> I was mistaken, now I'm sure,
> When I withheld myself from him.
> My grief is deep, my days are dim,
> And life itself has no allure.
>
> I wish my knight might sleep with me
> And hold me naked to his breast.
> On my own form to take his rest,
> And grieve no more, but joyous be.
> My love for him surpasses all

Minstrels playing the harp, the flute, and the pipe and tabor.

The loves that famous lovers knew.
My soul is his, my body, too,
My heart, my life, are at his call.

My most beloved, dearest friend,
When will you fall into my power?
That I might lie with you an hour,
And love you 'til my life should end!

My heart is filled with passion's fire.
My well-loved knight, I grant thee grace,
To hold me in my husband's place,
And do the things I so desire.

Not all the lyric poems of Southern France took love or life quite so seriously. In some, one encounters a refreshing lightness and wit. The following verses, by Duke William IX of Aquitaine (1071–1127), typify the vivacious spirit of the South and contrast sharply with the serious, heroic mood of the *chansons de geste:*

I'll make some verses just for fun,
Not of myself or anyone,
Nor of great deeds that knights have
    done
Nor lovers true.
I made them riding in the sun,
My horse helped, too.

When I was born, I'm not aware,
I'm neither gay nor in despair,
Nor stiff, nor loose, nor do I care,
Nor wonder why.
Since meeting an enchantress fair,
Bewitched am I.

Living for dreaming I mistake,
I must be told when I'm awake,
My mood is sad, my heart may break,
Such grief I bear!
But never mind, for heaven's sake,
I just don't care.

I'm sick to death, or so I fear,
I cannot see, but only hear.
I hope that there's a doctor near,
No matter who.
If he can heal me, I'll pay dear,
If not, he's through.

My lady fair is far away,
Just who, or where, I cannot say,
She tells me neither yea nor nay,

Yet I'm not blue,
So long as all those Normans stay
Far from Poitou.

My distant love I so adore,
Though me she has no longing for,
We've never met, and furthermore—
To my disgrace—
I've other loves, some three or four,
To fill her place.

This verse is done, as you can see,
And by your leave, dispatched 'twill be
To one who'll read it carefully
In far Anjou.
Its meaning he'd explain to me
If he but knew.

These verses, only a brief sampling of the fascinating lyrics of
Southern France—and distorted by translation—may provide some
feeling for the rich and delightful civilization that flourished there in
the twelfth century and disintegrated with the savage horrors of the
Albigensian Crusade.

THE ROMANCE

Midway through the twelfth century, the Southern tradition of
courtly love was brought northward to the court of Champagne and
began to spread rapidly across France, England, and Germany. As
its influence grew, the Northern knights discovered that more was
expected of them than loyalty to their lords and a life of carefree
slaughter. They were now expected to be gentlemen as well—to be
courtly in manner and urbane in speech, to exhibit delicate and
refined behavior in feminine company, and to idolize some noble
lady. Such, briefly, were the ideals of courtly love. Their impact on
the actual behavior of knights was distinctly limited, but their effect
on the literature of Northern Europe was revolutionary. Out of the
convergence of vernacular epic and vernacular lyric, there emerged
a new poetic form known as the romance.

Like the *chanson de geste*, the romance was a long narrative poem,
but like the Southern lyric, it was exceedingly sentimental and

imaginative. It was commonly based on some theme from the remote past: the Trojan War, Alexander the Great, and, above all, King Arthur—the half-legendary sixth-century British king. Arthur was transformed into an idealized twelfth-century monarch surrounded by charming ladies and chivalrous knights. His court at Camelot, as described by the great French poet, Chrétien de Troyes, was a center of romantic love and refined religious sensitivity where knights worshipped their ladies, went on daring quests, and played out their chivalrous roles in a world of magic and fantasy.

In the *chanson de geste* the great moral imperative was loyalty to one's lord; in the romance it was love for one's lady. Several romances portray the old and new values in direct conflict. An important theme in both the Arthurian romances and the twelfth-century romance of *Tristan and Iseult* is a love affair between a vassal and his lord's wife. Love and feudal loyalty stand face to face, and love wins out. Tristan loves Iseult, the wife of his lord, King Mark of Cornwall. King Arthur's beloved knight Lancelot loves Arthur's wife, Guinevere. In both stories the lovers are ruined by their love, yet love they must—they have no choice—and although the conduct of Tristan and Lancelot would have been regarded by earlier standards as nothing less than treasonable, both men are presented sympathetically in the romances. Love destroys the lovers in the end, yet their destruction is romantic—even glorious. Tristan and Iseult die together, and in their very death their love achieves its deepest consummation.

Alongside the theme of love in the medieval romances, and standing in sharp contrast to it, is the theme of Christian purity and dedication. The rough-hewn knight of old, having been taught to be courteous and loving, was now taught to be holy. Lancelot was trapped in the meshes of a lawless love, but his son, Galahad, became the prototype of the Christian knight—pure, holy, and chaste. And Perceval, another knight of the Arthurian circle, quested not for a lost loved one but for the Holy Grail of the Last Supper.

The romance flourished in twelfth- and thirteenth-century France and among the French-speaking nobility of England. It spread also into Italy and Spain, and became a crucial factor in the evolution of vernacular literature in Germany. The German poets, known as minnesingers, were influenced by the French lyric and romance, but developed these literary forms along highly original lines. The minnesingers produced their own deeply sensitive and mystical versions of the Arthurian stories which, in their exalted symbolism and profundity of emotion, surpass even the works of Chrétien de Troyes and his French contemporaries.

AUCASSIN ET NICOLETTE; THE ROMANCE OF THE ROSE

As the thirteenth century drew toward its close, the French romance tended to become conventionalized and drained of inspiration. The love story of *Aucassin et Nicolette*, which achieved a degree of popularity, was actually a satirical romance in which the hero was much less heroic than heroes usually are, and a battle is depicted in which the opponents cast pieces of cheese at each other. Based on earlier Byzantine material, *Aucassin et Nicolette* makes mortal love take priority over salvation itself. Indeed, Aucassin is scornful of Heaven:

> For into Paradise go only such people as these: There go those aged priests and elderly cripples and maimed ones who day and night stoop before altars and in the crypts beneath the churches; those who go around in worn-out cloaks and shabby old habits; who are naked and shoeless and full of sores; who are dying of hunger and of thirst, of cold and of misery. Such folks as these enter Paradise, and I will have nothing to do with them. I will go to Hell. For to Hell go the fair clerics and comely knights who are killed in tournaments and great wars, and the sturdy archer and the loyal vassal. I will go with them. There also go the fair and courteous ladies who have loving friends, two or three, together with their wedded lords. And there go the gold and silver, the ermine and all rich furs, the harpers and the minstrels, and the happy folk of the world. I will go with these, so long as I have Nicolette, my very sweet friend, at my side.

Another important product of thirteenth-century vernacular literature, the *Romance of the Rose*, was in fact not a romance in the ordinary sense but an allegory of the whole courtly love tradition in which the thoughts and emotions of the lover and his lady are transformed into actual characters. Thus, Love, Reason, Jealousy, Fair-

Welcome, and similar personifications all have their roles to play. Begun by William of Lorris as an idealization of courtly love, the *Romance of the Rose* was completed after William's death by Jean de Meun, a man of limited talent and bourgeois origin. Jean's contribution was long-winded and encyclopedic, and the poem as a whole lacks high literary distinction, yet it appealed to contemporaries and enjoyed a great vogue.

FABLIAUX AND FABLES

Neither epic, lyric, nor romance had much appeal below the level of the landed aristocracy. The inhabitants of the rising towns had a vernacular literature all their own. From the bourgeoisie came the high medieval *fabliaux*, short satirical poems, filled with vigor and crude humor, which devoted themselves chiefly to ridiculing conventional morality. Priests and monks were portrayed as lechers, merchants' wives were easily and frequently seduced, and clever young rascals perpetually made fools of sober and stuffy businessmen.

Medieval urban culture also produced the fable, or animal story, an allegory in the tradition of Aesop in which various stock characters in medieval society were presented as animals—thinly disguised. Most of the more popular fables dealt with Renard the Fox and were known collectively as the *Romance of Renard*. These tales constituted a ruthless parody of chivalric ideals in which the clever, unscrupulous Renard persistently outwitted King Lion and his loyal but stupid vassals. Thus, paradoxically, the medieval town, which produced such powerful waves of piety, was responsible for literary forms characterized chiefly by secularism, immorality, and the ridiculing of customs and conventions. To balance the impression conveyed by the *fabliaux* and fables we must consider the great Romanesque and Gothic cathedrals, the *Song of Brother Sun* composed by that illustrious son of a medieval merchant, St. Francis of Assisi, and the deeply religious poetry of the Florentine Dante.

DANTE

Vernacular poetry matured late in Italy, but in the works of Dante (1265–1321) it achieved its loftiest expression. Dante wrote on a wide variety of subjects, sometimes in Latin, more often in the

Tuscan vernacular. He composed a series of lyric poems celebrating his love for the lady Beatrice, which are assembled, with prose commentaries, in his *Vita Nuova* (*The New Life*). Dante's lyrics reflect a more mystical and idealized love than that of the troubadours:

> A shining love comes from my lady's eyes,
> All that she looks on is made lovelier,
> And as she walks, men turn to gaze at her,
> Whoever meets her feels his heart
>   arise . . . .
> Humility, and hope that hopeth well,
> Come to the mind of one who hears her
>   voice,
> And blessed is he who looks on her a
>   while.
> Her beauty, when she gives her slightest
>   smile
> One cannot paint in words, yet must
>   rejoice
> In such a new and gracious miracle.

Firmly convinced of the literary potential of the Tuscan vernacular Dante urged its use in his *De Vulgari Eloquentia*, which he wrote in Latin so as to appeal to scholars and writers who scorned the vulgar tongue. And he filled his own vernacular works with such grace and beauty as to convince by example those whom he could not persuade by argument. In his hands, the Tuscan vernacular became the literary language of Italy.

Dante was no mere disembodied writer, but a man deeply immersed in the politics of his age. His experience brought him to the opinion that Italy's hope for peace lay in imperial domination and in divorcing the papacy from politics. Although rather futile and anachronistic in view of the Empire's impotence in Dante's time, these views were expressed forcefully in his great political essay, *On Monarchy*.

Dante's masterpiece was the *Divine Comedy*. Written in the Tuscan vernacular, it is a magnificent synthesis of medieval literature and thought. It abounds in allegory and symbolism, and encompasses in one majestic vision the entire universe of medieval man. Dante tells of his own journey through hell, purgatory, and paradise to the very presence of Almighty God. This device permits the poet to make devastating comments on past and contemporary history by placing all those of whom he disapproved—from local politicians to popes— in various levels of hell. Virgil, the archetype of ancient rationalism, is Dante's guide through hell and purgatory; the lady Beatrice, a symbol of purified love, guides him through the celestial spheres of paradise; and St. Bernard, the epitome of medieval sanctity, leads him to the threshold of God. The poem closes with Dante alone in the divine presence:

> Eternal Light, thou in thyself alone
> Abidest, and alone thine essence knows,
> And loves, and smiles, self-knowing and
>   self-known . . . .
> Here power failed to the high fantasy,
> But my desire and will were turned—as
>   one—
> And as a wheel that turneth evenly,
> By Holy Love, that moves the stars and
>   sun.

THE ROMANESQUE STYLE

The High Middle Ages is one of the great epochs in the history of Western architecture. Stone churches, large and small, were built in prodigious numbers: in France alone, more stone was quarried during the High Middle Ages than by the pyramid and temple builders of ancient Egypt throughout its 3000-year history. Yet the real achievement of the medieval architects lay not in the immense scope of their activities but in the splendid originality of their aesthetic vision. Two great architectural styles dominated the age: the Romanesque style evolved in the eleventh century, rose to maturity in the early twelfth, and during the middle decades of the twelfth century gave way gradually to the Gothic style. From about 1150 to 1300 the greatest of the medieval Gothic cathedrals were built. Thereafter the Gothic style lost some of its inspiration as it became overly elaborate and increasingly showy, but during the High Middle Ages it constituted one of humanity's most audacious and successful architectural experiments.

High medieval architecture was deeply affected by two of the basic cultural trends of the period. First, the great cathedrals were products of the urban revolution and the rise of intense urban piety. Second, the evolution from Romanesque to Gothic closely parallels the shift which we have already observed in literature and piety toward emotional sensitivity and romanticism. Romanesque architecture, although characterized by an exceeding diversity of expression, tended in general toward the solemnity of earlier Christian piety and the uncompromising masculinity of the *chansons de geste*. Gothic architecture, on the other hand, is dramatic, upward-reaching, and, in a certain sense, feminine. A vast number of Gothic cathedrals were dedicated to Notre Dame—Our Lady.

The development from Romanesque to Gothic can be understood, too, as an evolution in the principles of structural engineering. The key architectural ingredient in the Romanesque churches was the round arch, which appears in their portals, their windows, their arcades, and the massive stone vaulting of their roofs. Romanesque roof design was based on various elaborations of the round arch, such as the barrel vault and the cross vault (see Figures a and b). The immense downward and outward thrusts of these heavy stone roofs required massive pillars and thick supporting walls with windows that were necessarily small.

The mosaic decoration and wooden roofs, which characterized the churches of late-Roman, Byzantine, and Carolingian times, gave way to the domination of stone as the key material in both Romanesque architecture and Romanesque sculpture. Indeed, the inventive, fantastic religious sculpture of the age—ornamenting the capitals of Romanesque columns and the semicircular areas between the lintels and round arches of the doors (the *tympana*)—were totally architectonic—completely fused into the structure of the church itself.

A church in the fully developed Romanesque style conveys a feeling of artistic unity and earthbound solidity. Its sturdy arches, vaults, and walls, and its somber, shadowy interior give the illusion of mystery and otherworldliness, yet suggest at the same time the steadfast might of the universal Church.

THE GOTHIC STYLE

During the first half of the twelfth century new structural elements began to be employed in the building of Romanesque churches:

Romanesque exterior: Sainte-Foy in Conques (*c.* 1050–*c.* 1120).

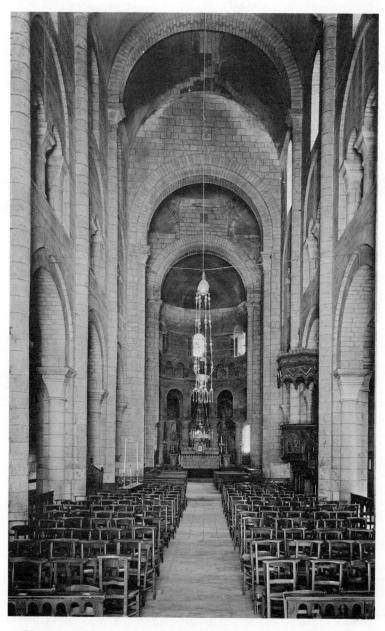

Romanesque interior: Saint-Etienne in Nevers (*c*. 1083–1097).

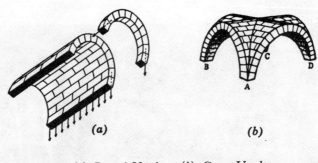

(a) Barrel Vault.   (b) Cross Vault.

first, ribs of stone that ran along the edges of the arched cross vaults and helped to support them; next, pointed arches that permitted greater flexibility and height in the vaulting. By the middle of the century these novel features—vault rib and pointed arch—were providing the basis for an entirely new style of architecture, no longer Romanesque but Gothic. They were employed with such effect by Abbot Suger in his new abbey church of Saint-Denis near Paris, around 1140, that Saint-Denis is often regarded as the first true Gothic church.

French Gothic churches of the late twelfth century such as Notre Dame of Paris disclose the development of vault rib and pointed arch into a powerful and coherent style. During these exciting years, every decade brought new experiments and opened new possibilities in church building, yet Notre Dame of Paris and the churches of its period and region retain some of the heaviness and stolidity of the earlier Romanesque. Not until the thirteenth century were the full potentialities of Gothic architecture realized. The discovery of the vault rib and pointed arch, and of a third Gothic structural element —the flying buttress—made it possible to support weights and stresses in a totally new way. The traditional building, of roof supported by walls, was transformed into a radically new kind of building—a skeleton—in which the stone vault rested not on walls but on slender columns and graceful exterior supports. The wall became structurally superfluous, and the vast areas between the supporting pillars could be filled with glass. Concurrent with this architectural revolution was the development, in twelfth- and thirteenth-century Europe, of the new art of stained-glass making. The glorious colored windows created in these two centuries, with episodes from the Bible

Romanesque tympanum: Sainte-Foy in Conques.

and religious legend depicted in shimmering blues and glowing reds, have never been equalled.

During the first half of the thirteenth century all the structural possibilities of Gothic skeleton design were fully exploited. In the towns of Central and Northern France there now rose churches of delicate, soaring stone with walls of lustrous glass. Never before in history had windows been so immense or buildings so lofty; and never since has European architecture been at once so assured and so daringly original.

Gothic sculpture, like Romanesque, was intimately related to architecture, yet the two styles differed markedly. Romanesque fantasy, exuberance, and distortion gave way to a serene, self-confident naturalism. Human figures were no longer crowded together on the capitals of pillars; often they stood as statues—great rows of them—in niches on the cathedral exteriors: saints, prophets, kings, and angels, Christ and the Virgin, depicted as tall slender figures, calm yet warmly human, or as lovely young women, placid and often smiling. The greatest Gothic churches of thirteenth-

"Adoration of the Magi," Cloister capital, Moissac (1100).

ROMANESQUE CAPITALS

Nave capital, Anzy-le-Duc (late eleventh century).

Detail of right portal, Vezelay (begun 1120).

Cloister capital, Moissac (1100).

255

Nave looking east (showing vault ribs), Notre Dame in Paris
(begun 1163).

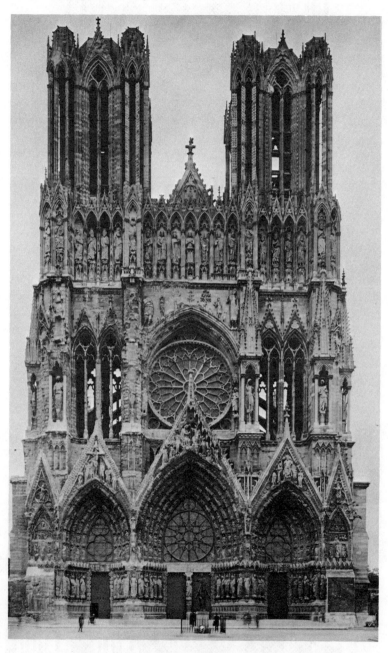

Gothic exterior: Reims Cathedral (1211–1290).

Gothic interior: Bourges Cathedral (begun *c.* 1195).

Gothic exterior (showing flying buttresses with angels): Reims
Cathedral.

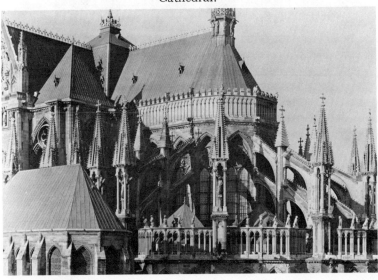

Gothic sculpture: *Visitation*, west portal
of Reims Cathedral.

century France—Bourges, Chartres, Amiens, Reims, Sainte-
Chapelle—are superb syntheses of many separate arts. Their interiors convey a striking illusion of graceful stone vaulting springing
up from walls of luminous colored glass. The pictures in the glass,
the sculpture, and the architecture of the buildings themselves are
all fused and directed to a single end: the expression and illumination of a deep, vital faith.

14

The World of Intellect

THE RISE OF UNIVERSITIES

Like the Gothic cathedral, the university was a product of the medieval town. The urban revolution of the eleventh and twelfth centuries brought about the decline of the old monastic schools which had done so much to preserve culture over the previous centuries. They were superseded north of the Alps by cathedral schools located in the rising towns, and in Italy by semi-secular municipal schools. Both the cathedral schools and the municipal schools had long existed, but it was only in the eleventh century that they rose to great prominence. Many of these schools now became centers of higher learning of a sort that Europe had not known for centuries. Their enrollments increased steadily and their faculties grew until, in the twelfth century, some of them evolved into universities.

In the Middle Ages, *university* was an exceedingly vague term. A university was simply a group of persons associated for any purpose. The word was commonly applied to the merchant guilds and craft guilds of the rising towns. A guild or university of students and scholars engaged in the pursuit of higher learning was given the more specific name, *studium generale*. When we speak of the medieval university, therefore, we are referring to an institution that would have been called a *studium generale* by a man of the thirteenth century. It differed from lesser schools in three significant respects: (1) the

260

studium generale was open to students from many lands, not simply those from the surrounding districts; (2) the *studium generale* was a large school with a number of teachers rather than merely one omnicompetent master; and (3) the *studium generale* offered both elementary and advanced curricula. It offered a basic program of instruction in the traditional "seven liberal arts": astronomy, geometry, arithmetic, music, grammar, rhetoric, and dialectic; and also instruction in one or more of the "higher" disciplines: theology, law, and medicine. Upon the successful completion of his liberal arts curriculum, the student could apply for a license to teach, but he might also wish to continue his studies by specializing in medicine, theology, or—most popular of all—civil or canon law. Legal training offered as its reward the promise of a lucrative administrative career in royal government or the Church.

Fundamentally, the medieval university was neither a campus nor a complex of buildings, but a guild—a privileged corporation of teachers, or sometimes of students. With its classes normally held in rented rooms, it was a highly mobile institution, and on more than one occasion, when a university was dissatisfied with local conditions, it won important concessions from the townsmen simply by threatening to move elsewhere.

In the thirteenth century, flourishing universities were to be found at Paris, Bologna, Naples, Montpellier, Oxford, Cambridge, and elsewhere. Paris, Oxford, and a number of others were dominated by guilds of instructors in the liberal arts. Bologna, on the other hand, was governed by a guild of students which managed to reduce the exorbitant local prices of food and lodgings by threatening to move collectively to another town, and which established strict rules of conduct for the instructors. Professors had to begin and end their classes on time and to cover the prescribed curriculum; they could not leave town without special permission. It is important to point out that Bologna specialized in legal studies and that its pupils were older professional students for the most part—men who had completed their liberal arts curriculum and were determined to secure sufficient training for successful careers in law.

The students of the medieval universities were, on the whole, rowdier and more exuberant than students of American universities today, more imaginative in their pranks, and more hostile toward the surrounding towns. Thus the history of medieval universities is punctuated by frequent town-gown riots. New students were hazed unmercifully; unpopular professors were hissed, shouted down, and even pelted with stones. Most of the students were of relatively humble origin—from the towns or the ranks of the lesser nobility—but they were willing to spend their student days in abject poverty if necessary in order to acquire the new knowledge and prepare themselves for the rich social and economic rewards that awaited many graduates.

Despite the enormous differences between medieval and modern university life, it should be clear that the modern university is a direct outgrowth of the institution that came into being in high medieval Europe. We owe to the medieval university the concept of a formal teaching license, the custom—unknown to antiquity—of group instruction, the idea of academic degrees, the notion of a liberal arts curriculum, the tradition of professors and students dressing in clerical garb (caps and gowns) on commencement day, student riots, and other university traditions. Even the letters written by medieval students to their parents or guardians have a curiously modern ring:

> This is to inform you that I am studying at Oxford with the greatest diligence, but the matter of money stands in the way of my promotion, as it is now two months since I spent the last of what you sent me. The city is expensive and makes many demands; I have to rent lodgings, buy necessities, and provide for many other things which I cannot now specify. Wherefore I respectfully beg your paternity that by the promptings of divine pity you may assist me, so that I can complete what I have well begun. For you must know that without Ceres and Bacchus, Apollo grows cold.

MEDICINE AND LAW

The chief medical school of medieval Europe was the University of Salerno. Here, in a land of vigorous cultural intermingling, scholars were able to draw from the medical heritage of Islam and Byzantium. In general, medieval medical scholarship was a bizarre medley of cautious observation, common sense, and gross superstition. In one instance we encounter the good advice that a person should eat and drink in moderation. But we are also instructed that onions will cure baldness, that the urine of a dog is an admirable cure for warts, and that all one must do to prevent a woman from conceiving is to bind her head with a red ribbon. Yet in the midst of this nonsense, important progress was being made in medical science. The writings of the great second-century scientist Galen, which constituted a synthesis of classical medical knowledge, were studied and digested, as were the important works of Arab students of medicine. And to this invaluable body of knowledge European scholars were now making their own original contributions on such subjects as the curative properties of plants and the anatomy of the human body. It is probable that both animal and human dissections were performed by the scholars of twelfth-century Salerno. These doctors, their crude and primitive methods notwithstanding, were laying the foundations on which western European medical science was to rise.

Medieval legal scholarship addressed itself to two distinct bodies of material: civil law and canon law. The legal structure of early medieval society was largely Germanic in inspiration and custom-based, particularly in Northern Europe where Roman law had almost entirely disappeared. Customary law remained strong throughout the High Middle Ages: it governed the relationships among the feudal aristocracy and determined the manorial obligations of the medieval peasantry. It limited the feudal prerogatives of kings, and underlay Magna Carta. But from the late eleventh century on, Roman law was studied in Bologna and other European universities. Christendom was now exposed to a distinctly different legal tradition—coherent and logical—which began to compete with Germanic law, to rationalize it, and in some instances to replace it.

The foundation of medieval Roman law was the *Corpus Juris Civilis* of Justinian which was unknown in the West throughout most of the Early Middle Ages but reappeared at Bologna in the last quarter of the eleventh century. Italy remained the center of Roman legal studies throughout the High Middle Ages, for the traditions of Roman law had never entirely disappeared there, and the Italian peninsula therefore provided the most fertile soil for their revival. From Italy, the study of Roman law spread northward. A great school of law emerged at Montpellier in Southern France, and others flourished at Orleans, Paris, and Oxford. But Bologna remained the most notable center of Roman legal scholarship. There, able scholars known as "glossators" wrote analytical commentaries on the *Corpus Juris*, elucidating difficult points and reconciling apparent contradictions. Later on they began to produce textbooks and important original treatises on the *Corpus* and to reorganize it into a coherent sequence of topics. Eventually such an extensive body of supplementary material existed that the glossators turned to the task of glossing the glosses—elucidating the elucidations. Around the mid-thirteenth century the work of the earlier glossators was brought to a climax with a comprehensive work by the Bolognese scholar Accursius, the *Glossa Ordinaria*, which was a composite synthesis of all previous commentaries on the *Corpus Juris*. Thereafter the *Glossa Ordinaria* became the authoritative supplement to the *Corpus Juris* in courts of Roman law.

The impact of the glossators was particularly strong in Italy and Southern France where elements of Roman law had survived as local custom. By the thirteenth century Roman law was beginning to make a significant impact in the North as well, for by then civil lawyers trained in the Roman tradition were achieving an increasingly dominant role in the courts of France, Germany, and Spain. These men devoted themselves wholeheartedly to the royal service and used their legal training to exalt their monarchs in every possible way. Although the Roman legal tradition had originally contained a strong element of constitutionalism, it inherited from Justinian's age an autocratic cast which the court lawyers of the rising monarchies put to effective use. Thus, as Roman law gained an increasingly firm hold in the states of continental Europe, it tended to make their governments at once more systematic and more absolute. In France, for example, civil lawyers played an important part in the gradual transformation of the early Capetian feudal monarchy into the royal autocracy of later times. And the development and durability of the parliamentary regime in England owed much to the fact that a strong monarchy, founded on the principles of Germanic law with its custom-based limitations on royal authority, was already well established before Europe felt the full impact of the Roman-law revival.

Canon law developed alongside Roman law and derived a great deal from it. Methods of scholarship were quite similar in the two fields—commentaries and glosses were common to both—and the ecclesiastical courts borrowed much from the principles and procedures of Roman law. But whereas Roman law was based on the single authority of Justinian's *Corpus Juris*, canon law drew from many sources: the Bible, the writings of the ancient Church fathers, the canons of Church councils, and the decretals of popes. The *Corpus Juris*, although susceptible to endless commentary, was fundamentally complete in itself; popes and councils, on the other hand, continued to issue decrees, and canon law was therefore capable of unlimited development.

Canon law, like civil law, first became a serious scholarly discipline in eleventh-century Bologna and later spread to other major centers of learning. The study of canon law was strongly stimulated by the Investiture Controversy and subsequent Church-state struggles, for the papacy looked to canon lawyers to support its claims with cogent, documented arguments and apt precedents. But the medieval scholars of canon law were far more than mere papal propagandists. They were grappling with the formidable problem of systematizing their sources, explaining what was unclear, reconciling what seemed contradictory—in other words, imposing order on the immense variety of dicta, opinions, and precedents upon which their discipline was based.

The essential goal of the canon lawyers was to assemble their diverse sources—their canons—into a single coherent work. It was up to them, in short, to accomplish the task that Justinian had performed for Roman law back in the sixth century. The civil lawyers had their *Corpus Juris Civilis;* it was up to the canon lawyers to create their own "Corpus Juris Canonici." The first attempts to produce comprehensive canonical collections date from the Early Middle Ages, but it was not until the eleventh-century revival at Bologna that serious scholarly standards were applied to the task. The definitive collection was completed around 1140 by the great Bolognese canon lawyer, Gratian. Originally entitled *The Concordance of Discordant Canons*, Gratian's work is known to posterity as the *Decretum*.

Gratian not only brought together an immense body of canons from a bewildering variety of sources; he also framed them in a logical, topically-organized scheme. Using scholarly methods that were just beginning to be employed by scholastic philosophers and logicians, he raised questions, quoted the relevant canons, endeavored to reconcile those that disagreed, and thereby arrived at firm conclusions. The result was an ordered body of general legal principles derived from particular passages from the Bible, the fathers, and papal and conciliar decrees. The *Decretum* became the authoritative text in ecclesiastical tribunals and the basis of all future study in canon law.

As time passed, and new decrees were issued, it became necessary to supplement Gratian's *Decretum* by collecting the canons issued subsequent to 1140. The first collection was made in 1234 under the direction of the lawyer-pope Gregory IX, another in the pontificate of Boniface VIII, and still others in later generations. Together, the *Decretum* and the supplementary collections were given the title, *Corpus Juris Canonici*, and became the ecclesiastical equivalent of Justinian's *Corpus*. These two great compilations, ecclesiastical and civil, symbolize the parallel growth of medieval Europe's two supreme sources of administrative and jurisdictional authority: Church and monarchy.

BACKGROUND OF HIGH MEDIEVAL PHILOSOPHY

It is only to be expected that an age which witnessed such sweeping economic and political changes and such vigorous creativity in religious and artistic expression would also achieve notable success in the realm of abstract thought. Medieval philosophy is richly variegated and marked by boundless curiosity and heated controversy. Although every important philosopher in the High Middle Ages was a churchman of one sort or another, ecclesiastical authority did not stifle speculation. Catholic orthodoxy, which hardened noticeably at the time of the Protestant Reformation, was still relatively flexible in the twelfth and thirteenth centuries, and the philosophers of the age were far from being timid apologists for official dogmas. If some of them were impelled by conviction to provide the Catholic faith with a logical substructure, others asserted vigorously that reason does not lead to the truth of Christian revelation. And among those who sought to harmonize faith and reason there was sharp disagreement as to what form the logical substructure should take. All were believers—all were Catholics—but their doctrinal unanimity did not limit their diversity or curb their adventurous spirit.

The high medieval philosophers drew nourishment from five earlier sources: (1) From the Greeks they inherited the great philosophical systems of Plato and Arisotle. At first these two Greek masters were known in the West only through a handful of translations and commentaries dating from late Roman times. By the thirteenth century, however, new and far more complete translations were coming into Christendom from Spain and Sicily, and Aristotelian philosophy became a matter of intense interest and controversy in Europe's universities. (2) From the Islamic world came a flood of Greek scientific and philosophical works which had long before been translated from Greek to Arabic and were now translated from Arabic into Latin. These works came into Europe accompanied by extensive commentaries and original writings of Arab philosophers and scientists, for the Arabs had come to grips with Greek learning long before the advent of the High Middle Ages. Islamic thought made its own distinctive contribution to European science; in philosophy it was important chiefly as an agency for the transmission and interpretation of Greek thought. (3) The early Church fathers, particularly the Latin Doctors, had been a dominant influence on the thought of the Early Middle Ages and their authority remained strong in the twelfth and thirteenth centuries. Saint Augustine retained his singular significance, and was, indeed, the chief vessel of Platonic and Neoplatonic thought in the medieval universities. No philosopher of the High Middle Ages could ignore him, and some of the most distinguished of them were conscious and devoted Augustinians. (4) The early medieval scholars themselves contributed significantly to the high medieval intellectual revival. Gregory the Great, Isidore of Seville, Bede, Alcuin, Raban Maur, John the Scot, and Gerbert of Aurillac were all studied seriously in the new universities. The original intellectual contributions of these men were less important, however, than the fact that they and their contemporaries had kept learning alive, fostered and perpetuated the classical tradition in Europe, and created an intellectual climate that made possible the reawakening of philosophical speculation in the eleventh century. Although stimulated by contacts with other civilizations, the intellectual surge of the High Middle Ages was fundamentally an internal phenomenon with roots in Ottonian, Carolingian, and pre-Carolingian Europe. (5) The high-medieval philosophers looked back beyond the scholars of the Early Middle Ages, beyond the fathers of the early Church, to the Hebrew and primitive Christian religious traditions as recorded in Scripture. Among medieval theologians the Bible, the chief written source of divine revelation, was quite naturally the fundamental text and the ultimate authority.

Such were the chief elements—Greek, Islamic, Patristic, early medieval, and scriptural—that underlay the thought of the scholastic philosophers of the High Middle Ages. Narrowly defined, "scholasticism" is simply the philosophical movement associated with the high-medieval schools—the cathedral and monastic schools, and later the universities. More basically it was a movement concerned above all with exploring the relationship between rationalism and theism—reason and revelation. All medieval scholastics were theists; all were committed, to some degree, to the life of reason. Many of them were immensely enthusiastic over the intellectual possibilities inherent in the careful application of Aristotelian logic to basic human and religious problems. Some believed that the syllogism was the master key to a thousand doors, and that, with sufficient methodological rigor, with sufficient exactness in the use of words, the potentialities of human knowledge were all but limitless.

The scholastics applied their logical method to a vast number of problems. They were concerned chiefly, however, with matters of basic significance to human existence: the nature of man, the purpose of human life, the existence and attributes of God, the fundamentals of human morality, the ethical imperatives of social and political life, the relationship between God and man. It would be hard to deny that these are the most profound sorts of questions that philosophers can ask, although many thinkers of our own day are inclined to reject them as unanswerable. Perhaps they are, but the scholastics, standing near the beginning of Europe's long intellectual journey and lacking the modern sense of disillusionment, were determined to make the attempt.

RELATIONSHIP OF FAITH AND REASON

Among the diverse investigations and conflicting opinions of the medieval thinkers, three central issues deserve particular attention: (1) the degree of interrelationship between faith and reason, (2) the relative merits of the Platonic-Augustinian and the Aristotelian intellectual traditions, and (3) the reality of the Platonic archetypes or, as they were called in the Middle Ages, "universals."

The issue of faith *versus* reason was clearly the most far-reaching of the three. Ever since Tertullian in the third century, there had been Christian writers who insisted that God so transcended reason that any attempt to approach him intellectually was useless and, indeed, blasphemous. It was the mystic who knew God, not the theologian. Tertullian had posed the rhetorical questions,

> What has Athens to do with Jerusalem? What concord is there between the Academy and the Church? . . . Let us have done with all attempts to produce a bastard Christianity of Stoic, Platonic, and dialectic composition! We desire no curious disputation after possessing Christ Jesus, no inquisition after enjoying the Gospel!

Tertullian had many followers in the Middle Ages, who insisted that God cannot be bound or even approached by logic. Saint Bernard denounced and hounded his brilliant rationalist contemporary Peter Abelard. St. Francis regarded intellectual speculation as irrelevant and perhaps even dangerous to salvation. A later spiritual Franciscan, Jacopone da Todi, expressed the antirational position in verse:

> Plato and Socrates may oft contend,
> And all the breath within their bodies spend,
> Engaged in disputations without end.
> What's that to me?
> For only with a pure and simple mind
> Can one the narrow path to heaven find,
> And greet the King; while lingers far behind,
> Philosophy.

The contrary view was just as old. Third-century theologians such as Clement and Origen in the school of Alexandria had labored to provide Christianity with a sturdy philosophical foundation and did not hesitate to elucidate the faith by means of Greek—and particularly Platonic—thought. The fourth-century Latin Doctors, Ambrose, Jerome, and Augustine, had wrestled with the problem of whether a Christian might properly use elements from the pagan classical tradition in the service of the Faith, and all three ended with affirmative answers. As Augustine expressed it,

If those who are called philosophers, and especially the Platonists, have said aught that is true and in harmony with our faith, we must not only not shrink from it, but claim it for our own use from those who have unlawful possession of it.

Such is the viewpoint that underlies most of high medieval philosophy—that reason has a valuable role to play as a servant of revelation. St. Anselm, following Augustine, declared, "I believe so that I may know." Faith comes first, reason second; faith rules reason, but reason can perform the useful service of illuminating faith. Indeed, faith and reason are separate avenues to a single body of truth. By their very nature they cannot lead to contradictory conclusions, for truth is one. Should their conclusions ever *appear* to be contradictory, the philosopher can be assured that some flaw exists in his logic. Reason cannot err, but man's use of it can, and revelation must therefore be the criterion against which reason is measured.

This, in general, became the common position of later scholastic philosophers. The intellectual system of St. Thomas Aquinas was built on the conviction that reason and faith were harmonious. Even the arch-rationalist of the twelfth century, Peter Abelard, wrote: "I do not wish to be a philosopher if it means resisting St. Paul; I do not wish to be Aristotle if it must separate me from Christ." Abelard believed that he could at once be a philosopher and a Christian, but his faith took first priority.

Among some medieval philosophers the priorities were reversed. Averroës, a profound Islamic Aristotelian of twelfth-century Spain, boldly asserted the superiority of reason over faith. He affirmed the truth of several propositions which were logical byproducts of Aristotle's philosophy but were directly contrary to Islamic and Christian doctrine. Averroës taught, for example, that the world had always existed and was therefore uncreated—that all human actions were determined—that there was no personal salvation. In the thirteenth century a Christian philosophical school known as Latin Averroism became active at the University of Paris and elsewhere. Latin Averroists such as Siger of Brabant took the position that reason and revelation led to radically contrary conclusions. As Christians they accepted the teachings of the Church as ultimate truth, but as scholars they insisted that the conclusions of Aristotle

and Averroës, being logically air-tight, were "philosophically necessary." This position came to be called the doctrine of the "two-fold
truth."

The Latin Averroists shared with antirationalists the belief that
reason did not lead to the truth of revelation; they shared with
Anselm and Aquinas the conviction that ultimate truth was revealed
truth. Yet unlike most scholastics they abandoned altogether the
effort to harmonize reason and revelation, and unlike the antirationalists they did not reject philosophy but made it their profes-
sion. As believers they conceded the supremacy of dogma; as philosophers they insisted on the supremacy of reason. And although
Siger of Brabant and most of his contemporaries appear to have
held this awkward position in full sincerity, some of their successors
became outright religious skeptics and only paid the necessary lip
service to Christian doctrine. The fourteenth-century Latin Averroist John of Jaudun, for example, never lost an opportunity to
poke subtle fun at any Christian dogma that seemed to him contrary to reason. On the subject of the Creation, John points out
that according to reason the world has always existed. He concludes
—with tongue in cheek—that as Christians we must nevertheless
believe that God created the world; "Let it be added that creation
very seldom happens; there has been only one, and that was a very
long time ago."

PLATONISM-AUGUSTINIANISM
VERSUS ARISTOTELIANISM

Thus medieval thought produced a diversity of views on the
proper relationship of reason and revelation. The same is true of
the other two issues that we are to consider: the rivalry between
Platonism and Aristotelianism, and the controversy over universals.
The conflict between the intellectual systems of Plato-Augustine and
Aristotle did not emerge clearly until the thirteenth century when
the full body of Aristotle's writings came into the West in Latin
translations from Greek and Arabic. Until then, most efforts at
applying reason to faith were based on the Platonic tradition transmuted and transmitted by Augustine to medieval Europe. Saint
Anselm, for example, was a dedicated Augustinian, as were many
of his twelfth-century successors. The tradition was carried on bril-

liantly in the thirteenth century by the great Franciscan, St. Bona-venture. Many thoughtful Christians of the thirteenth century were deeply suspicious of the newly recovered Aristotelian writings, and the rise of Latin Averroism served to deepen their apprehensions. They regarded Aristotle as pagan in viewpoint and dangerous to the Faith. Other thirteenth-century intellectuals, such as St. Thomas Aquinas, were much too devoted to the goal of reconciling faith and reason to reject the works of a man whom they regarded as antiquity's greatest philosopher. Saint Thomas sought to Christian-ize Aristotle much as Augustine had Christianized Plato and the Neoplatonists. In the middle decades of the thirteenth century, as high medieval philosophy was reaching its climax, the Platonic and Aristotelian traditions flourished side by side, and in the works of certain English scientific thinkers of the age they achieved a singu-larly fruitful fusion.

THE CONFLICT OVER UNIVERSALS

The contest between Platonism and Aristotelianism carried with it the seeds of yet another controversy: the argument over arche-types or universals. Plato had taught that ideas such as "dog," "man," or "cat" not only described particular creatures but also had reality in themselves—that individual cats are imperfect reflec-tions of a model cat, an archetypal or universal cat. Similarly, there are many examples of circles, squares, or triangles. Were we to measure these individual figures with sufficiently refined instru-ments we would discover that they were imperfect in one respect or another. No circle in this world is absolutely round. No square or triangle has perfectly straight sides. They are merely crude approximations of a perfect "idea." In "heaven," Plato would say, the perfect triangle exists. It is the source of the concept of triangu-larity that lurks in our minds and of all the imperfect triangles that we see in the phenomenal world. The heavenly triangle is not only perfect but *real*. The earthly triangles are less real, less significant, and less worthy of our attention. To take still another example, we call certain acts "good" because they partake, imperfectly, of a universal good which exists in heaven. In short, these universals—cat, dog, circle, triangle, beauty, goodness, etc.—exist apart from the multitude of individual dogs, cats, circles, triangles, and beautiful and good things in this world. And the person who seeks knowledge ought to meditate on these universals rather than study the world of phenomena in which they are only imperfectly reflected.

St. Augustine accepted Plato's theory of universals but not without amendment. Augustine taught that the archetypes existed in the mind of God rather than in Plato's abstract "heaven." And whereas Plato had ascribed our knowledge of the universals to dim memories from a prenatal existence, Augustine maintained that God puts a knowledge of universals directly into our minds by a process of "divine illumination." Plato and Augustine agreed, however, that the universal existed apart from the particular and, indeed, was *more real* than the particular. In the High Middle Ages, those who followed the Platonic-Augustinian approach to universals were known as *realists*—they believed that universals were real.

The Aristotelian tradition brought with it another viewpoint on universals: they existed, to be sure, but only in the particular. Only by studying particular things in the world of phenomena could men gain a knowledge of universals. The human mind drew the universal from the particular by a process of abstraction. The universals were real, but in a sense less real—or at least less independently real —than Plato and Augustine believed. Accordingly, medieval philosophers who inclined toward the Aristotelian position have been called *moderate realists.*

Medieval philosophers were by no means confined to a choice between these two points of view. Several of them worked out subtle solutions of their own. As early as the eleventh century the philosopher Roscellinus declared that universals were not real at all. They were mere names that men gave to arbitrary classes of individual things. Reality was not to be found in universals but rather in the multiplicity and variety of objects which we can see, touch, and smell in the world around us. Those who followed Roscellinus in this view were known as *nominalists*—for them, the universals were *nomina*—"names." Nominalism remained in the intellectual background during the twelfth and thirteenth centuries but was revived in the fourteenth. Many churchmen regarded it as a dangerous doctrine, since its emphasis on the particular over the universal seemed to suggest that the Church was not, as Catholics believed, a single universal body but rather a vast accumulation of individual Christians.

ST. ANSELM

Having examined these three significant issues of high medieval philosophy—the relationship of reason to revelation, the relative validity and relevance of the Platonic-Augustinian and Aristotelian systems of thought, and the problem of universals—let us now see how they developed in the minds of individual philosophers between the eleventh and fourteenth centuries.

The scholastic philosophers first made their appearance in the later eleventh century. They were products of the general reawakening that Europe was just then beginning to undergo. The earliest important figure in scholastic philosophy was St. Anselm (c. 1034–1109), an Italian intellectual who came to Normandy and later became archbishop of Canterbury. During his eventful career he found time to write profoundly on a variety of philosophical and theological subjects.

As an Augustinian, Anselm took the realist position on the problem of universals. It was from Augustine, too, that he derived his attitude on the relationship of faith and reason. He taught that faith must precede reason, but that reason could serve to illuminate faith. His conviction that reason and faith were compatible made him a singularly important pioneer in the development of high medieval rationalism. He worked out several proofs of God, and in his important theological treatise, *Cur Deus Homo*, subjected the doctrines of the incarnation and atonement to rigorous logical analysis.

Anselm's emphasis on reason, employed within the framework of a firm Christian conviction, set the stage for the significant philosophical developments of the following generations. With Anselm, Western Christendom regained at last the intellectual level of the fourth-century Latin Doctors.

ABELARD

The twelfth-century philosophers, intoxicated by the seemingly limitless possibilities of reason and logic, advanced boldly across new intellectual frontiers at the very time that their contemporaries were pushing forward the territorial frontiers of Europe. The most brilliant and audacious of these twelfth-century Christian rationalists was Peter Abelard (1079–1142), an immensely popular teacher, dazzling and egotistical, whose meteoric career ended in tragedy and defeat.

Abelard is perhaps best known for his love affair with the young Heloise, an affair that ended with Abelard's castration at the hands of thugs hired by Heloise's enraged uncle. The lovers then separated permanently, both taking monastic vows, and in later years Abelard wrote regretfully of the affair in his autobiographical *History of My Calamities*. There followed a touching correspondence between the two lovers in which Heloise, now an abbess, confessed her enduring love and Abelard, writing almost as a father confessor, offered her spiritual consolation but nothing more. Abelard's autobiography and the correspondence with Heloise survive to this day, providing modern students with a singularly intimate and tender picture of romance and pathos in a society far removed from our own.

Abelard was the supreme logician of the twelfth century. Writing several decades before the great influx of Aristotelian thought in Latin translation, he anticipated Aristotle's position on the question of universals by advocating a theory rather similar to Aristotle's moderate realism. Universals, Abelard believed, had no separate existence, but were derived from particular things by a process of abstraction. In a famous work entitled *Sic et Non (Yes and No)*, Abelard collected opinions from the Bible, the Latin fathers, the councils of the Church, and the decrees of the papacy on a great variety of theological issues, demonstrating that these hallowed authorities very often disagreed on important religious matters. Others before him had collected authoritative opinions on various theological and legal issues, but never so thoroughly or systematically. Abelard, in his *Sic et Non*, employed a method of inquiry that was developed and perfected by canon lawyers and philosophers over the next several generations. We have already seen how the canonist Gratian, in his *Decretum*, used the device of lining up conflicting authorities. But Abelard's successors sought to reconcile the contradictions and arrive at conclusions, whereas Abelard left most of the issues unresolved and thereby earned the enmity of his more conservative contemporaries. Abelard was a devoted Christian, if something of an intellectual show-off, but many regarded him as a dangerous skeptic. Thus he left himself open to bitter attacks by men such as St. Bernard who were deeply hostile to the Christian rationalist movement which he so flamboyantly exemplified. The brilliant teacher was hounded from one place to another. At length, his opinions were condemned by an ecclesiastical council in 1141. He died at Cluny, on his way to Rome to appeal the condemnation.

PETER LOMBARD AND HUGH OF SAINT-VICTOR

But twelfth-century rationalism was far more than a one-man affair, and the persecution of Abelard failed to halt its growth. His student Peter Lombard (*c.* 1100–1160), for example, produced an important theological text, the *Book of Sentences*, which set off conflicting opinions on the pattern of the *Sic et Non*, but which, like Gratian's *Decretum*, took the further step of reconciling the contradictory authorities. Lombard's *Book of Sentences* remained for centuries a fundamental text in schools of theology.

The Augustinian tradition was best represented in Abelard's time at the school of Saint-Victor in Paris, and in particular by the distinguished scholar, Hugh of Saint-Victor (d. 1141). Hugh was a Christian rationalist, but he believed that reason was only the first step in man's approach to God. Beyond reason lay mysticism, and God could not be circumscribed by logic alone. Hugh and his school emphasized the subordination of the material to the spiritual, and—drawing on the ancient tradition of Biblical allegory—interpreted the entire natural world as a vast multitude of symbols pointing to spiritual truths.

JOHN OF SALISBURY

The intellectual mood of the twelfth century was one of immense excitement at the possibilities of logic or dialectic. In this atmosphere, the remaining liberal arts—and especially the study of humanistic disciplines such as Latin literature—began to lose out in the competition. The cathedral school of Chartres was an important center of literary studies in the eleventh century and remained so throughout much of the twelfth. But as the century closed it began to fade before the onslaught of dialectic and the shift of students to the urban universities. The accomplished twelfth-century English scholar, John of Salisbury (*c.*1115–1180), had studied under Abelard and also under the masters at Chartres. A master of Greek and a well-trained logician, John of Salisbury was above all a humanist—a student of classical literature. He approved of dialectic but regretted the fact that it was growing to the exclusion of all else; he complained that the schools were tending to produce narrow logicians rather than broadly educated men.

In his *Policraticus* (1159), John of Salisbury made a notable contribution to medieval political philosophy. Drawing on the thought of Classical Antiquity and the Early Middle Ages, he stressed the divine nature of kingship but emphasized equally its responsibilities and limitations. The king drew his authority from God, but was commissioned to rule for the good of his subjects rather than himself. He was bound to give his subjects peace and justice and to protect the Church. If he abused his commission and neglected his responsibilities he lost his divine authority, ceased to be a king, and became a tyrant. As such he forfeited his subjects' allegiance and was no longer their lawful ruler. Under extreme circumstances, and if all else failed, John of Salisbury recommended tyrannicide. A good Christian subject, although obliged to obey his king, might kill a tyrant. Apart from the highly original doctrine of tyrannicide, the views expressed in the *Policraticus* reflect the general political attitudes of the twelfth century—responsible limited monarchy and government in behalf of the governed. These theories, in turn, were idealizations of the actual feudal monarchies of the day which were deterred from autocracy by the power of the nobility, the authority of the Church, and ancient custom.

THE NEW TRANSLATIONS

In the later twelfth and early thirteenth centuries the movement of Christian rationalism was powerfully reinforced by the arrival of vast quantities of Greek and Arabic writings in Latin translation. Significant portions of the philosophical and scientific legacy of ancient Greece now became available to European scholars. Above all, the full Aristotelian corpus now came into the West through the labors of translators in Spain, Sicily, and the Latin Empire of Constantinople.

These translations were by no means fortuitous. They came in answer to a deep hunger on the part of Western thinkers for a fuller knowledge of the classical heritage in philosophy and science. The introduction of certain new Aristotelian works provoked a crisis in Western Christendom, for they contained implications which seemed hostile to the Faith. And with them, as we have seen, came the skeptical and intellectually impressive works of the Spaniard Averröes which gave rise to the corrosive doctrine of the "twofold truth." For a time it seemed as though reason and revelation were sundered, and the Church reacted in panic by condemning certain of Aristotle's writings. It was one of the major goals of St. Thomas Aquinas to refute the Latin Averroists—to rescue Aristotle and, indeed, reason itself for Western Christianity.

THE SHAPE OF THIRTEENTH-CENTURY THOUGHT

The thirteenth century—the century of St. Thomas—differed sharply in spirit from the twelfth. The philosophers of the twelfth century were intellectual pioneers undertaking a great adventure, advancing across new frontiers into virgin soil. They were daring, original, and often radical; their mood was one of youthful exploration. The thirteenth century, although by no means lacking in intellectual originality, was preeminently an age of consolidation and synthesis. Its scholars digested the insights and conclusions of the past and cast them into great comprehensive systems of thought. The characteristic products of the age were encyclopedias and summas. Vincent of Beauvais (d. 1264), attempted in his *Speculum Majus* to bring together all knowledge of all imaginable subjects into one immense compendium. At a much higher level, theologians such as Alexander of Hales (d. 1245), Albertus Magnus (1193–1280), and Thomas Aquinas (1225–1274) produced great systematic treatises on theology known as summas in which they gave majestic structure and unity to the theological speculations of theirs and past ages.

ST. BONAVENTURE

The thought of Aristotle loomed large in the thirteenth-century schools, but the Platonic-Augustinian tradition was well represented, too. There was a tendency for the Dominican scholars to espouse Aristotle, and the Franciscans to follow Plato and Augustine. Thus the outstanding thirteenth-century exponent of Platonism-Augustinianism was the Franciscan St. Bonaventure (1221–1274), an Italian of humble origin who rose to become a cardinal of the Church and minister-general of the Franciscan order.

Bonaventure was at once a philosopher and a mystic. Following in the Augustinian tradition, he was a realist on the matter of universals and a rationalist who stressed the subordination of reason to faith. He accepted the nature symbolism of Hugh of Saint-Victor, and visualized the whole physical universe as a vast multitude of symbols pointing to God and glorifying Him. For example, he regarded everything in the natural world that could possibly be divided into three parts as a reflection of the Holy Trinity. Bonaventure's universe was eternally reaching upward toward the Divine Presence.

Bonaventure, like many of his intellectual predecessors and contemporaries, regarded the cosmos as an immense series of transparent concentric spheres. At its periphery, beyond the range of mortal eyes, were the nine spheres of angels. According to medieval theology, the angels were divided into nine ranks arranged hierarchically into three major groups, each containing three subgroups. As might be imagined, Bonaventure interpreted these three angelic triads as multiple symbols of the Trinity. Inside the spheres of angels was the sphere of stars which whirled daily round the earth. Within the stellar sphere were the spheres of the planets, sun, and moon. Such, in essence, had been Plato's conception of the universe, and Bonventure remained faithful to it.

At the center of all the celestial spheres was the earth itself, and on the earth was man—the ultimate reason for the physical universe. Man was a creature of immense dignity and importance—the lord of the earth, the master of all lower creatures. The cosmos was created for man—to sustain him and, through its myriad symbols, to lead him to God. Indeed, it was for man that God himself died on the cross.

Man was at the fulcrum of creation. His body gave him kinship with beasts; his soul gave him kinship with the angels. The human soul was created in the image of the Trinity, with three components: intellect, will, and memory. Man perceived the physical universe through his senses, but he knew the spiritual world—the world of universals—through the grace of divine illumination. The road to God and to truth, therefore, lay in introspection, meditation, and worship, not in observation and experiment.

Bonaventure's philosophy is not coldly intellectual but warm, emotional, and deeply spiritual. His discussion of God's attributes becomes a litany—an act of worship. His emphasis is less on knowledge than on love, and his entire system of thought can be regarded as a prayer in praise of God.

THE NEW ARISTOTELIANISM; ST. ALBERTUS MAGNUS

While Bonaventure was bringing new dimensions to traditional Platonism-Augustinianism, several of his contemporaries were coming to grips with the great Aristotelian-Averroistic challenge to orthodox Christian rationalism. The conflicting intellectual currents of the age were brilliantly represented by philosophers and theologians on the faculty of the University of Paris. There, teaching concurrently, were the Augustinian Bonaventure, the Latin Averroist Siger of Brabant, and the orthodox Aristotelians Albertus Magnus and Thomas Aquinas.

Albertus and his student, Thomas Aquinas, were both Dominicans, and both devoted themselves wholeheartedly to the reconciliation of reason and faith through the fusion of Aristotelianism and Christianity. They sought to confound the Latin Averroists by demonstrating that reason and revelation pointed to one truth, not two. A product of Germany, Albert Magnus was a scholar of widely ranging interests who made important contributions to natural science—especially biology—as well as to philosophy and theology. He was a master of Aristotelian philosophy and a summa writer, whose goal was to purge Aristotle of the heretical taint of Averroism and transform his philosophy into a powerful intellectual foundation for Christian orthodoxy. This audacious goal was brilliantly achieved, not by Albertus Magnus himself but by his still more gifted student, Thomas Aquinas.

ST. THOMAS AQUINAS

Saint Thomas was born of a Norman-Italian noble family in 1225. His family intended him to become a Benedictine, but in 1244 he shocked them by joining the radical new Dominican Order. He went to the University of Paris in 1245 and spent the remainder of his life traveling, teaching, and writing. Unlike Augustine he had no youthful follies to regret. Unlike Anselm, Bernard, and Bonaventure, he played no great role in the political affairs of his day. His biography is agonizingly dull except for an incident late in his life in which he abandoned his theological work, asserted that all his writings were worthless, and devoted his remaining days to mysticism. Shortly before his death he is reported to have risen off the ground while in a mystical trance. This act of levitation, if we can accept it, was a particularly noteworthy miracle in view of St. Thomas' marked corpulence during his later years. At his death, the priest who heard his final confession described it as being as innocent as that of a five-year-old child.

From the standpoint of intellectual history St. Thomas is a figure of singular interest and significance. In his copious writings—particularly his great comprehensive work, the *Summa Theologica*—he explored all the great questions of philosophy and theology, political theory and morality, using Aristotle's logical method and Aristotle's categories of thought but arriving at conclusions that were in complete harmony with the Christian faith. Like Abelard, St. Thomas assembled every possible argument, pro and con, on every subject that he discussed, but unlike Abelard he drew conclusions and defended them with cogent arguments. Few philosophers before or since have been so generous in presenting and exploring opinions contrary to their own, and none has been so systematic and exhaustive.

Saint Thomas created a vast, unified intellectual system, ranging from God to the natural world, logically supported at every step. His theological writings have none of the fiery passion of St. Augustine, none of the literary elegance of Plato; rather, they have an *intellectual* elegance, an elegance of system and organization akin to that of Euclid. His *Summa Theologica* is organized into an immense series of separate sections, each section dealing with a particular philosophical question. In part I of the *Summa*, for example, Question II takes up the problem of God's existence. The *Question* is subdivided into three Articles: (1) "Whether God's existence is self-evident" (St. Thomas concludes that it is not), (2) "Whether it can be demonstrated that God exists" (St. Thomas concludes that it can be so demonstrated), and (3) "Whether God exists" (here St. Thomas propounds five separate proofs of God's existence).

In each article. St. Thomas takes up a specific problem and subjects it to a rigorous formal analysis. First, he presents a series of *Objections* (*Objection I, Objection II*, etc.) in which he sets forth as effectively as he possibly can all the arguments *contrary* to his final conclusion. For example, *Question II, Article III*, "Whether God exists," begins with two *Objections* purporting to demonstrate that God does not exist. One of them runs as follows:

> Objection I. It seems that God does not exist, because if one of two contraries can be infinite, the other would be altogether destroyed. But the name "God" means that He is infinite goodness. Therefore, if God existed there would be no evil discoverable; but there is evil in the world. Therefore God does not exist.

After presenting the *Objections*, St. Thomas then turns to the second step in his analysis, the appeal to authority. This appeal is always introduced by the phrase, *On the contrary*, followed by a quotation from Scripture or from some authoritative patristic source which supports St. Thomas' own opinion on the subject. In the *Article* on God's existence, the *Objections* are followed by the statement, "On the contrary, It is said in the person of God: 'I am Who I am' (Exodus iii, 14)." Having cited his authority, St. Thomas next appeals to reason and subjects the problem to his own logical scrutiny, beginning always with the formula, *I answer that* . . . . For example, "I answer that, The existence of God can be proved in five ways," followed by a presentation of the five proofs of God:

> The fifth way is taken from the governance of the world. We see that things which lack knowledge, such as natural bodies, act for an end, and this is evident from their acting always or nearly always in the same way, so as to obtain the best result. Hence it is clear that they achieve their end not only by chance but by design. Now whatever lacks knowledge cannot move toward an end unless it be directed by some being endowed with knowledge and intelligence, as the arrow is directed by the archer. Therefore some intelligent being exists by whom

all natural things are directed to their end; and this being we call God.

The analysis concludes with refutations of the earlier *Objections:*

> *Reply to Objection I.* As Augustine says, "Since God is the highest good, He would not allow any evil to exist in His works unless His omnipotence and goodness were such as to bring good even out of evil." This is part of the infinite goodness of God, that He should allow evil to exist, and out of it to produce good.

Having completed his analysis, St. Thomas then turns to the next *Article* or the next *Question* and subjects it to precisely the same process of inquiry: *Objections, On the contrary, I answer that,* and *Reply to Objections.* And as in Euclidian geometry, so in Thomistic theology, once a problem is settled the conclusion can be used in solving subsequent problems. Thus the system grows, problem by problem, step by step, as St. Thomas' wide-ranging mind takes up such matters as the nature and attributes of God, the nature and destiny of man, human morality, law, and political theory. The result is an imposing, comprehensive intellectual edifice embracing all major theological issues.

As the Gothic cathedral was the artistic embodiment of the high medieval world, so the philosophy of Aquinas was its supreme intellectual expression. Both were based on clear and obvious principles of structure. St. Thomas shared with the cathedral builders the impulse to display rather than disguise the structural framework of his edifice. Like the boldly executed Gothic flying buttress, the Thomistic *Questions, Articles, and Objections* allowed no doubt as to what the builder was doing, where he was going, or how he was achieving his effects. The scholastics were nothing if not systematic— they loved to exhibit the underlying principles of their organization —and none carried this tendency farther than St. Thomas. It is not without reason that the *Summa Theologica* has been called a cathedral of thought.

As a devoted Christian and Aristotelian, Aquinas contended against both the Augustinians, who would reject Aristotle altogether, and the Latin Averroists, who would make a heretic of him. St. Thomas distinguished carefully between revelation and reason but endeavored to prove that they could never contradict one another.

Since human reason was a valid avenue to truth, since Christian revelation was undoubtedly authoritative, and since truth was one, then philosophy and Christian doctrine had to be compatible and complementary. "For faith rests upon infallible truth, and therefore its contrary cannot be demonstrated." This was the essence of St. Thomas' philosophical position. This was the conviction that separated him so radically from the Latin Averroists.

As against the Augustinianism of St. Anselm, Hugh of Saint-Victor, and St. Bonaventure, Aquinas emphasized the reality of the physical world as a world of things rather than symbols. Embracing the moderate realism of Aristotle, he declared that universals were to be found in the world of phenomena and nowhere else—that knowledge came from observation and analysis, not from divine illumination. Whereas Augustine, following Plato, had emphasized the *duality* of matter and spirit, earth and heaven, body and soul, Aquinas emphasized the *unity* of God's creation. He asserted the unity of ideas and phenomena—the universal was not outside the particular but within it—and thus he shared with St. Francis and others the notion that the physical world was deeply significant in itself, that matter mattered. He affirmed the unity of intellectual knowledge and sensation, maintaining that knowledge is acquired by a gradual ascent from things to concepts, from the visible to the invisible world. He stressed the unity of man, declaring that a human being was not a soul using a body or a spirit imprisoned in flesh, as the Platonists suggested, but an inseparable composite of body and soul. The human body, although a source of temptation, was good in itself and was an essential part of man.

Similarly, the state, which previous Christian thinkers had commonly regarded as a necessary evil—an unfortunate but indispensable consequence of the Fall of Adam—was accepted by Aquinas as a good and natural outgrowth of man's social impulse. He echoed Aristotle's dictum that "Man is a political animal," and regarded the justly governed state as a fitting part of the Divine Order. Like John of Salisbury, St. Thomas insisted that kings must govern in their subjects' behalf and that a willful, unrestrained ruler who ignored God's moral imperatives was no king but a tyrant. Just as the human body could be corrupted by sin, the body politic could be corrupted by tyranny. But although the Christian must reject both sin and tyranny, he should nevertheless revere the body, the state, and indeed all physical creation as worthy products of God's will, inseparable from the world of the spirit, and essential ingredients in the unity of existence.

Such was the Thomistic vision. In binding together matter and spirit, the concrete and the abstract, body and soul, God and man, Aquinas was seeking to encompass the totality of being in a vast existential unity. At the center of this majestic system was God, the author of physical and spiritual creation, the maker of heaven and earth, who himself assumed human form and redeemed mankind on the Cross, who discloses portions of the truth to man through revelation, permits him to discover other portions through the operation of his intellect, and will lead him into all truth through salvation. Ultimately, truth is God himself, and it is man's destiny, upon reaching heaven, to stand unshielded in the divine presence—to love and to know. Thus the roads of St. Thomas, St. Bonaventure, St. Bernard, and Dante, although passing over very different terrain, arrive finally at the same destination. It is not so very surprising, after all, that in the end St. Thomas rejected the way of the philosopher for the way of the mystic.

CRITICS OF ST. THOMAS

To this day there are men of keen intelligence who accept the philosophy of St. Thomas. On the other hand, many of his own thirteenth-century contemporaries rejected it in whole or in part, and it remained a source of intense controversy in the centuries that followed. Franciscan intellectuals such as Bonaventure were particularly suspicious of the intellectual *tour de force* of this gifted Dominican. Bonaventure was a rationalist, but in a far more limited sense than was Aquinas, and Bonaventure's Franciscan successors came increasingly to the opinion that reason was of little or no use in probing metaphysical problems. The Scottish Franciscan, Duns Scotus (d. 1308), undertook a rigorous and subtle critique of St. Thomas' theory of knowledge. And in the philosophy of the astute English Franciscan, William of Ockham (*c.* 1300–1349), reason and revelation were divorced altogether. Christian doctrine, Ockham said, could not be approached by reason at all but had to be accepted on faith. The Thomist synthesis was a mirage. Reason's province was the natural world and that alone.

SCIENCE

The Ockhamist position represents a distinctive combination of empiricism and mysticism. Both these elements had been present among the Franciscans of the thirteenth century. The mysticism of a Bonaventure represents one pole of Franciscan thought. At the other pole stands a group of important scientific thinkers who applied their logical tools to the humble but significant task of investigating the natural world. Thirteenth-century Oxford became the leading center of scientific investigation, and it was here that western European science came of age.

The key figure in the development of medieval science was the great English scholar, Robert Grosseteste (1168–1253), who, although not a Franciscan himself, was chief lecturer to the Franciscans at Oxford. Grosseteste was on intimate terms with Platonic and Neoplatonic philosophy, Aristotelian physics, and the rich scientific legacy of Islam. At bottom, he was a Platonist and an Augustinian, but he wrote important commentaries on the scientific works of Aristotle and was able to draw on both traditions. From Plato he derived the notion that mathematics is a basic key to understanding the physical universe; the fundamental importance of numbers is very much in keeping with the Platonic realist interpretation of universals, and Plato himself had once asserted that "God is a mathematician." From Aristotle he learned the importance of abstracting knowledge from the world of phenomena by means of observation and experiment. Thus, bridging the two great traditions, Grosseteste brought together the mathematical and experimental components that together underlie the rise of modern science. More than that, drawing on the suggestive work of his Islamic predecessors he worked out a far more rigorous experimental procedure than is to be found in the pages of Aristotle. An outstanding pioneer in the development of scientific method, he outlined a system of observation, hypothesis, and experimental verification that was elaborated by his successors into the methodological technique which modern physical scientists still employ.

Like other pioneers, Grosseteste followed many false paths. He was better at formulating a scientific methodology than in applying it to specific problems, and his explanations of such phenomena as heat, light, color, comets, and rainbows were rejected in later centuries.

But the experimental method which he formulated was to become, in time, a powerful intellectual tool. The problem of the rainbow, for example, was solved by the fourteenth-century scientist Theoderic of Freiburg who employed a refined version of Grosseteste's experimental methodology. The great triumphs of European science lay far in the future, but with the work of Robert Grosseteste the basic scientific tool had been forged. Grosseteste's career illustrates not that science was born in the thirteenth century but rather that scientific thought evolved gradually from antiquity to modern times, and that the High Middle Ages contributed markedly to its development.

Grosseteste's work was carried further by his famous disciple, the Oxford Franciscan Roger Bacon (c. 1214–1294). The author of a fascinating body of scientific sense and nonsense, Roger Bacon was more an advocate of experimental science than a consistent practitioner of it. He dabbled in the mysteries of alchemy and astrology, and his boundless curiosity carried him along many strange roads. He led a turbulent life, at times enjoying the friendship of the papacy, at other times imprisoned by his own Franciscan order which suspected him of practicing magic. Roger Bacon was critical of the deductive logic and metaphysical speculations that so intrigued his scholastic contemporaries: "Reasoning," he wrote, "does not illuminate these matters; experiments are required, conducted on a large scale, performed with instruments and by various necessary means."

At his best, Roger Bacon was almost prophetic:

> Experimental science controls the conclusions of all other sciences. It reveals truths which reasoning from general principles would never have discovered. Finally, it starts us on the way to marvelous inventions which will change the face of the world.

One such marvelous invention, the telescope, was not to be invented for another three centuries, yet Roger Bacon described it in astonishing detail:

> We can give such figures to transparent bodies, and dispose them in such order with respect to the eye and the objects, that the rays will be refracted and bent toward any place we please, so that we will see the object near at hand or at a distance,

under any angle we wish. And thus from an incredible distance we may read the smallest letters, and may number the smallest particles of dust and sand, by reason of the greatness of the angle under which we see them . . . . The sun, moon, and stars may be made to descend hither in appearance, and to be visible over the heads of our enemies, and many things of a like sort which persons unacquainted with such matters would refuse to believe.

THE MEDIEVAL INTELLECTUAL ACHIEVEMENT

Thus the intense intellectual activity of the thirteenth century produced both the supreme synthesis of Christian rationalism in the philosophy of St. Thomas and the genesis of a new method of scientific inquiry in the thought of Robert Grosseteste and his successors. In the realm of the intellect, as in so many others, the thirteenth century was both synthetic and creative.

With the coming of the fourteenth century, the growth of scientific thought was accompanied by the gradual erosion of the Thomist synthesis. Universal systems such as that of St. Thomas have seldom been lasting, but for a few brief years Thomism represented, for many, the perfect fusion of intellect and belief. As such, it takes its place alongside the Gothic cathedral, the *Divine Comedy* of Dante, and the piety of St. Francis as a supreme and mature expression of high medieval culture.

CONCLUSION

The world of the High Middle Ages is described in some outworn textbooks as stagnant, gloomy, and monolithic. At the other extreme, it has been portrayed as an ideally constituted society, free of modern fears and tensions, where men of all classes could live happily and creatively, finding fulfillment in their service to the common good. In reality, it was an age of vitality, of striking contrasts, of dark fears and high hopes, of poverty that was often brutal yet gradually diminishing. Above all, it was an age in which Europeans awoke to the rich variety of possibilities that lay before them. A thirteenth-century poet, in his celebration of springtime, captured perfectly the spirit of this awakening:

The earth's ablaze again
With lustrous flowers.
The fields are green again,
The shadows, deep.
Woods are in leaf again,
And all the world
Is filled with joy again.
This long-dead land
Now flames with life again.
The passions surge,
Love is reborn,
And beauty wakes from sleep.

Suggested Readings

The asterisk indicates a paperback edition.

GENERAL WORKS

R. W. Southern, *The Making of the Middle Ages* (*Yale). A brilliant, sympathetic interpretation of the eleventh and twelfth centuries.

Frederick Heer, *The Medieval World* (*Mentor). Heer contrasts twelfth-century expansion with thirteenth-century stabilization.

ECONOMIC HISTORY AND THE FRONTIERS

Henri Pirenne, *Economic and Social History of Medieval Europe* (*Harvest). A compact, richly interpretive survey by a great scholar.

Henri Pirenne, *Medieval Cities* (*Anchor). Brief, lucid, and highly original.

Sidney Painter, *Medieval Society* (*Cornell). A short, introductory essay.

Steven Runciman, *A History of the Crusades* (3 vols., Cambridge University Press; Vol. I: *Harper). Comprehensive and authoritative.

EMPIRE AND PAPACY

Geoffrey Barraclough, *Medieval Germany, 911–1250* (2 vols., Blackwell). Volume I is a valuable introductory essay; Volume II consists of specialized studies by German scholars in English translation.

Gerd Tellenbach, *Church, State and Christian Society* (Blackwell). The finest analysis of the Investiture Controversy in English.

Walter Ullmann, *The Growth of Papal Government in the Middle Ages* (Methuen). An intellectual history of the medieval papal ideology.

Ernst Kantorowicz, *Frederick II*. An excellent biography. Kantorowicz's conclusions should be compared with those of Barraclough in his *Origins of Modern Germany* (*Capricorn).

Innocent III, Vicar of Christ or Lord of the World?, J. M. Powell (Ed.) (*Heath). Essays by historians representing diverse viewpoints.

ENGLAND AND FRANCE

For high medieval England, the appropriate volumes of the monumental Oxford History are authoritative but rather heavy:

A. L. Poole, *From Domesday Book to Magna Carta.*

F. M. Powicke, *The Thirteenth Century.*

For a lighter treatment of the period see especially:

Christopher Brooke, *From Alfred to Henry III* (Thomas Nelson).

Helen M. Cam, *England Before Elizabeth* (*Harper).

C. Warren Hollister, *The Making of England* (*Heath).

Robert Fawtier, *The Capetian Kings of France* (*St. Martin's). A short, masterful treatment, highly recommended.

Amy Kelly, *Eleanor of Aquitaine* (*Vintage). Sound and entertaining.

CHRISTIANITY IN THE HIGH MIDDLE AGES

Norman F. Cantor, *Medieval History* (Macmillan). A recent, highly interpretive textbook, particularly strong on matters ecclesiastical.

Summerfield Baldwin, *The Organization of Medieval Christianity* (Holt). A short introductory essay.

Steven Runciman, *The Medieval Manichee* (*Compass Books). A penetrating investigation of medieval heresy.

Paul Sabatier, *St. Francis of Assisi* (Scribners). A masterly older study, deeply sympathetic to St. Francis.

Dom David Knowles, *From Pachomius to Ignatius* (Oxford). A very brief but authoritative account of the organization of religious orders, emphasizing the period from the rise of Cluny to the death of St. Dominic.

THOUGHT, LETTERS, AND THE ARTS

F. C. Copleston, *Medieval Philosophy* (*Harper). A popular introduction by a leading scholar.

Gordon Leff, *Medieval Thought* (*Penguin). A survey which emphasizes the development of metaphysics.

C. H. Haskins, *The Rise of the Universities* (*Cornell). Short and highly competent; a pleasure to read.

C. H. Haskins, *The Renaissance of the Twelfth Century* (*Meridian). An epoch-making book, particularly strong in the area of Latin literature.

Erwin Panofsky, *Gothic Architecture and Scholasticism* (*Meridian). A challenging study which endeavors to demonstrate lines of connection between these two great medieval enterprises.

C. H. McIlwain, *The Growth of Political Thought in the West* (Macmillan). The preferred one-volume account of medieval political theory.

Walter Ullmann, *A History of Political Thought: The Middle Ages* (*Penguin). A short, provocative summary by a leading modern authority on medieval political theory.

SOURCES

The Portable Medieval Reader, tr. J. B. Ross and M. M. McLaughlin (*Viking).
   Like Cantor's *Medieval World*, a useful, well-chosen selection of medieval
   sources in translation.
Documents of the Christian Church, tr. Henry Bettenson (Oxford). A useful
   collection running from antiquity to the present.
The Little Flowers of St. Francis, tr. L. Sherley-Price (*Penguin). A fascinating
   collection of sources relating to the life of St. Francis.
Otto of Freising, *The Deeds of Frederick Barbarossa*, tr. C. C. Mierow and
   R. Emery (Columbia). A good example of medieval historical writing.
Memoirs of the Crusades: Villehardouin and de Joinville, tr. Sir Frank Marzials
   (Everyman). Excellent contemporary accounts of the Fourth Crusade
   and the crusading adventures of St. Louis.
The Portable Dante, tr. Paolo Milano (*Viking). Good translations of the
   Divine Comedy and other works.
Introduction to St. Thomas Aquinas, tr. Anton C. Pegis (Modern Library).
   Intelligently chosen selections together with a stimulating introduction.

Part 3

THE LATE MIDDLE AGES:

The Ordeal of Transition

15

Church and State in the Fourteenth and Fifteenth Centuries

THE DECLINE OF THE HIGH-MEDIEVAL SYNTHESIS

Like most eras of transition, the fourteenth and fifteenth centuries were violent and unsettled, marked by a gradual ebbing of the self-confidence on which the high-medieval synthesis had rested. Prosperity gave way to depression, optimism to disillusionment, and the thirteenth-century dream of fusing the worlds of matter and spirit came to an end. Social behavior ran to extremes—to rebellion, sensualism, flagellation, cynicism, and witchcraft. Powerful creative forces were at work in these centuries, but they were less evident to most contemporary observers than the forces of disintegration and decay. The shrinking of Europe's economy, population, and territorial frontiers was accompanied by a mood of pessimism and claustrophobia, exploding periodically into frenzied enthusiasm or blind rage. The literature and art of the period disclose a preoccupation with fantasy, eccentricity, and death. England and France were torn by war, and both were ruled for a time by madmen. The Black Death struck Europe in the mid-fourteenth century and returned periodically to darken men's spirits and disrupt society.

These varied symptoms of social neurosis were associated with a gradual shift in Western Europe's political orientation—from a

Christian commonwealth to a constellation of territorial states. The Roman Catholic Church fared badly during the Late Middle Ages. The Western kingdoms were racked by civil and external war and, at times, by a near breakdown of royal government, yet during the final half-century of the period (c. 1450–1500) strong monarchies emerged in England, France, and Spain. These three states were destined to dominate Western European politics far into the future. By 1500 the monarchy was coming to replace the Church as the object of men's highest allegiance. The pope had become mired in local Italian politics, and medieval Christian cosmopolitanism was breaking up into sovereign fragments.

THE CHURCH IN THE LATE MIDDLE AGES

The late-medieval evolution from Christendom toward nationhood was not so much a transformation as a shift in balance. Even during the High Middle Ages the ideal of a Christian commonwealth, guided by pope and clergy, had never approached realization. At best, popes could win momentary political victories over kings and achieve an uneasy equilibrium between royal and clerical authority within the European kingdoms. And by the end of the thirteenth century, the balance was already tipping in favor of monarchs such as Edward I of England and Philip the Fair of France. Two centuries later, in 1500, the papacy was far weaker as an international force and the monarchies stronger, but "nationhood," by any strict definition, had not yet come. Still, papal authority over the churches within the various kingdoms, which had been a significant reality in the High Middle Ages, was becoming tenuous by 1500. The princely electors of Germany had long before denied the papacy any role in imperial elections or coronations, and papal influence in the appointment of French, English, and Spanish prelates had ebbed. More important still, the Late Middle Ages witnessed a collapse of papal spiritual prestige and a widening chasm between Christian piety and the organized Church.

MYSTICS AND REFORMERS

Christianity did not decline noticeably during this period; it merely became less ecclesiastical. The powerful movement of lay piety, which had been drifting away from papal leadership all through the High Middle Ages, now became increasingly hostile to ecclesiastical wealth and privilege, increasingly individualistic, and increasingly mystical. The wave of mysticism that swept across late-medieval Europe was not, for the most part, openly heretical, but by stressing the spiritual relationship between the individual and God the mystics tended to deemphasize the role of the ordained clergy and the sacraments as channels of divine grace. The mystic, although not denying the efficacy of the Holy Eucharist, devoted himself chiefly to the direct mystical apprehension of God, for which no clerical hierarchy, no popes, and no sacraments were needed.

Mysticism had always been an element in the Christian devotional life, and it was well known to the High Middle Ages. But with the breakdown of the high-medieval synthesis, and with the growth of complacency and corruption within the Church, mysticism became, for the first time, a large-scale movement among the laity. Early in the fourteenth century, the great Dominican mystic, Meister Eckhart (d. 1327), taught that man's true goal is utter separation from the world of the senses and absorption into the Divine Unknown. Eckhart had many followers, and as the century progressed several large mystical brotherhoods took form. The greatest of them, the Brethren of the Common Life, was founded about 1375 by the Flemish lay preacher Gerard Groot, a student of one of Eckhart's disciples. The Brethren of the Common Life devoted themselves to unpretentious lives of preaching, teaching, and charitable works. Their popularity in fifteenth-century Northern Europe approached that of the Franciscans two centuries before, but the Brethren, unlike the Franciscans, took no lifetime vows. Their schools were among the finest in Europe and produced some of the leading mystics, humanists, and reformers of the fifteenth and sixteenth centuries. Erasmus and Luther were both products of the Brethren's schools, as was St. Thomas à Kempis (d. 1471) whose *Imitation of Christ* stands as the supreme literary expression of late-medieval mysticism. *
The Imitation of Christ typifies the mystical outlook in its emphasis on adoration over speculation, inner spiritual purity over external "good works," and direct experience of God over the sacramental avenues to divine grace. *The Imitation* remained well within the

---

*Although most scholars attribute *The Imitation of Christ* to Thomas à Kempis the attribution is not certain.

bounds of Catholic orthodoxy, yet it contained ideas that had great appeal to the sixteenth-century Protestant reformers. The emphasis on individual piety, common to all the mystics, tended to erode the medieval Christian commonwealth by transforming the Catholic Church into a multitude of individual souls, each groping upward alone.

This element of Christian individualism was carried at times to the point of outright heresy. John Wyclif (d. 1384), a professor at Oxford, anticipated the later Protestants by placing the authority of Scriptures over the definitions of popes and councils. Pushing the implications of contemporary mysticism to their limit, he stressed the individual's inner spiritual Odyssey toward God, questioned the real presence of Christ in the Holy Eucharist, deemphasized the entire sacramental system, and spoke out strongly against ecclesiastical wealth. This last protest had been implicit in the thirteenth-century Franciscan movement—although St. Francis showed his devotion to apostolic poverty by living it rather than forcing it on others. The compromises of later Franciscanism on the matter of property had given rise to a zealous splinter group—the "Spiritual Franciscans"—whose insistence on universal ecclesiastical poverty had turned them anticlerical and antipapal. John XXII (1316–1334), the shrewd Avignonese "financier-pope," had been obliged in 1323 to denounce the doctrine of apostolic poverty as heretical. And Wyclif, more than half a century later, was stripped of his professorship and convicted of heresy. Owing to his powerful friends at court, and to the unpopularity of the papacy in fourteenth-century England, he was permitted to die peacefully, but his followers, the Lollards, were less fortunate. Their fate is suggested by the title of a parliamentary act of 1401: "The Statute on the Burning of Heretics." There were no Lollards around to celebrate King Henry VIII's break with Rome in the 1530s.

English Lollardy represented an extreme expression of a growing discontent with the official Church. Wyclif's doctrines spread to far-away Bohemia where they were taken up by the reformer John Hus. The Hussites used Wyclif's anticlericalism as a weapon for Czech independence from German political and cultural influence. John Hus was burned at the stake at the Council of Constance in 1415, but his followers survived into the Reformation era as a dissident national group. Both Wyclif and Hus represented, in their opposition to the organized international Church, a reconciliation of personal religious faith and the idea of national sovereignty. If Christianity was an individual affair, then the political claims of popes and prelates were meritless, and secular rulers might govern without ecclesiastical interference. Thus the radical thrust of late-medieval Christianity, by its very anticlericalism, tended to support the growing concept of secular sovereignty. Ardent religious spirits such as John Hus—and Joan of Arc, burned as a heretic in 1431—could fuse Christian mysticism with the beginnings of patriotism.

POPES AND COUNCILS

The mystics and reformers, implicitly or explicitly, rejected the pope as the mediator between God and the Christian community. And the late-medieval papacy did little to merit this awesome responsibility. Between 1309 and 1376 the popes ruled from the papal city of Avignon on the Rhone, officially outside the domains of France yet always in their shadow. The Avignon popes were subservient to the French crown only to a degree. They were capable of independent action, particularly at times when France was ruled weakly, but their very location suggested to non-Frenchmen that they were no longer an impartial international force. There were attempts to return the papacy to Rome, but until 1376 they were foiled by the insecurity and violent factionalism of the holy city. The Avignon popes were not evil men, but they carried to its ultimate degree the thirteenth-century emphasis on administrative and fiscal efficiency. Englishmen and Germans resented paying high taxes to a seeming tool of the French crown. And the immense, mildly corrupt bureaucracy of papal Avignon could hardly be expected to inspire mystics and reformers. As the wealth of the papacy grew, its spiritual capital declined alarmingly.

In 1376 Pope Gregory XI moved his headquarters from Avignon to Rome. Chagrined by the turbulent conditions he encountered there, he made plans to return but died in 1378 before he could carry them out. Urged on by a Roman mob, the cardinals—most of whom were homesick Frenchmen—grudgingly elected an Italian to the papal throne. The new pope, Urban VI, had previously been a colorless functionary in the ecclesiastical establishment. Now, to everyone's surprise, he became a zealous reformer and began taking steps to reduce the cardinals' revenues and influence. The French cardinals fled Rome, quashed their previous election on the grounds of mob intimidation, and elected a French pope who returned with them to Avignon. Back in Rome, Urban VI appointed new cardinals, and for the next thirty-seven years the universal Church was torn by schism. When the rival popes died, their cardinals elected rival successors. Excommunications were hurled to-and-fro between Rome and Avignon, and the states of Europe chose their sides according to their interests. France and her allies supported Avignon, England and the Empire backed Rome, and the Italian states shifted from one side to the other as it suited their purposes. Papal prestige was falling in ruin, yet in the face of age-long papal claims to absolute spiritual authority, there seemed no power on earth that could claim to arbitrate between two rival popes. The Church was at an impasse.

As the schism dragged on, increasing numbers of Christians became convinced that the only solution was the convening of a general Church council. Both popes argued that councils were inferior to them and could not judge them, and Christians were perplexed as to who, if not the popes, had the authority to summon a council. At length the cardinals themselves, in both camps, called a council to meet in Pisa. There, in 1409, a group of 500 prelates deposed both popes and elected a new one. Since neither pope recognized the conciliar depositions, the effect of the Council of Pisa was to transform a two-way schism into a three-way schism. The situation was ceasing to be scandalous and was becoming ludicrous. Finally the Holy Roman Emperor, drawing on the ancient precedent of the Emperor Constantine, summoned the prelates of Europe to the Council of Constance (1415–1418). Here, at last, the depositions of all three popes were voted and enforced, and the schism was healed by the election of a conciliar pope, Martin V (1417–1431).

To many thoughtful Christians, the healing of the schism was not enough. The papacy stood discredited, and it was argued that future popes should be guided by general councils meeting regularly and automatically. The role of councils and assemblies was familiar enough to contemporary secular governments. Why should not the Church, too, be governed "constitutionally"? Such views had been urged by political philosophers such as Marsilius of Padua in the fourteenth century and Nicholas of Cusa in the fifteenth, and they were widely accepted among the prelates at Constance. The essential conservatism of these delegates is suggested by their decision to burn John Hus who came to Constance with an imperial promise of safe conduct. Yet the Council of Constance made a genuine effort to reform the constitution of the Church along conciliar lines. The delegates affirmed, against papal objection, the ultimate authority of councils in matters of doctrine and reform, and they decreed that thenceforth general councils would convene at regular intervals.

These broad principles, together with a number of specific reforms voted by the Council, met with the firm opposition of Pope Martin V and his successors who took their stand on the principle of absolute papal supremacy. The popes reluctantly summoned a council in 1423 and another in 1431 but worked to make them ineffective. The last of the medieval councils—the Council of Basel (1431–1449)—drifted gradually into open schism with the recalcitrant papacy and petered out ingloriously in 1449. By then Europe's enthusiasm for conciliarism was waning, and no further councils were summoned until after the Reformation. The Conciliar Movement was dead, and a single pope ruled unopposed once more in Rome.

The popes between the dissolution of Basel (1449) and the opening of the Reformation (1517) were radically different from their high-medieval predecessors. Abandoning much of their former jurisdiction over the international Church, they devoted themselves to the beguiling culture and bitter local politics of Renaissance Italy. Struggling to strengthen their hold on the Papal States, maneuvering through the shifting sands of Italian diplomacy, they conceded to northern monarchs an extensive degree of control over Church and clergy in return for a formal recognition of papal authority and an agreed division of Church revenues between pope and king.

The fifteenth century ended with the pontificate of the Borgia pope, Alexander VI (1492–1503), whose scandalous behavior was sufficient even to raise eyebrows in high-Renaissance Italy. Alexander's pontificate is a caricature of all that ailed the papacy at the end of the Middle Ages. He divided his time between ruthless political aggrandizement and sensual pleasures. Contemporary rumor had it that he numbered his own illegitimate daughter Lucretia among his mistresses. However this may be, he gave full support to the unprincipled military and diplomatic activities of his son, Caesar, who used assassination, treachery, and force to carve out a great Borgia state in central Italy. As the Borgia pontificate vividly illustrates, the papacy, by 1500, had ceased to be an international spiritual power. Fourteen years after Alexander VI's death, the Protestant Reformation began, and the tremendous popular response to Luther's rebellion bespeaks the failure of the late-medieval popes. Europeans were not prepared to abandon Christianity, but they were willing, in large numbers, to desert tarnished Rome.

CHRONOLOGY OF THE LATE-MEDIEVAL CHURCH

1309–1376:	Avignon papacy prior to the Great Schism
1316–1334:	Pontificate of John XXII, the "financier pope"
1327:	Meister Eckhart dies
c. 1375:	Gerard Groot founds the Brethren of the Common Life
1378–1415:	Great Schism: Rome versus Avignon
1384:	John Wyclif dies
1409:	Council of Pisa: three-way schism
1415–1418:	Council of Constance: schism healed, beginning of conciliarism
1415:	John Hus burned at the stake
1417–1431:	Pontificate of Martin V
1431–1449:	Council of Basel: waning of conciliarism
1492–1503:	Pontificate of Alexander VI, the Borgia pope
1517:	Outbreak of Lutheran Reformation

THE WESTERN MONARCHIES

The late-medieval trend from international Catholicism toward secular sovereignty found forceful expression in Marsilius of Padua's important treatise, the *Defensor Pacis* (1324). Here the dilemma of conflicting sovereign jurisdictions, secular and ecclesiastical, was resolved uncompromisingly in favor of the state. The Church, Marsilius argued, should be stripped of political authority, and the state should wield sovereign power over all its subjects, lay and clerical alike. Thus the Church, united in faith, would be divided politically into a multitude of state churches obedient to their secular rulers and not to the pope. In its glorification of the sovereign state, the *Defensor Pacis* foreshadowed the evolution of late-medieval and early-modern politics.

Not until after 1450, however, were the Western monarchies able to assert their authority with any consistency over the particularistic nobility. Between the early fourteenth century and the mid-fifteenth century, the high-medieval trend toward royal centralization seemed to have reversed itself. The major Iberian powers—Aragon, Castile, and Portugal—were tormented by sporadic internal upheavals and made no progress toward reducing Granada, the remaining Islamic enclave in the peninsula. England and France, through most of the period, were involved in the Hundred Years' War (1337–1453) which drove England to the brink of bankruptcy and ravaged the French countryside and population.

ENGLAND

The unwritten English constitution developed significantly during these years. In the course of the fourteenth century, Parliament grew from an occasion to an institution and split into Lords and Commons. The House of Commons, consisting of representative townsmen and shire knights, bargained with a monarchy hard-pressed by the expenses of the Hundred Years' War. Commons traded its fiscal support for important political concessions, and by the century's end it had gained the privilege of approving or disapproving all uncustomary taxation. With control of the royal purse strings secured, Commons then won the power to legislate. Adopting the motto, "redress before supply," it refused to pass financial grants until the king had approved its petitions, and in the end, Commons petitions acquired the force of law.

Without belittling these constitutional advances, we must recognize that the late-medieval Commons was largely controlled by the force or manipulation of powerful aristocrats. Elections could be rigged; representatives could be bribed or overawed. And although Parliament deposed two English kings in the fourteenth century—Edward II in 1327 and Richard II in 1399—in both instances it was simply ratifying the results of aristocratic power struggles. It is significant that such parliamentary ratification should seem necessary to the nobility, but we must not conclude that Parliament had yet become an independent agent. Symbolically, it represented the will of the English community; actually, it remained sensitive to aristocratic force and tended to affirm decisions already made in castles or battlefields.

The Hundred Years' War, which proved such a stimulus to the growth of parliamentary privileges, also constituted a serious drain on English wealth and lives. Beginning in 1337, it dragged on fitfully for 116 years, with periods of savage warfare alternating with prolonged periods of truce. Broadly speaking, it was a continuation of the Anglo-French rivalry that dated from the Norman Conquest. Since 1066, England and France had battled on numerous occasions. In 1204 the Capetian crown had won the extensive northern French territories of the Angevin Empire. Normandy, Anjou, and surrounding lands had fallen more or less permanently into French royal hands, but the English kings retained a tenuous lordship over Gascony in the south. The English Gascon claim, cemented by a brisk commerce in Gascon wine and English cloth, gave rise to an expensive but inconclusive war (1294–1303) between Philip the Fair of France and Edward I of England, and competing English and French claims to jurisdiction in Gascony constituted one of several causes for the resumption of hostilities in 1337.

Another cause of the Hundred Years' War was the Anglo-French diplomatic struggle for control of Flanders which France needed to round out its territories and which England needed to secure its profitable wool trade. Tension mounted in 1328 when, on the death of the last French Capetian, King Edward III of England (1327–1377) laid claim to the throne of France. Edward III's mother was a daughter of Philip the Fair, but the French nobility, refusing to be governed by an English monarch, ruled that the succession could not pass through a female. Accordingly, they chose Philip V (1328–1350), the first king of the long-lived Valois dynasty. Edward III accepted the decision at first, but in 1337, when other reasons prompted him to take up arms, he revived his claim and titled himself king of France and England.

None of these causes can be considered decisive, and war might yet have been avoided had it not been that both Edward III and Philip V were chivalric, high-spirited romantics who longed for heroic clashes of arms. The same spirit infected the nobility on both sides, but the French knights lost their ardor when English longbowmen won smashing victories at Crécy (1346) and Poitiers (1356).

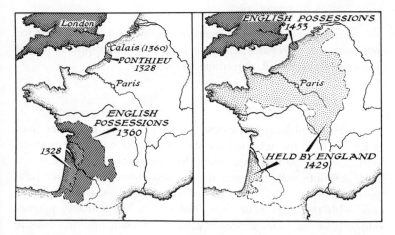

The English revered Edward III so long as English arms were victorious, but they deposed his successor, Richard II (1377–1399), who showed no interest in fighting Frenchmen. Henry V (1413–1422) revived hostilities and gained the adulation of his subjects by winning a momentous victory over the French at Agincourt in 1415. But Henry V's early death, and the subsequent career of Joan of Arc, turned the tide of war against the English. By 1453, when the long struggle ended at last, England had lost all of France except the port of Calais. The centuries-long process of Anglo-French disentanglement was completed, and Joan of Arc's vision was realized: her dauphin ruled France unopposed as King Charles VII.

The Hundred Years' War had been over for scarcely two years when England entered an era of civil strife between the rival houses of York and Lancaster. The Wars of the Roses, which raged off and on between 1455 and 1485, were the medieval English nobility's last orgy of violence. Common Englishmen were tired of endless bloodshed and longed for firm royal governance. They achieved it, to a degree, in the reign of the Yorkist Edward IV (1461–1483). And after a final burst of warfare, strong monarchy came permanently to England with the accession of the first Tudor king, Henry VII (1485–1509). Both Edward IV and Henry VII sought peace, a full treasury, and effective government, and by the late fifteenth century these goals were coming within reach. The economy was reviving, many of the more troublesome nobles had perished in the Wars of the Roses, and most Englishmen were willing to exchange violent independence for obedience and peace. All that was needed now was strong royal leadership, and that was supplied in full measure by the willful, determined Tudors.

FRANCE

The Hundred Years' War was a far greater trial to France than to England. All the fighting took place on French soil, and numerous mercenary companies, even when they were not engaged in actual warfare, continually pillaged the French countryside. King John the Good (1350–1364)—a very bad king indeed—was powerless to cope with the English or bring order to a demoralized, plague-ridden land. In 1356, a decade after the French military debacle at Crécy—and eight years after the onset of the Black Death—France was stunned by a crushing defeat at Poitiers. French nobles fell in great numbers, and King John himself was taken prisoner by the English.

The Estates General, meeting in Paris under the leadership of a dynamic Parisian cloth merchant, Etienne Marcel, momentarily assumed the reins of government. In 1357 they forced King John's son, the young dauphin Charles, to issue a radical constitutional statute known as the "Great Ordinance." This statute embodied the demands of the bourgeois-dominated Estates General to join with the monarchy in the governance of France. The Estates General were thenceforth to meet on regular occasions and to supervise the royal finances, courts, and administration through a small standing committee. The dauphin Charles, deeply hostile to this infringement of royal authority, submitted for a time, then fled Paris to gather royalist support in the countryside.

By 1358 the horrors of the plague and mercenary marauders had goaded the French peasantry into open revolt. The Jacquerie—as the rebellious peasants were called—lacked coherent goals and effective leaders, but they managed for a time to terrorize rural France. On one occasion, they are reported to have forced an aristocratic wife to eat her roasted husband, after which they raped and murdered her. But within a few months the aristocracy and urban élites succeeded in crushing the Jacquerie with a savagery worthy of the rebels themselves. The peasants' rebellion of 1358 evoked a widespread longing for law and order and a return to the ways of old. This conservative backlash resulted in a surge of royalism that doomed Etienne Marcel's constitutional movement in Paris. Marcel himself was murdered in midsummer, 1358, and the dauphin Charles returned to the city in triumph.

The Great Ordinance of 1357 became a dead letter after Marcel's fall, and not until 1789 did the Estates General again seriously threaten royal authority. In the centuries between, this representative body met less and less frequently. The dauphin Charles, who became the able King Charles V (1364–1380), instituted new tax measures which largely freed the monarchy from its financial dependence on assemblies and made it, potentially, the richest in Europe. The Estates General, unlike the English Parliament, failed to become an integral part of the government, and French kings reverted more and more to their high-medieval practice of dealing with their subjects through local assemblies. There were "Parlements" in France—outgrowths of the central and regional courts—but their functions remained strictly judicial; they did not deliberate on the granting of taxes, and they did not legislate. French national cohesion continued to lag behind that of England and, in the absence of an articulate national parliament, the only voice that could claim to speak for the French people was the voice of their king.

Charles V succeeded in turning the tide of war by avoiding pitched battles. His armies harassed the English unceasingly and forced them, little by little, to draw back. By Charles' death the French monarchy was recovering, and the English, reduced to small outposts around Bordeaux and Calais, virtually abandoned the war for a generation. But Charles V was succeeded by the incompetent Charles VI (1380–1422)—"Charles the Mad"—who grew from a weak child into an insane adult. His reign was marked by a bloody rivalry between the houses of Burgundy and Orleans, each controlling a strong group of fiefs. The duke of Orleans was Charles the Mad's brother; the duke of Burgundy was his uncle. In Capetian times, such powerful fief-holding members of the royal family had usually cooperated with the king, but now, with a madman on the throne, Burgundy and Orleans struggled grimly for control of the kingdom. In the course of the fifteenth century, the Orleanist faction became identified with the cause of the Valois monarchy, and Burgundy evolved into a powerful independent state between France and Germany. But at the time of Charles the Mad, all was uncertain. With France ravaged once again by murder and civil strife, King Henry V of England resumed the Hundred Years' War and, in 1415, won his overwhelming victory at Agincourt. At this, the Burgundians joined with the English, and Charles the Mad was forced to make Henry V his heir. Both kings died in 1422, and while Charles the Mad's son, Charles VII (1422–1461), carried on a half-hearted resistance, the Burgundians and English divided northern France between them and prepared to crush the remaining power of the Valois monarchy.

At the nadir of his fortunes, Charles VII, as yet uncrowned, accepted in desperation the military services of the peasant visionary, Joan of Arc. Joan's victory at Orleans, her insistence on Charles' coronation at Reims, and her capture and death on the stake in 1431 are well known. The spirit that she kindled raised French hopes,

CHRONOLOGY OF LATE-MEDIEVAL ENGLAND AND FRANCE

England		*France*	
1307–1327:	Reign of Edward II	1328–1589:	Valois Dynasty
1327–1377:	Reign of Edward III	1328–1350:	Reign of Philip V
1337–1453:	Hundred Years' War	1337–1453:	Hundred Years' War
1346:	Battle of Crécy	1346:	Battle of Crécy
1348–1349:	Black Death	1348–1349:	Black Death
		1350–1364:	Reign of John the Good
1356:	Battle of Poitiers	1356:	Battle of Poitiers
		1357:	The Great Ordinance
		1358:	Jacquerie Rebellion
1377–1399:	Reign of Richard II	1364–1380:	Reign of Charles V
1381:	Peasants' Revolt	1380–1422:	Reign of Charles the Mad
1413–1422:	Reign of Henry V		
1415:	Battle of Agincourt	1415:	Battle of Agincourt
		1422–1461:	Reign of Charles VII
		1429–1431:	Career of Joan of Arc
1455–1485:	Wars of the Roses		
1461–1483:	Reign of Edward IV	1461–1483:	Reign of Louis XI
1485–1509:	Reign of Henry VII. Beginning of Tudor Dynasty		

and in the two decades following her death Charles VII's armies went from victory to victory. The conquest of France had always been beyond English resources, and English successes in the Hundred Years' War were largely a product of wretched French leadership and paralyzing internal division. Now, as the war drew at last to a successful close, Charles VII could devote himself to the rebuilding of the royal government. He was supported in this task by secure tax revenues and a standing army, and by subjects who had had their fill of armed combat and civil turbulence.

Like the English, the French in the later fifteenth century longed for strong monarchy and effective government. And Charles VII and his Valois successors, like the Tudors, were prepared to govern firmly. By 1500 the French monarchy was ruling through a centralized administration of middle-class professional bureaucrats. The nobility was pampered but tamed, the towns were flourishing, and French armies, no longer forced to fight for survival, were carrying the dynastic claims of the Valois kings into foreign lands.

THE IBERIAN KINGDOMS

The course of Spanish history in the Late Middle Ages runs parallel to that of England and France, with generations of internal turmoil giving way in the later fifteenth century to political coherence and royal consolidation. As the high-medieval *Reconquista* rolled to a stop around 1270, the Iberian Peninsula contained two strong Christian kingdoms—Castile and Aragon—the weaker Christian kingdom of Portugal along the western coast, and Moslem Granada in the extreme south. Of the two major kingdoms, Castile was the larger but Aragon was the more urbanized and imperialistic. During the thirteenth and fourteenth centuries, Aragonese kings conquered the Mediterranean islands of Majorca, Minorca, Sardinia, and Sicily, and Aragonese merchants began to play a significant role in international commerce.

Aragon and Castile were both plagued by civil turbulence during the Late Middle Ages. The Aragonese monarchy strove with only limited success to placate the nobility and townsmen by granting significant concessions to the Cortes—the regional representative assemblies. A prolonged revolt by the mercantile class in the Aragonese province of Catalonia was put down in 1472 only with the greatest difficulty. Castile, in the meantime, was torn by constant aristocratic uprisings and disputed royal successions. Peace and strong government came at last with the marriage of Ferdinand of Aragon and Isabella of Castile in 1469. Isabella inherited her throne in 1474; Ferdinand inherited his in 1479; and thereafter, despite the continuation of regional cortes, tribunals, and customs, an efficient central administration governed the two realms and welded them into a single Kingdom of Spain.

In 1492 the new kingdom completed the long-delayed *Reconquista* by conquering Islamic Granada. Working tirelessly to enforce obedience, unity, and orthodoxy, the Spanish monarchy presented its Moslem and Jewish subjects with the choice of conversion or banishment, and the consequent Jewish exodus drained the kingdom of valuable mercantile and intellectual talent. The Catholic Inquisition became a tool of the state and, as an instrument of both political and doctrinal conformity, it brought the crown not only religious unity but lucrative revenues as well. The nobility was persuaded that its best interests lay in supporting the monarchy rather than opposing it, and regional separatism was curbed. With unity established, and with the immense wealth of the New World soon to be pouring in, Spain in 1500 was entering a period of rich cultural expression and international power.

The wealth of Spain and Portugal in the sixteenth century resulted from their strategic location at the extreme west of Europe, facing the Atlantic. Important advances in shipbuilding and navigation opened the way for long ocean voyages, and by 1500 European captains had traversed the Atlantic and Indian Oceans. The conquest of these seas brought Spain a New World empire and the wealth of the Incas and Aztecs. It brought Portugal a direct searoute to India and a vast commercial empire in the Far East. The first Atlantic explorations, however, were pioneered by Italian seamen who could draw on their experience in Mediterranean commerce. In the early fourteenth century, Venetian galley fleets were making yearly expeditions through the Straits of Gibraltar to England and Flanders, and Genoese merchants were trading with the Canary Islands. By the mid-fifteenth century the Canaries, Madeiras, Azores, and Cape Verde Islands had all passed into Spanish or Portugese hands, but the ships of the Iberian monarchies continued to depend often on the skill of Italian captains and crews.

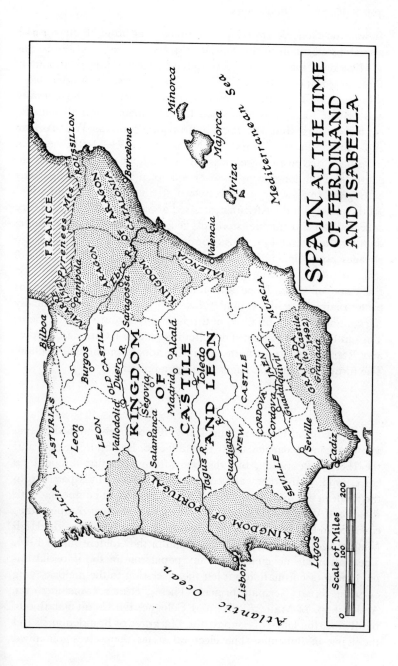

SPAIN AT THE TIME OF FERDINAND AND ISABELLA

Scale of Miles
0   100   200

It was the Genoese captain, Columbus, who brought the Spanish monarchy its claim to the New World.

Missionary zeal, curiosity, and greed were the mixed motives of these explorations. In the long run, greed was the primary consideration of both the sponsoring monarchies and the captains and private merchants who stood to make their fortunes from successful voyages. But the great patron of Portugese West-African exploration, Prince Henry the Navigator (1394–1460), seems to have been driven in large measure by the hope of Christian evangelism and the longing to discover unknown lands. From his court at Sagres, ships were sent westward to the Atlantic islands and southward down the African coast, and at Sagres itself Prince Henry collected an invaluable store of geographical and navigational data for the instruction of his captains. The Portugese West-African voyages continued intermittently after Prince Henry's death and reached their climax in 1497–1499 when Vasco da Gama rounded the Cape of Good Hope and reached India. The 6000 percent profit realized by da Gama's voyage demonstrated emphatically the commercial potentialities of this new, direct route to the Orient. The old trade routes were short-circuited, and the Ottoman Empire and Renaissance Italy both suffered gradual commercial decline. The future lay with the rising Atlantic monarchies.

GERMANY AND ITALY

Late-medieval Germany and Italy suffered from much the same sort of regional particularism that afflicted England, France, and the Iberian Peninsula, but the late fifteenth century brought no corresponding trend toward centralization. Both lands passed into the modern era divided internally and incapable of competing with the great Western monarchies. The weak elective Empire that emerged in Germany from the papal-imperial struggles of the High Middle Ages was given formal sanction in the Golden Bull of 1356. The Bull made no mention of any papal role in the imperial appointment or coronation but left the succession to the majority vote of seven great German princes. These "electors" included the Archbishops of Mainz, Trier, and Cologne, the Count Palatine of the Rhine, the Duke of Saxony, the Margrave of Brandenburg, and the King of Bohemia. The electoral states themselves remained

ITALY
C.1490

SWISS CONFEDERATION

SAVOY
Turin
Milan
MILAN
Genoa
GENOA

Tyrol
Trent
Verona
Padua
MANTUA
MODENA
FERRARA
Bologna
Lucca
Pisa
Florence
FLORENCE
Siena
SIENA
Umbria
PAPAL
STATES
Rome

Carinthia

Carniola

Venice
VENETIAN REPUBLIC

Dalmatia

Urbino
The Marches

Adriatic
Sea

Naples

KINGDOM

Otranto

OF THE

Palermo

TWO SICILIES

Scale of Miles
0   100   200

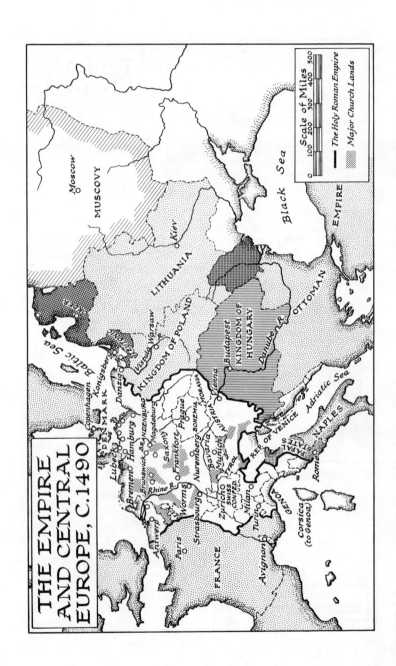

THE EMPIRE AND CENTRAL EUROPE, C.1490

Scale of Miles
0 100 200 300 400 500

—— The Holy Roman Empire
▨ Major Church Lands

Moscow
MUSCOVY

Black Sea

Kiev

LITHUANIA

Baltic Sea

Copenhagen
DENMARK
Königsberg
Danzig
Warsaw
Vistula
KINGDOM OF POLAND

OTTOMAN

Budapest
KINGDOM OF
HUNGARY
Danube R.

EMPIRE

Lübeck
Bremen
Hamburg
Brunswick
Magdeburg
Saxony
BRANDENBURG
Frankfort
Prague
BOHEMIA
MORAVIA
Nuremberg
Vienna
AUSTRIA
Bavaria
Munich
Tyrol
REP. OF VENICE
Adriatic Sea

Antwerp
Paris
Strasbourg
Worms
Rhine R.
Zurich
SWISS CONFED.
Milan
Turin
GENOA
NAPLES
PAPAL STATES
Rome

FRANCE

Avignon

Corsica
(to Genoa)

314

relatively stable, as did other large German principalities such as the Hapsburg duchy of Austria, but the Empire itself became power-less. Germany in 1500 was a Chinese puzzle of over 100 principali-ties—fiefs, ecclesiastical city-states, free cities, counties, and duchies —their boundaries shifting constantly through war, marriage, and inheritance. Imperial authority in Italian politics was as dead as papal authority in imperial elections. Germany and Italy were disengaged at last, but both suffered the prolonged consequences of their former entanglement.

The political crazy-quilt of late-medieval Italy evolved during the fifteenth century, through the domination of small states by larger ones, into a delicate power balance between five strong politi-cal units: the Kingdom of Naples, the Papal States, and the three northern city-states of Florence, Milan, and Venice. Naples was ruled by French or Aragonese dynasties. The Papal States were under tenuous papal control, compromised by the particularism of local aristocrats and the political turbulence of Rome itself. Milan, and later Florence, ceased to be republics and fell under the rule of self-made despots. And Venice remained a republic domi-nated by a narrow commercial oligarchy.

The despots, ruling without the sanction of royal anointment or legitimate succession, governed by their wits and by the realities of power, uninhibited by traditions or customs. They have often been regarded as symbols of the "new Renaissance man," but in fact their ruthlessness and opportunism were qualities well known to the northern monarchs, and their behavior would have sur-prised neither Frederick II nor Philip the Fair. Yet the very inse-curity of their positions, and the fragile equilibrium of the five major Italian powers, gave rise to a considerable refinement of traditional diplomatic practices. Ambassadors—skilled at compli-ments and espionage—were exchanged on a regular basis, and out of the tendency of two or three weaker states to combine against a stronger one came the policy of shifting alliances known as the "balance of power" principle. The balance of power had been practiced by rulers over the previous 5000 years, but the states of Renaissance Italy brought it to a point of perfection.

The Italian power balance was upset in 1494 when a powerful French army invaded the peninsula. For generations thereafter, Italy was a battleground for French-Spanish rivalries, and the techniques and concepts of Italian Renaissance diplomacy passed across the Alps to affect the relations of the northern kingdoms. The modern tendency to ignore moral limitations and ecclesiastical mediation—to base diplomacy on a calculated balance of force—was growing throughout late-medieval Europe, but it reached fruition first in Renaissance Italy.

EASTERN EUROPE

Eastern Europe was, in general, no more successful than Germany and Italy in achieving political cohesion. Scandinavia, Poland, Lithuania, and Hungary were all afflicted by aristocratic turbulence and dynastic quarrels. The Teutonic Knights were humbled by Slavic armies and internal rebellions, and most of the Balkan Peninsula was overwhelmed by the Ottoman Turks. Only the Russians and Ottomans were able to build strong centralized regimes, and both, by 1500, were uncompromisingly autocratic.

Poland had become a Catholic-Christian kingdom around A.D. 1000, but throughout the High Middle Ages it had been paralyzed by aristocratic factions and disputed successions. In 1386 it united temporarily with rapidly expanding Lithuania, and the Polish-Lithuanian state became the largest political unit in Europe. It was also, very possibly, the worst governed. Under the Lithuanian warrior-prince Jagiello (1377–1434), who converted from heathenism to Catholicism when he accepted the Polish crown, the dual state humbled the Teutonic Knights at the decisive battle of Tannenberg (1410). But even under Jagiello, Poland-Lithuania had no real central government, and her nobles would cooperate with their ruler only against the hated Germans—and even then, only momentarily. Stretching all the way from the Black Sea to the Baltic, incorporating many of the former lands of the Teutonic Order and most of the old state of Kievan Russia, Poland-Lithuania lacked the skilled administrators and political institutions necessary to govern her vast territories. Her nobles were virtually all-powerful, and her peasantry was slipping toward serfdom. Her hopeless political impotence guaranteed that no strong state would emerge between Germany and Russia during Europe's early modern centuries.

Russia had acquired its religion from Constantinople rather than from the West, and Byzantine Civilization was a determining factor in the development of Russian culture. This development was set back for a time by the Mongols, who had swept westward out of Asia between 1237 and 1242, crossing Russia and penetrating momentarily into the heart of Central Europe. The Mongols had quickly withdrawn from most of Europe, but they remained in Russia for about 240 years, allowing local autonomy to the Russian Christian princes but ruthlessly enforcing the collection of tribute.

During the centuries of Mongol domination, the Muscovite principality managed not only to survive but to expand and flourish. The Grand Princes of Moscow extended their influence in northern Russia by collaborating with their Mongol lords and winning the support of the Church. They were appointed sole collectors of the Mongol tribute, and on occasion they helped the Mongols crush the rebellions of other Russian princes. Moscow became the headquarters of Russian Orthodox Christianity, and when Constantinople fell in 1453, Moscow, the "Third Rome," claimed spiritual sovereignty over the Orthodox Slavic world. At first, the Muscovite princes spread their ascendency with the full backing of the Mongols, but toward the end of the fourteenth century Moscow began taking the lead in anti-Mongol resistance. At last, in 1480, Ivan III the Great, Grand Prince of Moscow and Czar of the Russians, repudiated Mongol authority altogether and abolished the tribute.

The Muscovite princes enjoyed a certain popular support in their struggle against the Mongols and their battles against the Roman Catholic Lithuanians, but their political philosophy was autocratic to a degree worthy of Byzantium itself. The beginnings of republicanism in city-states such as Novgorod were crushed with the expansion of Muscovite authority. The Grand Princes built a powerful, consolidated state inspired by Constantinople, without local or national assemblies and without an articulate middle class. Russia was to be a great power in modern Europe, but the process of westernization was slow in starting and imperfectly achieved.

THE OTTOMAN EMPIRE

The great outside threat to Eastern Europe came from the southeast where the Ottoman Turks pressed into the Balkans from Asia Minor. These Altaic tribesmen, driven from their Central Asian homeland by the Mongols, came into Asia Minor first as mercenaries, then as conquerors. Adopting the Islamic faith, the Ottomans subjected the greater part of Asia Minor to their rule, and in 1354, bypassing the diminutive Byzantine Empire, they invaded Europe. During the latter half of the fourteenth century, they crushed Serbia and Bulgaria and extended their dominion over most of the Balkan Peninsula.

By 1400 Constantinople was surrounded and apparently doomed, but ageless Byzantium was given another half century by virtue of an unexpected onslaught of Central-Asian invaders under the conqueror Tamerlane. Sweeping into Asia Minor, Tamerlane won a tremendous victory over the Ottomans in 1402 at the battle of Ankara. Immediately thereafter, he turned eastward toward China, and upon his death in 1405, his loose-knit empire collapsed. The Ottomans, however, required some time to recover from the blow. At length they returned to their Balkan aggressions, and at the decisive battle of Varna in 1444 they decimated an anti-Turkish crusading army and consolidated their hold on southeastern Europe. After the great Ottoman victory at Varna, the storming of Constantinople in 1453 was little more than a postscript. Yet all Europe recognized that the Sultan Mohammed II, in conquering the unconquerable city, had ended an era.

The Ottoman Empire endured until the twentieth century; as the Republic of Turkey it endures still. Like the Muscovite princes, the Ottoman sultans were autocrats. Slaves served in their administration and fought in their armies alongside mounted noblemen of the Ottoman landed aristocracy. And while the sultans were living in splendor on the Golden Horn, their repressive government was smothering Balkan culture and insulating southeastern Europe from the vital civilization of the West.

CHRONOLOGY OF LATE-MEDIEVAL EASTERN EUROPE

1237–1242:	Mongols invade Eastern Europe
1354:	Ottoman Turks invade Balkans
1377–1434:	Jagiello rules Lithuania
1386:	Union of Poland and Lithuania under Jagiello
1402:	Tamerlane defeats Ottomans at Ankara
1410:	Poland-Lithuania defeats Teutonic Knights at Tannenberg
1444:	Ottomans defeat Christians at Varna
1453:	Ottomans conquer Constantinople
1480:	Czar Ivan III the Great discontinues Mongol tribute

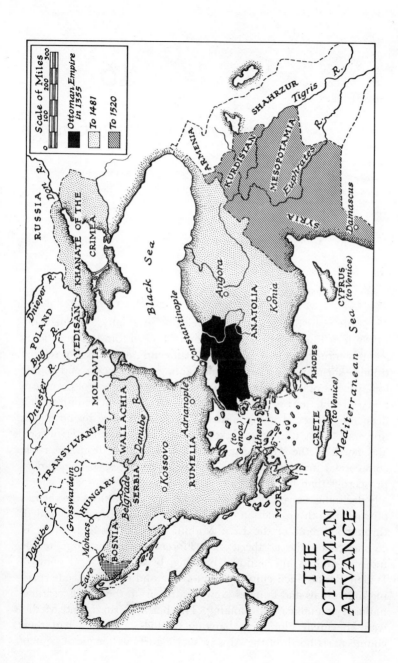

THE
OTTOMAN
ADVANCE

Scale of Miles
0 100 200 300
Ottoman Empire in 1355
To 1481
To 1520

RUSSIA
Don R.
Dnieper R.
Bug R.
POLAND
Dniester R.
YEDISAN
MOLDAVIA
KHANATE OF THE CRIMEA
Black Sea
Constantinople
Adrianople
RUMELIA
Kossovo
TRANSYLVANIA
Grosswardein
Danube R.
WALLACHIA
SERBIA
Belgrade
HUNGARY
Mohacs
BOSNIA
Save R.
Danube
MOREA
Athens
(to Genoa)
ANATOLIA
Angora
Konia
ARMENIA
SHAHRZUR
KURDISTAN
Tigris R.
MESOPOTAMIA
Euphrates R.
SYRIA
Damascus
CYPRUS (to Venice)
RHODES
CRETE (to Venice)
Mediterranean Sea

16

Economic and Cultural Change

TOWNS AND COMMERCE

The shift from boom to depression came gradually and unevenly to Western Europe in the years around 1300. From the early fourteenth century through much of the fifteenth, a number of related trends—shrinking population, contracting markets, an end to the long process of land reclamation, and a creeping mood of pessimism and retrenchment—resulted in a general economic slump and a deepening of social antagonisms. These trends were by no means universal. They were less marked in northern Italy than elsewhere, and north of the Alps certain localities, profiting from favorable commercial situations or technological advances, became more prosperous than before. At a time when English towns were generally declining, Coventry and a few others grew wealthy from the rise of woolen cloth production. The Flemish town of Bruges remained, throughout most of the Late Middle Ages, a bustling center of commerce on the northern seas. Florence, with its large textile industry and its international banking, became the focal point of Italian Renaissance culture. In Florence and elsewhere, enterprising individuals and families grew wealthy from the profits of international commerce and banking. The Bardi, Peruzzi, and Medici were the great Florentine banking families, and they had their counterparts north of the Alps in such figures as Jacques Coeur of

Bourges—financier of the fifteenth-century French monarchy—
and the Fuggers of Augsburg. But such great financiers as these
were exceedingly insecure in the turbulent years of the Late Middle
Ages. The Bardi and Peruzzi houses collapsed in the mid-fourteenth
century, and Jacques Coeur was ruined by his royal debtor, King
Charles VII. And even though some fortunes continued to grow, the
total assets of late-medieval bankers fell considerably below the
assets of their thirteenth-century predecessors. The success of families
such as the Medicis and Fuggers illustrates the late-medieval tendency toward an increasingly unequal distribution of wealth. The
other side of the picture is to be seen in intensified urban strife and
peasants' rebellions.

The late-medieval depression began well before the coming of
the Black Death (1348–1349). The fundamental trends of demo-
graphic and economic decline were not set off by the plague, but
they were enormously aggravated by it. Carried by fleas that in-
fested black rats, the bubonic plague entered Europe along the
trade routes from the East and spread with frightening speed. The
death toll cannot be determined with any precision. The best esti-
mate would probably be $\frac{1}{4}$ to $\frac{1}{3}$ of Europe's population. In many
crowded towns the mortality rate may well have exceeded 50 per-
cent, whereas isolated rural areas tended to be spared. Consequently, the most progressive, most enterprising, and best-trained
Europeans were hit the hardest. Few urban families can have been
spared altogether. Those who survived the terrible years 1348–1349
were subjected to periodic recurrences of the plague over the next
three centuries. Fourteenth-century medical science was at a loss to
explain the process of infection, and fourteenth-century urban
sanitation was so primitive as to only encourage its spread. Some
people fled their cities, some gave way to religious frenzy or stark
hedonism, and some remained faithfully at their posts, hoping for
divine protection against the pestilence. But none can have emerged
from the ordeal unaffected.

The towns of late-medieval Europe, confronted with shrinking
markets and decreasing opportunities, lost their earlier social mobility and buoyancy. Privileged classes closed their ranks and guarded
their monopolies, and heredity became the chief avenue to the status
of guild master. In their grim efforts to retain their share of declining markets, guilds struggled with one another, with the district

nobility, and with the increasingly desperate urban proletariat—its class consciousness growing as its upward mobility was choked off. Few towns of late-medieval Europe escaped being torn by class violence. Many of the Italian cities, as we have seen, evolved from oligarchic republics to despotisms. Florence, for example, ravaged by the Black Death, terrorized by a workers' rebellion in 1378, and impoverished by decades of inconclusive warfare, passed in 1434 from oligarchic rule to the rule of the Medicis. Over a century before, Milan had fallen under the control of the ambitious Visconti family which gave way in 1450 to still another dynasty of despots— the Sforzas. In general, the commercial and mercantile élites retained their privileged economic status in the face of lower-class pressure by sharing their political authority with great magnates or kings, or by abdicating it to despots. They usually were able, through political control or manipulation, to keep down wages in the face of the plague-induced labor shortage, and to smash the resulting lower-class uprisings.

THE LANDED NOBILITY AND PEASANTRY

The rural nobility of Western Europe, like the urban élite, managed to survive the turbulent socio-economic changes of the Late Middle Ages. Faced with a continued shift from a status-based society to an income-based society, the nobles were able—with some exceptions—to hold their extensive lands and preserve much of their wealth. They responded to the decline in grain prices by accelerating the high-medieval processes of leasing demesne lands to peasants and commuting customary peasant services to fixed money payments. In this way, aristocratic incomes were protected against deflation so long as peasants could manage the agreed payments. The peasantry continued to rise in legal status from land-bound serfs to free tenant farmers until, by 1500, serfdom had essentially disappeared from Western Europe. But the passing of serfdom was by no means accompanied by increased peasant prosperity. On the contrary, the declining population and the contracting grain market resulted in abandoned fields and a growing class of landless paupers. In some instances, rural noblemen retained direct control of their land and hired workers to farm it, or converted it from grain crops to the more profitable wool growing.

In general, then, the peasant passed from his earlier manorial status of rights and services to a new status based on cash, whether as a rent-paying tenant or as a landless wage-earner. And the nobleman dealt in receipts and expenditures instead of in the exploitation of customary services. These trends had begun in the High Middle Ages and were largely completed by 1500. At times of drastic population decline, such as in the decades following the Black Death, the resulting labor shortage tended to force up wages, and the nobility fought this tendency either through collective conspiracy or through legislation. In England, for example, the Statutes of Laborers of 1351 and thereafter were aimed at freezing wages in the wake of the plague. They succeeded only to a point, but they created among the peasantry a deep sense of grievance which contributed to the abortive English Peasants' Revolt of 1381. This confused and bloody uprising was merely one of a considerable number that terrorized late-medieval Europe. Like the Jacquerie rebellion in France, and like many similar peasant insurrections of the period, it bore witness to an unbalanced society in which classes struggled bitterly for their share of a declining wealth.

In Eastern Europe the peasant's lot was even worse than in the West, for the eastern nobility was reducing its peasantry to serfdom at the very time that western peasants were achieving legal freedom. The late-medieval landed nobility of both Eastern and Western Europe jealously guarded its privileges against peasantry and monarchy and, for a time, in both East and West, it seemed to be reversing the high-medieval trend toward stronger royal government. Eastern monarchies made no real progress against their nobles except in Russia, but by the later fifteenth century, western monarchies were beginning to curb the fractious independence of the landed aristocracy. The new Tudor monarchy in England tended to favor the mercantile class, but in Spain and France the nobility was rewarded for its political submissiveness by economic favoritism and privileged positions in the royal administration, the army, and the Church.

Thus, the western nobility was evolving from robber baron toward silk-clad courtier. Its traditional role of mounted knight in the feudal host was a thing of the past, for monarchs were now fighting with mercenaries, and foot soldiers were winning most of the major battles. Moreover, the increasing use of gunpowder

Chivalric Burgundian shield.

was making knightly armor redundant and knightly castles highly vulnerable. But while the feudal knight was vanishing from European armies, he was becoming ever more prominent in art, literature, and court ceremonial. The fifteenth century was an age of elaborate shining armor, fairy-tale castles, coats of arms, and extravagant tourneys. Knighthood, driven from the battlefield, took refuge in fantasy, and an age of ruthless political cynicism saw the full flowering of a romantic code of chivalric ethics. Behind this fanciful façade, the landed aristocracy retained as before its privileged position atop the social order.

ECONOMIC RECOVERY

The consolidation of royal authority in late fifteenth-century Western Europe coincided with a general economic upsurge following a long age of depression. Europe's population in 1500 may well have been lower than in 1300, but it was climbing again. Commerce was quickening and towns were growing. Technological progress

324

had never ceased, and now water-driven fulling mills were increasing wool production while water-driven pumps were draining mines. With advances in mining technology, Europe was increasing her supply not only of silver but of the various metals essential to her rising industries: iron, copper, alum, and tin. The development of artillery and movable-type printing depended not merely on the inventive idea but also on long generations of progress in the metallurgical arts. And advances in ship design and navigation lay behind the Atlantic voyages that would soon bring a torrent of wealth into Western Europe. By 1500 the long economic crisis had passed. Europe had entered upon an era of economic growth and world expansion that would far outstrip her earlier surge in the High Middle Ages.

GROWTH AND DECAY

Printing and gunpowder were the two most spectacular technological novelties of the Late Middle Ages. Gunpowder came first, and by the fifteenth century it was being used with some effect in the Hundred Years' War, the Turkish conquests and, indeed, most of the military engagements of Europe. Printing from movable type was developed midway through the fifteenth century, and although its effect on European culture was immense, the full impact was not felt until after 1500. Even among the "new men" of the Italian Renaissance, printed books were regarded as vulgar imitations of handwritten originals. This fact should warn us against viewing late-medieval Europe—and even Renaissance Italy—exclusively in terms of new beginnings. There was, to be sure, a strong sense of the new and "modern" among many creative Europeans of the period, but there was also a perpetuation of medieval ways, styles, and habits of thought. Often one encounters a sense of loss over the fading of medieval ideals and institutions—a conviction that civilization was declining. The Renaissance humanist Aeneas Sylvius—later Pope Pius II (d. 1464)—could look at the Turkish threat and the strife among Christian states and conclude that there was nothing good in prospect. The generation living after 1500, aware of the voyages of exploration and of the growing prosperity and political consolidation, might well be hopeful of the future, but between 1300 and 1500 a gloom hung over much of

Europe. The rise of modern civilization was less apparent than the decay of the Middle Ages.

Beneath the gloom, we find a sense of nervous unrest, a violent emotionalism and hyper-romanticism that gives dramatic intensity to late-medieval works of art but robs them of the balanced serenity characteristic of the best thirteenth-century creations. Society was unravelling and, in an era of depression, plague, and disorder, the high-medieval synthesis could no longer hold together. Unity was giving way to diversity.

The breakdown of hierarchy and order expressed itself in a hundred ways—in the intensifying conflict between class and class, in the architectural shift from organic unity to flamboyant decoration, in the schism between knightly function and chivalric fantasy, in the evolution from Christian Commonwealth to territorial states, and in the disintegration of the Thomist fusion of faith and reason. The high-medieval dream of a city of God on earth achieved its highest intellectual embodiment in Aquinas' hierarchical ordering and reconciliation of matter and spirit, body and soul, logic and revelation. And the fading of that dream is nowhere more evident than in the attacks of fourteenth-century philosophers on the Thomist system.

LATE-MEDIEVAL THOUGHT

St. Thomas' *Summa Theologica*, like the cathedral of Chartres, is a superb unification of religious aspiration and logical order, based on the conception of an omnipotent God who is both loving and rational. The fourteenth-century attack on this reconciliation was founded on two related propositions: (1) To ascribe rationality to God is to limit his omnipotence by the finite rules of human logic. Thus, the Thomist God of reason gave way to a God of will, and the high-medieval notion of a logical divine order was eroded. (2) Human reason, therefore, can tell us nothing of God; logic and Christian belief inhabit two separate, sealed worlds.

The first steps toward this concept of a willful, incomprehensible God were taken by the Oxford Franciscan, Duns Scotus (d. 1308), who produced a detailed critique of St. Thomas' theory of knowledge. Duns Scotus did not reject the possibility of elucidating revealed truth through reason, but he was more cautious in his use of logic than Aquinas had been. Whereas St. Thomas is called "The Angelic Doctor," Duns Scotus is called "The Subtle Doctor," and the extreme complexity of his thought prompted men in subsequent generations to describe anyone who bothered to follow Duns' arguments as a "dunce." The sobriquet is unfair, for Duns Scotus is an important and original figure in the development of late scholasticism. Yet we are tempted to draw a parallel between the intricacies of his intellectual system and the decorative elaborations of late-Gothic Churches. A Christian rationalist of the most subtle kind, he nevertheless made the first move toward dismantling the Thomist synthesis and withdrawing reason from the realm of theology.

Another Oxford Franciscan, William of Ockham (d. 1349), attacked the Thomist synthesis on all fronts. Ockham argued that God and Christian doctrine, utterly undemonstrable, must be accepted on faith alone, and that human reason must be limited to the realm of observable phenomena. In this unpredictable world of an unpredictable Creator, one can reason only about things that one can see or directly experience. Ockham's radical empiricism ruled out all metaphysical speculations—all rational arguments from an observable diversity of things to an underlying unity of things. And out of this great divorce between reason and faith came two characteristic expressions of late-medieval thought: the scientific manipulation of material facts, and pietistic mysticism unsullied by logic. In Ockham and many of his followers, we find empiricism and mysticism side by side. For since the two worlds never touched, they were in no way contradictory. An intelligent Christian could keep one foot in each of them.

The Ockhamist philosophy served as an appropriate foundation for both late-medieval mysticism and late-medieval science. Some mystics, indeed, regarded themselves as empiricists. For the empiricist is a person who accepts only those things that he experiences, and the mystic, abandoning the effort to *understand* God, strove to *experience* him. Science, on the other hand, was now freed of its theological underpinnings and could proceed on its own. Nicholas Oresme, teaching in the fourteenth-century University of Paris, attacked the Aristotelian theory of motion and proposed that the apparent daily rotation of the celestial sphere might be explained by assuming the daily rotation of the earth. Oresme's theories probably owed more to thirteenth-century scientists such as Robert

Grosseteste than to Ockham, but his willingness to tinker with the traditional physical structure of God's universe is characteristic of an age in which scientific speculation was being severed from revealed truth.

Many late-medieval philosophers rejected Ockham's criticism and remained Thomists, but owing to the very comprehensiveness of Aquinas' achievement, his successors were reduced to detailed elaboration or minor repair work. Between the tedious niggling of late Thomism and the drastic limitations imposed by Ockham on the scope of philosophical inquiry, many of Europe's finest minds shunned philosophy altogether for the more exciting fields of science, mathematics, and classical learning. When the philosopher John Gerson (d. 1429), chancellor of the University of Paris, spoke out in his lectures against "vain curiosity in the matter of faith," the collapse of the faith-reason synthesis was all but complete.

The fifteenth century witnessed a revival of Platonism and Neoplatonism, in Renaissance Italy and in the north as well. The two leading philosophers of the Italian Renaissance, Marsilio Ficino (d. 1499) and Pico della Mirandola (d. 1494), were both Platonists. They were able to draw from an extensive body of Plato's writings which had been unknown to the high-medieval West, yet neither Ficino nor Pico was a first-echelon figure in the history of Western thought. Neither possessed the acumen of the best high-medieval philosophers, and neither approached the profundity of their great contemporary north of the Alps, Nicholas of Cusa (d. 1464).

Educated by the mystical Brethren of the Common Life, Nicholas of Cusa became first a conciliarist and later an ardent papist. He agreed, up to a point, with Ockham's view that human reason is limited to the disconnected phenomena of the physical universe. But he insisted that the contradictions and diversity of the material world were reconciled and unified in an unknowable God. Nicholas of Cusa regarded God as beyond rational apprehension and approachable only through a mystical process which he termed "learned ignorance." Like Aquinas, he believed in an underlying universal order, but like Ockham he denied that any such order could be grasped by human reason. Yet his concept of an unknowable God was derived from a tradition far older than Ockhamism. It was rooted in the late-Roman Neoplatonism of the pagan Plotinus and his Christian followers—a tradition that had run as an underground

current through the entire Middle Ages. Like the older Neoplatonists, Nicholas of Cusa conceived of the universe as a ceaseless creative
unfolding of the infinite God. But going far beyond his Neoplatonic
predecessors, he reasoned that a universe emanating from an infinite
deity cannot be limited by human concepts of space and time. In
short, God's created universe was, potentially, infinite. And since a
universe without bounds is a universe without a physical center,
Nicholas of Cusa concluded that neither the earth nor the sun occupied any special position in it. The earth was not at the center, nor
was it stationary, for in an infinite universe position and motion are
entirely relative. God was at the center, Christ was at the center, but
only in the sense of metaphysical priority, not in the sense of physical
location.

In his emphasis on mysticism and the limitation of human reason,
Nicholas of Cusa was in tune with his age. In his synthetic vision of
an ordered cosmos, he echoed the thirteenth century. And in his
bold conception of a non-geocentric infinite universe, he anticipated
modern philosophy and astronomy. Bruno, Spinoza, Leibniz,
Newton, even Einstein, were indebted, directly or indirectly, to the
last great philosopher of the Middle Ages.

ARTS AND LETTERS

The change from high-medieval synthesis to late-medieval
diversity is clearly evident in the field of art. The high-Gothic
balance between upward aspiration and harmonic proportion—
between the vertical and the horizontal—was shifting in the cathedrals of the later thirteenth century toward an ever-greater emphasis
on verticality. Formerly, elaborate capitals and horizontal stringcourses had balanced the soaring piers and pointed arches of the
Gothic cathedrals, creating a sense of tense equilibrium between
heaven and earth. But during the Late Middle Ages, capitals disappeared and stringcourses became discontinuous, leaving little
to relieve the dramatic upward thrust from floor to vaulting. Late-
medieval churches achieved a fluid, uncompromising verticality—
a sense of heavenly aspiration that bordered on the mystical.

By about the mid-thirteenth century, the basic structural potentialities of the Gothic style had been fully exploited. Windows were
as large as they could possibly be, vaultings could be raised no

Nave of Amiens Cathedral, begun 1220, showing the capitals and decorated stringcourse.

Choir of Saint-Étienne at Beauvais, 1506-c. 1550, showing the
absence of capitals, inconspicuous and interrupted stringcourse,
and elaborate vaulting.

Tomb of Margaret of Austria with the choir stalls in the background in the church at Brou, 1516–1532.

An example of fan vaulting from "The New Building," Peterborough Cathedral, England.

High Gothic sculpture: *Le
beau dieu*, west portral of
Amiens Cathedral.

Three Mourners from the tomb of Philip the Bold of Burgundy, by
Claus Sluter and Claus de Werve.

333

The Madonna of the Chancellor Rolin, by Jan van Eyck.

higher without structural disaster, and flying buttresses were used with maximum efficiency. The fundamental Gothic idea of a skeletal stone framework with walls of colored glass had been embodied in cathedrals of incomparable nobility and beauty. During the Late Middle Ages, cathedrals changed in appearance as tastes changed, but the originality of post-thirteenth-century Gothic architects was inhibited by their devotion to a style that had already achieved complete structural development. Accordingly, the evolution of late-Gothic architecture consisted chiefly in new and more elaborate decoration, with the result that many late-medieval churches are, to some modern tastes, overdecorated sculptural jungles. Unrestrained verticality and unrestrained decorative elaboration were

334

Sistine Madonna, by Raphael.

the architectural hallmarks of the age, and both reflected a decline of rational unity and balance. Like Ockham's universe, the fourteenth- and fifteenth-century church became a fascinating miscellany of separate elements. Thus, the "flamboyant Gothic" style emerged in late-medieval France, while English churches were evolving from the "decorated Gothic" of the fourteenth century to the "perpendic-

335

The Golden Virgin, from the south portal of Amiens Cathedral.

David, by Michelangelo.

Venus, by Titian.

Interior of S. Andrea at Matua, by Alberti.

ular Gothic" of the fifteenth and sixteenth centuries, with its lacelike
fan vaulting, its sculptural profusion, and its sweeping vertical lines.
In the course of the sixteenth century, Gothic architecture, having
reached its decorative as well as its structural limits, gave way
throughout Northern Europe to the classical Greco-Roman style
which had been revived and developed in fifteenth-century Italy
and flowed north with the spread of Renaissance humanism.

Sculpture and painting, like architecture and thought, evolved
during the Late Middle Ages toward multiformity. The serene,
idealized humanism of thirteenth-century sculpture gave way to
heightened emotionalism and an emphasis on individual peculiar-
ities. Painting north of the Alps reached its apogee in the mirrorlike
realism of the Flemish school. Painters such as Jan van Eyck (d.
1440), pioneering in the use of oil paints, excelled in reproducing
the natural world with a devotion to detail that was all but photo-
graphic. Critics of the style have observed that detail seems to compromise the unity of the total composition, but in a world viewed
through Ockham's eyes, such is to be expected. It was Italy, again,

The Madonna of the Rocks, by Leonardo da Vinci.

that developed a new style of painting and sculpture, based on the classical canon of realism subordinated to a unifying idea. And the Italian Renaissance style of painting, like Renaissance architecture, streamed northward in the sixteenth century to bring a new vision to transalpine artists.

The decay of high-medieval forms of expression is vividly demonstrated in the late-medieval romance, which had once served as a vital literary form but now became sentimentalized, formalized, and drained of inspiration. Much of the popular literature of late-medieval Europe is beyond redemption, and writers could achieve vitality only by turning from warmed-over chivalry to graphic realism. Geoffrey Chaucer (d. 1400), in his *Canterbury Tales*, combines rare psychological insight with a descriptive skill worthy of the Flemish painters or the late-Gothic stone carvers. And François Villon (d. 1463), a brawling Parisian vagabond, expressed in his poems an anguished, sometimes brutal realism that captures the late-medieval mood of insecurity and disorientation.

ITALIAN RENAISSANCE CLASSICISM

These northern moods and movements stood in sharp contrast to the growing, self-confident classicism of Renaissance Italy. Here the late-medieval economic depression was less severe and less prolonged, and although endemic interurban warfare made conditions just as insecure as in the North, the civic spirit of the independent north-Italian communes encouraged innovation and novel forms of expression. Italy had never been entirely at ease with Gothic architecture, and the triumphs of high-medieval culture were more characteristically French than Italian. England and France had enjoyed relative peace during much of the thirteenth century, whereas Italy had been battered by papal-imperial wars. Italy, in short, harbored no fond memories of the High Middle Ages, and the coming of the Renaissance was not so much the advent of a new epoch in European history as a reassertion of Italian culture over French. By the time Renaissance ideas were significantly affecting transalpine Europe, Renaissance Italy was already in sharp decline.

In an age of French arms and French culture, such as the thirteenth century had been, Italians could return in memory to the days when Rome ruled the world. Roman monuments and Roman sculpture were all around them, and when, in the fourteenth and fifteenth centuries, they abandoned the Gothic style and the intellectual habits of Paris theologians, it was to their indigenous classical heritage that they turned for inspiration. In sculpture, the calm spiritual nobility of stone saints gave way to a classical emphasis on the human body. The slender young Virgins of the High Middle Ages suddenly turned voluptuous. Architects, abandoning the Gothic spire and pointed arch, created buildings with domes and round arches and elegant classical façades. Scholars abandoned Aristotle and St. Thomas for the delights of Greco-Roman belles lettres. And painters, with few actual classical models to follow, pioneered in techniques of linear and atmospheric perspective and imposed a classical unity upon their lifelike figures and landscapes.

The Italian Renaissance, while rebelling against the Middle Ages, retained much that was medieval. In 1492, while a worldly Borgia was acceding to the papacy and Columbus was discovering America, high-Renaissance Florence was passing under the influence of the austere Christian revivalist, Savonarola. Renaissance humanism was always an élitist phenomenon, restricted to urban nobilities and favored artists and leaving the Italian masses unchanged. Yet for all that, the Renaissance style represents a profound shift from the forms and assumptions of the Middle Ages. St. Thomas and his contemporaries had studied the Greek philosophers, but men of the Renaissance looked back on classical antiquity with a fresh perspective, seeing not a collection of ideas that might be used but a total culture that deserved to be revered and revived. It was this vision that underlay the new art and the new classical learning of early modern Europe.

THE GENESIS OF MODERN EUROPE

Historians of the past have probably overemphasized the impact of the Renaissance on the development of modern civilization. The Renaissance contributed much to art and classical studies, and to habits of intellectual precision which had been cultivated by Italian literary scholars. It contributed to the evolution of diplomatic techniques, but scarcely at all to constitutional development. Renaissance humanists were essentially scholars of the "humanities" and were no more interested in science than, say, a modern professor of

English literature or Latin. Modern science grew out of the medieval universities, and modern legislatures—even if they meet in domed, round-arched buildings—are outgrowths of medieval representative assemblies.

In the Europe of 1500, Italian Renaissance ideas were beginning to move across the Alps. But the promise of the future did not depend on the Renaissance alone. All across Europe commerce was thriving again and the population was growing. New non-Renaissance inventions—gunpowder, the three-masted caravel, the windmill, the water pump, and the printing press—were changing the ways men lived. The papacy had degenerated into a local principality, but England, France, and Spain had achieved stable, centralized governments and were on the road toward nationhood. European ships had reached America and India, and the first cargo direct from the Orient had arrived in Portugal. The late-medieval gloom was lifting and the world lay open to European enterprise.

Suggested Readings

The asterisk indicates a paperback edition.

GENERAL WORKS ON THE LATE MIDDLE AGES

Wallace K. Ferguson, *Europe in Transition, 1300–1520* (Houghton Mifflin). An excellent recent textbook; the best one-volume general account.

The two relevant volumes in the thorough and well-written Langer series in Modern European history are:
Edward P. Cheney, *The Dawn of a New Era, 1250–1453* (*Harper).
Myron P. Gilmore, *The World of Humanism, 1453–1517* (*Harper). Both these volumes have good bibliographies.

CHRISTIANITY AND THE CHURCH

G. Mollat, *The Popes at Avignon, 1305–1378* (*Harper). An older account written originally in French, treating the Avignon papacy thoroughly and skillfully.

Brian Tierney, *Foundations of the Conciliar Theory* (Cambridge). An excellent modern work by a gifted American historian of the medieval Church.

J. M. Clark, *The Great German Mystics* (Oxford). A perceptive study of Meister Eckhart and two of his followers, John Tauler and Henry Suso.

A. S. Atiya, *The Crusade in the Later Middle Ages* (Methuen). An account of late-medieval crusaders and crusading propaganda.

THE LATE-MEDIEVAL STATES

Several books noted in previous bibliographies cover this era as well as earlier ones. These books include Ostrogorsky, *History of the Byzantine State;* Hitti, *History of the Arabs;* Barraclough, *Origins of Modern Germany;* Hollister, *Making of England;* and Cantor, *Medieval History.*

The appropriate volumes in the Oxford History of England are:
May McKisack, *The Fourteenth Century.*
E. F. Jacob, *The Fifteenth Century.*

E. Perroy, *The Hundred Years' War* (*Capricorn). A comprehensive account, particularly illuminating on the history of late-medieval France.

342

J. H. Mariejol, *The Spain of Ferdinand and Isabella* (Rutgers University Press). Written originally in French in the nineteenth century, this valuable work has been edited and updated by B. Keen.

Gene A. Brucker, *Florentine Politics and Society, 1343–1378* (Princeton University Press). This scholarly study, based on a thorough investigation of Florentine archives, provides a valuable case history of political and social tensions in a major Italian city of the early Renaissance.

Garrett Mattingly, *Renaissance Diplomacy* (J. Cape, London). A thoughtful and original investigation of Italian diplomatic representation and dynastic politics.

P. Witteck, *The Rise of the Ottoman Empire* (Royal Asiatic Society). An interpretive study which explores the causes of Ottoman growth.

G. Vernadsky, *The Mongols and Russia* (Yale). An excellent, detailed treatment.

ECONOMIC HISTORY

Henri Pirenne, *Early Democracies in the Low Countries* (*Harper). A provocative examination of urban politics, institutions, and class struggles.

The Renaissance: Six Essays (Harper). The chapter on economic developments is perceptive and up-to-date. This book also contains useful sections on Renaissance art, literature, science, religion, and politics.

Raymond de Roover, *The Rise and Decline of the Medici Bank, 1397–1494* (*Norton). An authoritative study which elucidates the policies and methods of this great financial institution in the context of both Florentine local politics and the fifteenth-century European economy.

Richard Ehrenberg, *Capital and Finance in the Age of the Renaissance* (Harcourt). A product of German scholarship which deals with the role of the Fuggers in the European economic system.

Two books noted in previous bibliographies and useful here are Lynn White, *Medieval Technology and Social Change;* and Henri Pirenne, *Economic and Social History of Medieval Europe.*

INTELLECTUAL AND CULTURAL HISTORY

Again, several previously-cited books extend into the Late Middle Ages: Copleston, *Medieval Philosophy;* Leff, *Medieval Thought* (particularly good on Ockham); and McIlwain, *Growth of Political Thought in the West.*

Jacob Burckhardt, *The Civilization of the Renaissance in Italy* (*2 vols., Harper). This classic treatment, now over a century old and in many respects outdated, remains a masterpiece of historical writing.

The important problem of changing historical interpretations of the Renaissance can be approached through:

Wallace K. Ferguson, *The Renaissance in Historical Thought* (*Harper).
Tinsley Hilton, ed., *The Renaissance: A Reconsideration of the Theories of the Age* (University of Wisconsin Press).
Denys Hay, *The Renaissance Debate* (*Holt).

P. O. Kristeller, *Renaissance Thought* (*Harper). A brief, lucid interpretation, particularly interesting on the meaning of Renaissance humanism.

George Sarton, *Six Wings: Men of Science in the Renaissance* (*University of Indiana Press). A beautifully written work by a major scholar in the history of science.

Whitney S. Stoddard, *Monastery and Cathedral in France* (Wesleyan University Press). A splendidly illustrated guide to French medieval architecture, sculpture, and related arts, covering the entire Middle Ages.

Johan Huizinga, *The Waning of the Middle Ages* (*Doubleday). Concentrating on France and the Netherlands, this masterpiece of cultural history captures superbly the late-medieval mood.

SOURCES

Jean Froissart, *Chronicles of England, France, and Spain* (*Dutton). A contemporary bourgeois (d. 1410) treats the Hundred Years' War as a chivalric romance.

W. Langland, *Piers the Ploughman* (*Penguin). A profound allegorical poem of late fourteenth-century England.

The Imitation of Christ, attributed to Thomas à Kempis. Many editions.

Two good anthologies of contemporary literature are:

The Portable Chaucer, ed. T. Morrison (*Viking).
The Portable Renaissance Reader, ed. J. B. Ross and M. M. McLaughlin (*Viking).

Illustration Credits

Page 34: Anderson—Art Reference Bureau. Page 35: top, Alinari—Art Reference Bureau; bottom, Alinari—Art Reference Bureau. Page 37: Art Reference Bureau. Page 54: Copyright, British Museum. Page 67: Marburg —Art Reference Bureau. Page 73: The Pierpont Morgan Library. Page 82: Art Reference Bureau (Stiftsbibliothek, St. Gallen). Page 87: Marburg— Art Reference Bureau. Page 129: Model after drawings by Professor K. J. Conant; photograph courtesy of J. Combier. Page 150: Alinari—Art Reference Bureau. Page 151: Alinari—Art Reference Bureau. Page 177: Alinari— Art Reference Bureau (Lower Church of St. Francis, Assisi). Page 241: Historical Pictures Service—Chicago. Page 250: Marburg—Art Reference Bureau. Page 251: Marburg—Art Reference Bureau. Page 253: Marburg— Art Reference Bureau. Page 254: both, Marburg—Art Reference Bureau. Page 255: both, Marburg—Art Reference Bureau. Page 256: Marburg— Art Reference Bureau. Page 257: Marburg—Art Reference Bureau. Page 258: both, Marburg—Art Reference Bureau. Page 259: Marburg—Art Reference Bureau. Page 324: Historical Pictures Service—Chicago. Page 330: Courtesy of Professor Whitney S. Stoddard—Sandak, Inc. Page 331: Courtesy of Professor Whitney S. Stoddard—Sandak, Inc. Page 332: top, Courtesy of Professor Whitney S. Stoddard—Sandak, Inc.; bottom, Marburg—Art Reference Bureau. Page 333: top, Marburg—Art Reference Bureau; bottom, 40.128 Purchase from the J. H. Wade Fund, 58.66-67 Bequest of Leonard C. Hanna, Jr., The Cleveland Museum of Art. Page 334: Cliché des Musées Nationaux, Louvre. Page 335: The Dresden Museum. Page 336: upper left, Marburg—Art Reference Bureau; upper right, Alinari—Art Reference Bureau (Accademia, Florence); bottom, Alinari—Art Reference Bureau (Uffizi). Page 337: Alinari—Art Reference Bureau. Page 338: Cliché des Musées Nationaux, Louvre.

Index

347

Friars, 173, 174, 175, 182
Friars Minor, 179
Friars Preachers, 174
Frisians, 74, 75, 76
Frontiers, Byzantine, 39
  Carolingian, 83
  crusades, 153–157
  Eastern, 119
  internal, 143–146, 148–151
  pressure on, 16, 18, 21
  Sicilian and Southern Italian, 151–154
  Spanish, 146
Fuggers (Augsburg), 320
Fulda, Monastery of, 76, 79, 80, 90, 92

Galahad, 244
Galen, 66, 68, 263
Gascony, 304
Genoa, 140
Gentry, 221, 232
Gerbert of Aurillac, 122, 267
German Church, 76–77
Germania (Tacitus), 18
Germanic culture, 17, 18, 69, 120
German law, 18–19, 20, 37, 122, 199, 263
Germans, 8, 16, 18–25, 43, 53, 75
Germany, 69, 70, 171, 178, 226, 264, 280
  East Frankland, 97, 100, 101
  expansion of, 158–160
  Late Medieval, 312
  monarchy in, development of, 117–122
  relations of, with Roman Catholic Church, 76, 189, 190–203, 296–299
Gerson, John, 328
Gibraltar, Straits of, 22, 63, 310
Glossa Ordinaria (Accursius), 264
Glossators, 264
Golden Bull, 312
Gothic architecture, *see* Architecture
Gothic wars, 38
Granada, 147, 309, 310'
Grand Princes of Moscow, 317

Gratian, 265, 275
Great Mother Cult, 6
Great Ordinance, 306, 307
Greco-Roman culture, *see* classical culture
"Greek Fire," 61
Greek language, 32, 33, 39, 81, 93, 153, 267, 271, 277
Greenland, 104
Gregory I the Great, Pope, 44, 49, 51, 57, 267
Gregory VII, Pope, 1, 189, 190, 191, 194
Gregory IX, Pope, 180, 203, 206, 266
Gregory XI, Pope, 299
Gregory of Tours, St., 44
Groot, Gerard, 297
Grosseteste, Robert, 286, 288, 328
Guilds, 140, 141, 142, 260, 261, 320
Guinevere, Queen, 244
Gunpowder, 325

Hadrian IV, Pope, 194, 195, 196
Hamburg, 103
Hapsburgs, 315
Harness, tandem, 138
Harun-al-Rashid, Caliph, 64, 65
Hegira, 58
Heloise, 275
Henry I, King of England, 211, 212
Henry II, King of England, 191, 214, 216, 225, 226
Henry III, Emperor, 124, 130, 187, 188, 189, 193
Henry III, King of England, 218, 219, 220, 221, 228
Henry IV, Emperor, 189, 190, 191
Henry V, Emperor, 191, 192
Henry V, King of England, 305, 308
Henry VI, King of England, 197, 198, 200
Henry VII, King of England, 305
Henry the Lion, Duke of Saxony, 193, 197
Henry the Navigator, Prince, 312
Heraclius, Emperor, 40, 57, 60